In Pleasant Places

Joyce Grenfell

In Pleasant Places

M

© Joyce Grenfell 1979

SBN 333 27288 9

First published 1979 by

MACMILLAN LONDON LIMITED
*4 Little Essex Street London WC2R 3LF
and Basingstoke
Associated companies in Delhi, Dublin,
Hong Kong, Johannesburg, Lagos, Melbourne
New York, Singapore and Tokyo*

Printed in Great Britain by
BUTLER AND TANNER LIMITED
Frome and London

By the same author

JOYCE GRENFELL REQUESTS THE PLEASURE
GEORGE — DON'T DO THAT ...
'STATELY AS A GALLEON'

For Virginia

The lines are fallen unto me in pleasant places . . .
PSALM XVI: 6

Contents

List of Illustrations

Besides the photographers mentioned above, the publishers would like to make acknowledgement to any they have failed to trace or whose photographs they unwittingly reproduced. They would also like to thank Mr John Ward, R.A., for permission to reproduce his pictures, and Mr Peter Letts for copying photographs and pictures.

Foreword

WRITING about my childhood, my parents, my friends and relations, and my younger self, as I did in my first book of memories, was an indulgence. The pictures were sharp, set against steady blue skies. The 'I' of those days was far enough away to be looked at objectively as funny, foolish, touching and innocent. What happened to that 'I' was a kind of fairy story, unsought, unplanned and on the whole exciting, enjoyable and unexpected. The story-line was clear, events led on and opened up, and I found myself in a new enthralling world facing challenges that didn't – because I was ready for them – seem too difficult. Then a table-land was reached; the future brought developments but fewer startling 'first times'.

This second book is about these later years when life was less dramatic but richer. It has been interesting, more demanding and infinitely more rewarding. I can say with truth that – although I may be more selective and less easily enchanted than I used to be – when I am enchanted the delight is doubled. I believe the reason I enjoy such things as music, words, flowers, colour and above all friendship, even more than I did in the beginning, is that experience brings with it greater awareness and more appreciation.

And every new time is a first time. I once had the temerity to say to Walter de la Mare that I thought his line 'Look thy last on all things lovely every hour' should read 'Look thy first. . .' He said he had written the poem when he was young; had he written it later it might have been different.

The happiest – no, the most fulfilled – people I have met have all had one thing in common: an unending sense of discovery and wonder. And enthusiasm.

Thank God for zest.

The Countess of Coteley

CHAPTER ONE

Broadway

In 1954 my mother visited England while I was appearing in *Joyce Grenfell Requests the Pleasure* – a four-handed revue – the words written by me, the music by Dick Addinsell. It was my mother's dream to see me on the stage in America, and she was delighted when at last it was arranged for this little revue to go to Broadway. But she didn't live to see it happen; she died in 1955.

I had flown alone to America, in the spring of that year, to be with her. To say this was the happiest time I had known with her since I was a child must sound strange indeed; but there was a quiet closeness between us, and, as so often happens, we changed roles; she became the child and I the mother. We reached an unspoken recognition that the dividing past was over, wiped out, and the sadness spent. There was only *now*, and our love for each other. It was not an agonising time, nor an emotional one. I felt, at last, what I had long believed, that good is true and stays eternal; and, heaven knows, there had been plenty of good. Now I had the blessed experience of sensing, not just hoping, that the frail figure on the bed had little to do with the real identity of my mother. Her spiritual wholeness was untouched by what was happening to her body.

During my visit to her in Tryon, North Carolina, I went to New York for a few days to give an audition to the American producers. Because I had never before played in the United States I was free to draw on my complete repertoire, the fruit of fifteen years' work. I wanted to be sure which numbers travelled well and which suffered a sea-change, so – to give the producers a choice of items to select from for the October production – I was prepared to do many more numbers than would eventually go into the New York edition of *Joyce Grenfell Requests the Pleasure*.

Conditions for the audition were not very happy; a heat-wave raged, and the temperature stayed in the nineties, with deadening humidity. I had only two days to rehearse the songs with Stu Ross, a friendly pianist who didn't know my work. But he was reliable, encouraging and professional, and we managed to find an understanding in the short time available. I asked Lyn Austin and Tommy Noyes, who were looking after the show for the producers, Roger Stevens and Robert Whitehead, what lighting I could use. 'None,' they said; union rules did not allow any stage lighting unless a full stage staff was engaged for the evening.

'*None?*' I said.

Well, I could have a single top 'working' light.

I tried it out. Unless I stood high upstage against the back wall and kept my face lifted up no beam from the light could reach it.

My performance depended on an intimate relationship with the audience, and I always played downstage close to the footlights (when there were footlights), or was well lit by lights coming from the circle if that was the alternative. For this occasion I would have to abandon the thought of light and play in silhouette. I believe there were also union rules against a performer moving any furniture on stage without the aid of a complete stage crew, but as far as I remember I did shift the only chair I was allowed to use – a battered object – probably one of the lot used by the full complement of stagehands we were later compelled to hire for the run of the show, who spent their evenings smoking cigars and playing cards backstage since there was little work for them to do in a show without much scenery and few props. The upright piano was a poor thing, but on my insistence it had been tuned.

When I got into my black chiffon Victor Stiebel dress (I changed in a service flat on the Carlton House on Madison Avenue where my Astor cousins let me stay) I discovered to my horror that I could not pull up the back zip-fastener. The dress had a built-in bra, and, although I wore nothing under it but a girdle and a pair of brief panties, I got hotter and hotter as I struggled; and my fringe came out of curl. But it was no use. Eventually I got hold of a chambermaid who forced me into the dress, and left me pink and dripping and with my hair less bouffant than I wished.

A small audience was assembled in the dark auditorium of the Bijou theatre, where the show was eventually to play, and they seated themselves as far from each other as possible. (I am not easily thrown by adverse circumstances and I refused to be bullied by the handicaps that presented themselves that night, but it took a moment or two to find my calm and a sense of proportion.) My brother Tommy Phipps and his wife Mary did their loyal best to lift the atmosphere and turn the evening into an occasion; so did Stu Ross's wife Norah Howard, the English comedienne who was the first to sing A. P. Herbert's song, 'Other People's Babies', in a Cochran revue before the war. The three of them worked hard, laughed rather too loudly and too often, and applauded more than was really necessary, in an attempt to make up for the lack of enthusiasm of the others. I had met reluctant audiences before, but there was something strangely intangible about the atmosphere on that lead-heavy June night, and it took a lot of philosophy to overcome the apparent absence of interest shown by the silent few dotted about the stalls. Perhaps I had spoken too quickly in my unfamiliar English accents and rhythms. (My diary noted: 'After London the little audience seemed slow and very dull.') The thing that puzzled me was my own inability to know whether I was making contact or not. Not, I feared; and yet I didn't feel any hostility.

When it was all over and I had taken a couple of calls I waited for one of the producers to come and say something to me; but, instead, all four of them walked to the back of the theatre and stood there whispering together while I, astonished at being entirely ignored, was left standing by the piano making small talk to Stu Ross. My brother Tommy, Mary and Norah paused to see what was going to happen, and then came on stage, as baffled as I was by this curious behaviour. I had begun to think the whole evening had been a mistake and I had better fly back to London as soon as possible. But in my heart I knew the material had merit, and I hadn't performed it that badly. Tommy admitted he couldn't assess the situation either. Eventually Roger Stevens left his little group and came through the auditorium to where I was still standing on the stage. What he said was so unexpected that I could hardly believe my ears. 'I'm confident,' he said in a low voice as if he were about to break bad news, 'that the show is going to sweep New York.' The silent few now became vocal and even enthusiastic.

This bizarre evening went down, as so much has to, under the heading of Experience. The heavy heat was nobody's fault, but it was difficult not to resent what seemed to me then, and still seems to me now, a curious lack of imagination and manners on the part of the management; they were all agreeable, friendly people, and I like to think they were unaware of the way their behaviour appeared to the rest of us. I am not sure just what I learned – except that it is a mistake to think that clumsy behaviour necessarily signals antipathy.

When I returned to America, in September, with Beryl Kaye,

Paddy Stone and Irving Davies, the three dancers who shared the show with me, we had more run-throughs and conferences. The New Yorkers were afraid some of my numbers wouldn't work away from home. Roger and his co-producers wanted many changes; less dancing and more monologues. With a week to go before the opening the promoters seemed to lose their nerve, wanted even more changes and demanded broader treatment and harder hitting from me. 'Fear of the critics in New York is a sort of malady,' I wrote in my diary. 'So *much* money is involved; the show *must* be good. All right. But "they" must know when to stop *niggling*.' Our musical director in New York was George Bauer, a big, fair, good-humoured young man with an engaging laugh and a dimple. He has always looked years younger than he is and could have passed for my son. He is very musical, had plenty of experience playing for revues and had just finished a season with Carol Channing. He said I was far too easygoing with the management – '*You* know what you are doing – do it.' Easier said than done, with all that money involved in the enterprise and not much confidence being shown in my direction.

Different running orders were tried out, minds were changed daily, and the dancers looked unhappy or cheerful according to current decisions. I fought for their numbers, sometimes successfully, and though I accepted certain changes proposed for myself I suddenly decided that if the producers couldn't make up their minds I could; and I said so, loud and clear. I was encouraged when Al Hirschfeld, the distinguished caricaturist of the *New York Times*, came to draw me and said: 'Don't let them change *everything*. They *will* underestimate the New York public.' I could have hugged him. Then Reggie, Dick Addinsell, and Laurier Lister, who had directed the original production, arrived from London to back me up.

At the first dress rehearsal on Monday, 3 October, I managed to make the orchestra of eight players laugh. Afterwards two of the stage management staff gave me a yellow rose to encourage me. Things were looking up. There were previews from Wednesday to the end of the week, and I took back my opinion of New York audiences; it felt disloyal to say so, but I had to admit they were quicker and even more subtle than audiences in London.

We opened on Monday, 10 October, at the Bijou theatre on West 45th Street. My first-night cable from Virginia and Tony Thesiger read: 'BIJOU GOOD OR BIJOU BAD WE LOVE YOU.' And next day all the notices except one were good and some were even better. But the exception was the one that mattered most – Brooks Atkinson in the *New York Times*. He conceded that the programme was a success and that it would please theatregoers, but it wasn't his kind of show. Not tough enough; too 'special'. The management was downcast by this verdict, but I was grateful for the audience-reaction we were getting. The enthusiasm at the theatre kept us buoyant. In spite of this we ran for only eight happy weeks before the pre-Christmas slump finished us off. It seemed a very short season to me, but the producers confessed they had been pleasantly surprised that we had run for so long; after Atkinson's lukewarm notice they had feared we might only manage a month.

It is difficult to write about the generous offers made first by the orchestra and then by the stage crew to take cuts in order to keep the show running, without appearing to accept the gesture as a personal tribute, but I suppose that is what it was. I was flattered beyond measure, moved to actual tears and touched in a way I had not thought possible. Such things aren't supposed to happen on tough old Broadway.

As a result of my stage appearance I went on American television. It was during my first week at the Bijou (when I was going upstairs to change my dress for the second half) that the stage-door man called to me as I hurried by: 'Mr Sullivan is here to see you.'

'I can't see anybody in the interval, no time.'

'But it's Mr SULLIVAN,' he said in agony. 'He's *here*.'

A man came forward, the stocky Irish sports writer who had made history by presenting a variety show on Sunday night T.V. that the nation looked at week after week, year after year. Of course I had heard of him. The Ed Sullivan Show was *the* show to appear in, *the* shop-window for talent.

'Young lady,' he said (nice start), 'when are you coming on my show?'

I explained that eight performances a week were quite demanding, and Sunday was my only free day; could I perhaps wait till the run was over?

'You can come any time you want,' he said.

'Thank you,' I said. 'I'll let you know.'

When the management heard about his visit they said I must get on to him at once – go on the show next Sunday – any Sunday – whenever Ed Sullivan wants you.

'Oh,' I said, '*must* I?'

'You certainly must.'

They were quite right. I telephoned him to ask, if he still wanted me, when he would like me to be in his programme. Four weeks later I made my first nation-wide television appearance.

Ed was at the last night of the New York run, and as he had done on his first visit he came backstage to see me during the interval.

'Now I want you,' he said, 'to do a series on my show – tell the audience tonight.'

'Are you sure?'

'Absolutely.'

There was an affectionate gala feeling in the house, and the audience cheered the news. So did the loyal octet in the orchestra pit; on the stage the company felt as if it had been given a present. In the end the four of us gave two more T.V. performances, and, spread over the years, I made many solo return visits to the Sullivan Show.

Accepting Ed's invitation meant postponing my return home to London, but it was such an important and useful offer that I had to say yes, even though I was longing to be with Reggie. I had told Bertie Farjeon when he first asked me to be in his Little Revue that I would never let my job interfere with my private life, but I learned that if one is a pro there are times when work has to come first. This was the fourth time that we had been separated at Christmas.

I made some short trips to see old friends in the South, but most of the time I stayed in New York, and it was there I came to know better my sister-in-law Mary Phipps. I already liked her, but these weeks brought us much closer. She is not only enchanting to look at, tall, slim, fair, and with a perfect figure, but she is also elegant, sophisticated (in the flattering sense), domesticated and affectionate. Wherever she lives the rooms reflect her feeling for colour and gaiety. Her palette always includes pinks, reds, oranges and lemon yellow. She has been a top model since she was a girl, and now, at the time of writing, with both her children grown up, she is still in demand for work. Mary has humour and great sweetness; a quality not to be confused with anything sugary – a sound-as-a-nut wholeness that is universally recognised, and attracts.

I also got to know Tommy again. He had left England when he was seventeen, claimed his American citizenship (he was born in New York), and had not been an integral part of my life for many years. We saw a lot of each other in the winter of 1955 and it was a good time.

My brother Tommy

My sister-in-law Mary

Tommy looks a little like both our parents; he has our ma's fair colour-
ing and our pa's chin. I find him good company, loyal and handsome;
and he has an ageless charm. (I know he is my brother and one is not
supposed to boast about one's relations, but I am being objective – after
all none of his qualities is due to me.) Some wit once said 'all men are
born invited' and this is certainly true about T. W. Phipps. As our ma
was he is a social creature. He is, or was, gregarious. He was also a considerable beau and not the most home-loving of young men. When we
were young Tommy had been a great worry to his more strait-laced
sister; but he has become more conventional than she ever was.
Nothing like a spot of reformation. And since he married Mary he has
discovered, what Reggie and I have long known, the joy of *not* going
out.

19

An appearance on the Sullivan programme was seen by the biggest television audience in the world, and was naturally a great help in introducing me to a wider public than the few *aficionados* who patronised the art theatres and saw all the British comedy films, including those in which I had taken part. I had had no previous experience of the extraordinary power of peak-hour television. It is colossal. On my first appearance I did one of my nursery-school sketches. Next day, walking along Fifth Avenue, people stopped and asked me whether I was the English girl they had seen the night before on the Sullivan Show. A month later I appeared a second time. 'Hi – Miss Grenfell, saw you on the show last night!' After my third appearance it was 'Hi Joyce!' In my series of nursery-school sketches I always introduced a five-year-old character called George. He is apparently misbehaving and in every sketch I admonish him in that high, bright adult voice that is used to divert attention from some undesirable behaviour . . . 'George – don't do that . . .' The misdeed remains unspecified to this day. In America after I had done the sketches on television I was continually asked what was George doing, but I always answered that I thought it best not to know. And I didn't.

Before leaving America I agreed to return later in the year to give a concert-tour of one-night stands up and down the East Coast of the United States – based on what I had been doing in England with Viola Tunnard. Since 1945 Viola and I (who had made such long tours together during the war playing in military hospitals and isolated units all over the map) had continued to fit in our two-handed shows between my engagements in revue, playing to small special audiences, usually in music clubs; but I had not yet dared try out such a programme in a London theatre. By now Viola had begun to follow her own career as a 'straight music' accompanist and, though for several years we still gave occasional concerts together in England, she felt she could not play for me on this coming tour or during a theatre season. I fully understood her feelings; she was beginning to make a name for herself in her new field and it would have been foolish to break the continuity. In view of this I was glad to know that George Bauer would be in New York waiting to do the shows with me.

After the television programmes were over I sailed home to England. When I got back to London the old flat, where we had been happy for ten years, since the end of the war, looked shabby; the spring sunshine showed up the poverty of the wartime factory-waste tweed curtains I had been so pleased with when I put them up (blue-grey piped with sharp yellow braid). When I came in, laden with shopping, the three steep flights of lino-covered stairs seemed to rise up for ever. The noise of the traffic in the King's Road below was intolerable; I had to close the window before I could speak to anyone on the telephone. We must find somewhere quieter, more convenient, and preferably on one level. We didn't want to live in a modern block; but we knew Chelsea was turning old family houses, now too big for single families, into pleasant flats.

Harold Pearce, who, until my architect-father closed his office, had been my father's surveyor, was now the Borough Surveyor of the Chelsea Borough Council. I asked him if he knew of any available conversions in the district; were there any new ones coming up? He suggested Elm Park Gardens, where the Victorian houses, built at just the wrong period, are made of what I think of as public-lavatory yellow brick. 'Nothing,' I told Mr Pearce, 'would make me live in Elm Park Gardens.' He said the Council had taken over two of the streets; the yellow brick had gone grey from London soot; and he thought an excellent job had been made of turning the houses into flats. He knew of a two-floor conversion coming into the market and urged me to see it. To oblige him, but without a flicker of hope, I went.

The street looked as ugly as I remembered it, but the bricks had indeed gone greyer thanks to London soot – Lot's Road Power Station was less than a mile away, and it belched out plenty of grime. (Years later John Ward told us that when he and his brother were children they liked to walk through Elm Park Gardens because the grey houses reminded them of the stuffed elephant in the Natural History Museum, in Cromwell Road, which had a tiny stuffed mouse standing under it to emphasise its great size.)

Up on the third floor of No. 34 the rooms were well shaped, light and cheerful. The main windows faced east along the street at the southern end of the Gardens, and giant plane trees could be seen coming into leaf. The conversion was made laterally; flat number 8 must have been the nursery floors of two old family houses. The bedroom and kitchen faced west – the days had begun to get lighter, and that afternoon the sun poured in. A staircase at the end of the passage led to two attic rooms and a second bathroom. I liked it at once and began to visualise it furnished with our pictures, books and belongings.

Reggie was due back from South Africa where he went every January on a business visit, and the day after he got back I took him to look at

Reggie

No. 8. He liked it too. The deal was clinched; eighteen years left of a twenty-one-year lease.

Playing 'houses' is one of my great pleasures, and this was the first one I had had to play with since we went to Parr's Cottage nearly twenty years before. Our flat in the King's Road didn't count; it had been partly furnished when we took it over, and although by storing we got rid of most of the strange bits and pieces – including plum plush curtains with a mitre-shaped piece hanging down eighteen inches from the *middle* of the pelmet, and an antique wrought-iron lamp that didn't balance very well – we had only patched up the décor from

The new living-room in Elm Park Gardens

time to time because we did not expect to stay there for ever. With Reggie to work out the mathematics I made scale-drawings of the new rooms. I collected patterns for curtains and chair-covers, and we spent enjoyable evenings poring over the kitchen table, trying out different colour combinations, and juggling cut-out paper models of our sofas and chairs to fit the given spaces. We had huge turning-out sessions at 149 King's Road, where we had the luxury and fatal temptation of a box-room into which everything not immediately needed had been stowed. Mrs Gabe, who housekept for us for eighteen years until she remarried, found homes for a good many items; others were passed on to young couples we knew, who were setting up house for the first time. In the new flat there was no box-room, only a cupboard for suitcases. We were determined to reduce our belongings to fully employed pieces; no more keeping things 'in case of'; the place was to be kept beautifully free from clutter. Fond dream. You should see it now.

My second cousin, Elizabeth Winn (a child bridesmaid at our

23

wedding), is a freelance interior decorator, and when we had finally decided on what we wanted I asked her to help us. She is efficient and added her experience and knowledge to my hopes. We drew up detailed plans of everything, including door-knobs and lattice-work grilles to hide the ugly radiators (and, as we later found out, reduce their heat). When in September Reggie and I set off for my concert-tour in America, I left Elizabeth with a file full of instructions, working drawings, and my confidence, to complete the job. She did it well. Reggie would be returning to pack up the flat and move to Elm Park Gardens without me. We had worked it all out on paper, and I hoped all was in order for this big job. He was sure that with Mrs Gabe's help he could do it on his own, and he was proved right.

We had only been at 149 for ten years, but I tend to put down roots wherever I am happy, and I have been known to feel pangs when I leave a pleasant hotel room after only a few days. When I left the walk-up flat in the King's Road for the last time it was still furnished, and as I looked at its familiar run-down cosiness I was moved. I had feelings of guilt at quitting it, even though I hated the inconvenience of its draughts, all those stairs, the primitive icy bathroom, and the poorly planned kitchen. The pretty yellow-and-white patterned walls in the bedroom seemed to accuse me of treachery.

My career as an actress in revues was over. *Joyce Grenfell Requests the Pleasure* was the last show I ever did with other performers – apart from a pianist. Next would come solo programmes. I was on my way to give my first solo concert-tour – something I had long wanted to do.

CHAPTER TWO

Ships, Hats, Phippses and Parkers

On 18 September 1956 Reggie and I sailed to America on the S.S. *Mauretania*. Going by sea instead of by air greatly added to the pleasure of the trip. I have always preferred expectation to realisation, and the slowness of sea-travel prolonged the anticipation of the promised land that awaited us. Putting the clocks back an hour each night stretched the dream-time agreeably; just as the reverse on the way home to England made the return more exciting.

Part of the fun of travelling by sea was having cables, letters, flowers and presents delivered to one's cabin so soon after sailing that on outward journeys I managed to write my thank-you letters to special friends like Virginia Thesiger, Viola Tunnard and Dick Addinsell while we made the crossing to Cherbourg or Le Havre, in time to post them home from the French port. As a seasoned traveller I knew about reserving a quiet table in the dining-room, and a corner on deck for our hired chairs, where for most of the day we would be in the sun and out of the wind. These little jobs were the first thing we did after leaving port. When I was on my own it was pleasant to be invited to sit at one of the ship's officers' tables, but when we were together Reggie and I preferred to be alone.

There was no need to worry about over-weight luggage; women had tall, upright trunks that opened like cupboards, hanging space on one side and drawers for underclothes and shoes on the other; fat hat-boxes; and make-up cases fitted with glass bottles and jars and special places for brushes. This time Reggie and I had fifteen pieces of luggage including a trunk belonging to Constance Hardy, the English nanny I had engaged to look after Sally Phipps and the new baby Tommy and Mary were expecting in October.

As well as all the stage stuff and my own luggage I always took a hat-box. Indeed I seem to have had an obsession with hats. My diaries for the nineteen-fifties and early nineteen-sixties are full of visits to milliners to choose hats and fit hats, and of the pleasure of wearing

25

new hats. I wonder where I put them all. I have no recollection of special hat-shelves. Some of the hats must have been quite dashing. There were two draped velvet turbans bought at Bloomingdales in New York, one in clashing blues and greens and the other in clashing pinks and reds. I remember a large, three-cornered highwayman's number made of royal blue fur felt; cartwheel straws; a tiny black satin pill-box with a coarse-net eye-veil; and a huge snow-white rabbit-fur tam-o'-shanter. It makes me uneasy to think of them now. One Christmas Reggie had made for me what I thought was a very Anna Karenina cap made of astrakhan that I proudly wore for years. When I went to Australia, where winds blow in the winter months of July and August, I had head-hugging turbans designed for me by Simone Mirman. I whistled when I heard the price.

As I now seldom wear a hat and, for reasons of comfort rather than glamour, have taken to men's caps made in a variety of materials, I find this other self – the hat woman – an unfamiliar figure. But I still remember a little shiver of pleasure in putting on a fetching new hat that I thought did something for me. It gave me confidence; the hat seemed to go into the room ahead of me, and allow me time to adjust before facing a gathering of people I thought better dressed than I was. I no longer believe that a hat could provide me with the lift it once gave me.

There is a hat story that the actress Diana Wynyard, a beautiful English-rose type with great style, told about herself. She had bought a noticeable spring hat embellished by an outsize red rose, and was well pleased with it. Waiting one day at her table in the Apéritif restaurant for a friend to arrive, she looked up and saw a woman come through the door wearing the identical red-rose hat. Diana was a little taken aback, but decided to brazen it out, and waved to the woman, smiling as she pointed at her own hat and to that of the wearer, and she said, 'Snap!' The other woman looked alarmed and hurried away to the far end of the restaurant. It was only when she glanced into a mirror as she left an hour later that Diana realised she had not that day been wearing her red-rose hat.

I can't now remember which ship offered what amenities, but down the years Reggie and I availed ourselves of whatever was offered. We used the gymnasium, rode bone-shaking electric horses, pedalled on static bicycles, played deck-tennis and shuffleboard and competed in the ship's daily paper's crossword and general knowledge puzzles. We

Hat-fancier

went to the movies, walked a mile a day around the decks and ate our way through the menus. Even when we went Tourist (round trip fare £50) we changed for dinner every night. If there was a swimming pool I swam in it; Reggie never plunges except in a hot bath in which he stays for a minimum of twenty minutes. We borrowed books from the ship's library, read them in our hired deck-chairs under rented dark-blue Cunard rugs and enjoyed the hot chicken broth served on deck, with crisp Saltina biscuits, small, white and square, at mid-morning on all the transatlantic crossings I made – only I have an idea that in the later years the broth changed into beef-tea.

As a small child I crossed the ocean eight times before I was four. One of the delights I have never forgotten was being given by the steward a peeled orange on a fork. Did I bite straight into it? Must have been very messy. I only remember the shining wet look of a freshly peeled orange, sans pith and skin.

I haven't been on a liner for over twenty years, and, until I went on an Hellenic cruise, I did not think I would ever want to sail again. Now that I know it only takes a few hours to get from London to New York by air, the five-day sea-journey seems impractical and artificial; a refusal to accept the present. But progress has its drawbacks; sea-travel allowed time to recover from departure and prepare for arrival.

My concert-tour was to begin at the end of October, but before that I had to do two more Ed Sullivan programmes, to rehearse for the tour with George Bauer, pay some visits to friends in the country and spend time in New York with Tommy and Mary.

Mary's new baby took its time to arrive. We hoped it would come during our two weeks' stay in New York, but it didn't. After I had done the first Ed Sullivan show we set off on our holiday, partly spent in Tryon, North Carolina, and then with Frank and Elly Parker, two dear friends whom we had originally met over a quarter of a century earlier.

Elly, who is about ten years older than I am, came into my life when my mother remarried and lived for a time in an ugly, rented, Edwardian Tudoresque house (*so* unlike her taste – dark and over-furnished, with dull colours) in Greenwich, Connecticut. The Parkers' house was, in the American sense, 'right across the street'. Elly was my mother's new neighbour and younger friend. In fact the Parkers' handsome red brick house, built in the Georgian style, was the other side of a country road up a slope behind a little wood, just visible in the autumn when I was there, but hidden in summer. Elly was married to an intellectual lawyer, Frank Parker, and they had three attractive children of character who had taken to my mother, as children always did, and were in and out of the house all the time I was there. That Elly and I became friends is a minor miracle, because my mother's enthusiastic selling of us to each other before we met might well have put us off for ever. But any apprehensive feelings on our part faded when we came face to face; we found each other in our own way and have remained close.

Elly and Frank Parker

Over the open fireplace of Elly's living-room in Greenwich, Connecticut, hangs a picture of her, painted when she was about four years old. It shows a round-faced, round-eyed little girl with a big bow tying up her short, loose brown ringlets in the fashion of the early 1900s. She gazes directly from the canvas with the same gaze I know and love in the present-day Elly. This directness is an innate honesty – not of the blunt, bulldozing kind, but an honesty that is the central core of an instinctive, warm and loving human being.

When I first met her she was a short, slight, dark-haired young woman who stood (still stands) with her feet firmly planted and apart, while she decided her next move, physical or mental. To this day when we are out in the street she stops as she has always done to consider and question. In those days she was something of a rebel; she tended to argue with some feeling about the rights of minorities, and in the decidedly conventional, well-to-do 'establishment' society of Greenwich (in which she and Frank were only marginally involved) she was looked upon as very liberal. Even then this was a dangerous word; but with Elly as with me, liberalism was more an emotion than an active cause. She is not a political animal; neither am I. In my own way I was thought to be odd, and well left-of-centre. This didn't mean much; I have a normal instinct for fair shares for all, not in the dishonest, phoney Communist way of words without deeds (class and privilege probably exist more powerfully in Russia today than anywhere else in the world), but in the sense that everybody's potential should have opportunity for fulfilment. I was never a rebel – in the caring support of my parents and my happy childhood I had nothing to rebel against – but I was never entirely at ease in very grand circles, and was suspicious of great wealth; although I greatly benefited from the generosity of affluent aunts and cousins.

In many ways Elly and I are dissimilar. Our friendship is proof that it is not necessary for two people to share the same tastes in order fully to enjoy each other's company. She is more gregarious than I am. I think I probably like music, nature and reading more than she does. People come first with her at all times, and her friends range from children to her own contemporaries. She has a special rapport with the young still at school. I prefer people in small units. That is because I am not as large-hearted as she is, and more selfish.

I always thought of Frank as a typical New Englander of the old school. In fact he came from Michigan. Perhaps it was at Harvard, where he read law, that he acquired the appearance of a traditional bookish Yankee, spare and bony. He had a face I always wanted to draw. He wore button-down collars and sober suits in clerical grey and, like my pa, he was a bow-tie man. That endeared him to me from the start; so did his passion for the English language. When he came to London with his younger daughter Carol we took them to see Christopher Fry's play *The Lady's not for Burning*, and Frank responded as I had hoped he would to its imagery and poetic quality.

I saw the play thirteen times, not out of love for any of the performers, good as they were – John Gielgud, Pamela Brown, Claire Bloom, Richard Burton were some of the original cast – but for love of the play itself. I read it again the other day after an interval of twenty-five years or more and I still love it. For the record I recognised the enormous talent lurking in the playing of a tiny part by Richard Burton, and marked him down as an actor to be watched.

Frank was a collector. As other men collect butterflies, he collected hats. I had a number of hats myself, but I couldn't call them a collection for they came and went; Frank's stayed. I remember a Sherlock Holmes deer-stalker; a Russian fur pot of a hat; straw boaters; city homburgs;

fedoras; and a number of caps made of linen, denim, corduroy, tartan wool and synthetics. For week-end wood-chopping there was a bright red twill cap with ear-flaps. He also collected different blends of tea; and soaps.

Frank was an enjoyer. I shared in his taste for crossword puzzles and puns. He was also, as I know from experience, a good audience; when he laughed he shook and made a strange nasal whinny of appreciation. I found Frank an imaginative and sensitive companion.

Elly and I have been writing to each other since the early 1930s and we have managed to meet, either in America or in England, every two years or so – except during the war. Whenever I was in America I always spent some time enjoyably with her. After their children were grown up and had flown the nest Elly and Frank left the big house in the Deer Park and moved into a smaller white-painted clapboard farmhouse, with a red barn behind it, on the edge of stone-walled meadows, on Weaver Street. (In America quite rural areas are sometimes known by the names of roads, and roads over there are often called 'streets'.) The farmhouse was an early American building of charm and atmosphere. I loved the place. It reminded me of descriptions in stories I had read as a young schoolgirl in the American children's magazine *St Nicholas*, at a time when I was enamoured of all things American. My passion included gramophone records and, in particular, shoes. In London shoes were either plain, 'court', single-strapped or, for walking, lace-ups. American friends had the first elegant T-strapped, high-heeled shoes I had ever seen; and for evening some of them were made of coloured velvet. I dreamed of such delights, and when I was eighteen and my parents sent me to stay with my aunt and godmother, Irene Gibson, in America for some weeks, I bought myself three beautiful pairs of velvet evening sandals, in white – worn a year later at my wedding – red and bright green.

The Parkers took us twice to Vermont on what is known to the tourist trade as a 'foliage trip', both times in October, to see the leaves turn after the first frost, from green to a poster-paint brilliance of lemon yellow, coral, scarlet, rose-pink and orange. When you are near the trees they are vivid, but distance runs the colours together and they become a pale blur. Alfred Hitchcock filmed an early Shirley MacLaine movie, called *The Trouble with Harry*, in Vermont during the foliage season, and if you saw it you will remember the coloured splendour of the trees. For our magical journey Frank and Elly drove us up the New York State Turnpike – a great highway that runs north to the

Canadian border – through endless miles of low rolling tree-covered hills that look as if someone had flung over them countless pastel-patterned Persian rugs. New England countryside is largely farm land and comparatively unspoiled. We saw small settlements of white-painted wooden houses, and small townships set about broad streets planted with shade-trees – or there were shade-trees when we went that way, but Dutch elm disease had done terrible damage in America as it has in Europe.

Vermonters are reputed to be people of few words. There is something pleasing about legends that prove to be founded on fact. We lost ourselves one morning, and I wound down the car-window to ask a man working in a ditch if he knew the way to Stowe. He straightened up and said 'Yup', and went back to work in his ditch.

That trip, like the other one we made with the Parkers, was relaxed and fun. It was also memorable for Elly and me for the forgetfulness of our husbands. We had driven for two hours on the second day before Reggie realised he had left his overcoat hanging in the bedroom of the inn where we had spent the night. We turned round and went back to collect it. The next day, as if to make Reggie feel better about his lapse, Frank left his watch and chain under the pillow in the room he had occupied on the second night. Again we turned around and drove for two hours to retrieve his possessions. Elly and I couldn't help feeling a certain quiet satisfaction in knowing that for once the forget-fulness had not been feminine.

When Frank died I flew over to be with Elly and arrived on the evening of the funeral. In the little white house on Weaver Street the windows blazed with lights. It is an American practice to leave curtains unclosed; this is both welcoming and friendly, and I approve of it in principle, because I love being able to see into rooms as I pass by, but when I'm indoors I prefer privacy. The house was full of the Parker family, and the grandchildren were improvising an entertainment to cheer up their grandmother. As I was driven into the back yard I looked up to see one of the windows filled with giant coloured paper flowers parading past. Sounds of laughter and applause came from the living-room. The very naturalness of the happy atmosphere on such a day was a tribute to both Frank and Elly.

The next day Elly's devoted Dutch housekeeper, Sena, took time off and went to her home nearby, and Elly and I packed up Frank's clothes and cleared his cupboards – a task that would have distressed Sena. The collections presented a formidable challenge. The chief one was soap; two upstairs cupboards were full to bursting with the stuff in every conceivable form, much of it given to him by friends. As well as the more familiar cartoon figures of Mickey and Minnie Mouse, Donald Duck, and Thumper the Rabbit, there were soap fruits and flowers, eggs, a fire-engine, a ballet dancer, penguins, dominoes, and dogs, clowns, an aeroplane and a boxful of soap golf-balls. And more besides. Somehow we got them all into cardboard crates; where they eventually went I no longer remember. I know the cupboards were cleared and dusted before Sena came back next morning. Tea, enough to last a large family of tea-drinkers for at least ten years, was sorted and given away. The hats went to grandsons.

Elly left Weaver Street and now lives in a modern wooden house that time has already weathered to a soft pinky-grey, designed and built for her by Perry Duncan on a piece of lightly wooded land that borders a little river where it widens into a pond. She is still in Greenwich, near her many friends. When she is on her own much of her time is spent in her enviable big downstairs bed-living-room (as opposed to an upstairs bed-sitter), cross-lit by windows at either side. This new way of living, from choice not necessity, has much to recommend it. Several of our American friends, with the space to do so, have handed over the main living areas of their houses to their young adult children, and escaped to their own spacious bed-living-rooms. The important word is spacious. Successful versions of these bed-sitters have a living area at one end with armchairs, an open fireplace, a table to eat at and a desk. The sleeping area is part of the whole but, because the dressing-table and clothes cupboards are housed in a bath-dressing-room next door, it is uncluttered. When this arrangement is well planned it seems to me an attractive and convenient way of living. What is more you can watch television lying on or in the bed. In Britain more and more people are making kitchen-dining-rooms, but I haven't yet met with bed-living-rooms for choice, although doubtless they will soon be coming here.

Elly, too, has a collection of her own that she took with her to the new house in Bailiwick Road. Her family crest is a pineapple, and she has inherited, acquired and been given pineapples in many forms – not all of them exactly to her taste. As Frank found out, collecting, if it gets out of hand, can have its hazards. I have never been a serious collector of anything, but at different times I went through passing phases of accumulating objects, first with designs of ivy, then with strawberries on them. I had a set of coffee-cups decorated with ivy;

Winifred and her caravan

green enamel ivy-leaved coral drop ear-rings with a brooch to match; and for a time, during the war, I pinned sprays of fresh young ivy to my lapel, and arranged larger sprays, instead of flowers, in a pair of cornucopia vases on the mantelpiece. I managed to stem the flow of strawberry-decorated objects; but in my ivy time I didn't let it be known that I had plenty, thank you, before, Winifred Ashton (Clemence Dane the writer) heard that I had a fancy for ivy.

Winifred was a beautiful, statuesque woman whose gestures of heart and hand were, literally, wide. For part of the year she lived in a caravan resting in a field – evidently in the middle of ivy country. Her expansive generosity was on a scale to match her large heart. This sometimes turned out to be inconvenient for the recipients of her presents. One Christmas Day she and Olwen Bowen-Davies – who had another caravan in the same field – drove across country to have luncheon with Dick and Victor Stiebel, who was staying with Dick in his exquisite flat on the sea-front at Brighton. The flat was reached by a lacy, open-work lift just big enough to hold two passengers. Into this little wire cage Olwen and the taxi-driver had to manoeuvre an entire Yule log, collected by Winifred from a wood, and to which she had tied many Christmas presents, complete with its mosses, rich black earth and lichen, all of which fell off in bits as the log was dragged along the passage and on to the pale yellow wall-to-wall carpet in Dick's drawing-room where, wakened by the warmth of the room, a number of dazed little grey woodlice came out to join the party. Winifred telephoned me one afternoon to say she was sending round some freshly gathered sprays of ivy she had brought to London for me. We were still living in the King's Road. It took time to get the unwieldy parcel up to the top floor where I unpacked it in the kitchen. There was enough ivy to decorate a large village hall; six-foot lengths of it, with its little dangling tentacles, had been wrenched from walls and pulled off tree trunks. I cut it up, filled vases, packaged some to give our neighbours and was still left with yards and yards of it. Getting rid of it was not easy, but I rolled up what was left and dumped it near some dustbins at the back of the building where we lived. Another journey both ways down and up those awful stairs. With my thanks for her kind thought I gently let it be known that I now had all the ivy I was ever likely to need.

After we got back from our foliage trip with the Parkers, Tommy's second son, Lang, was born, on 10 October 1956. In later years I always arranged to spend some time in New York before the tours began, so that I could see and be with the Phipps family. I enjoyed watching the children grow up.

Sally, born just in time for my mother to enjoy her first grand-daughter, was a character from the beginning; a very definite indi-vidual, full of drive. My diaries record her development, her comedy and her appeal to my eye and heart. She liked being noticed, particu-larly by the opposite sex, and responded, as had her grandma (and a lot of other women before her) with sparkle and awareness to any atten-tion that came her way. Tommy and Mary brought anyone who happened to be visiting them to her bedside to say good-night. There Sally sat in bed, a row of battered dolls and stuffed animals ranged along the wall beside her, looking her best, rosy from the bath – smelling deliciously of talcum – with her fair hair brushed up into ducks' tails. I remember an evening when we found her thus, absorbed or pretending to be absorbed in a picture-book. She took no notice of the pilgrimage of admirers at the door; she was by now used to me. She liked variety, and, when she did look up and saw it was only family, she went back to her book – for a second – then she looked up again and said with heartfelt disappointment: 'Aren't there any men?'

When she was small she was sent to nursery-school. But, before she went, there was a form to be filled in. It was an earnest American document wanting to know about Sally's 'ability to relate to other people', her 'group awareness and general integration potential'; and, under the heading 'Toilet information', it asked what she was likely to say when she wanted to go to the lavatory. Mary hesitated for a moment and then, deciding that honesty was the best policy, wrote down 'Tinkle-tinkle' and 'Big-big phooey-phooey'.

At one time Sally had a Swiss French nurse who referred to Reggie and me as Ton Oncle and Ta Tante. This turned into an Americanised Konkl and Tanty. We are still called by those names and enjoy them. She was always an independent little girl, as wilful as her only aunt had been at the same age. Now we are thought by some to look like each other too, although she is fairer and slighter and has grown up to have a beautiful shape like her mother. It may be an echo of her grandmother Nora's inability to spell or get her words right that caused Sally to report that, 'Today at school a man came and played the organdi in the chaplin.'

Like me Sally dreamed dreams about dancing, and in the summer when the family came over for a holiday in London she was given a silver tinsel fairy costume with a wand, and she thundered up and down our not very large living-room in a way that was very like me at the same age in my early ballet phase. But unlike me Sally grew up to move gracefully, and at college she studied modern dance of the Martha Graham School and was good at it.

Lang was a blond, round-headed and beguiling little boy with a friendly nature and a natural talent for games. He was games-mad – as his pa had been before him – and he was slow to wrath. Just as Tommy had disturbed me when I was trying to paint (jiggling the table as he whizzed by on his little tricycle so that the paint-water spilled out of the the jam-jar) so Sally disturbed Lang by teasing him and insisting on playing *her* choice of records on the gramophone. His amiability was sorely tried, and one night, when his father went to say good-night, he saw on the bedside table a reminder Lang had written to himself in thick black felt pencil: REMEMBER TO HIT SALLY IN THE MORNING. Tommy swiped the note and sent it to me in England. Next day he asked Lang if he had remembered; Lang made the sort of face that is an alternative to swearing, and flicked his fingers to express regret at his omission. Wrath had not been vented; but it was over and forgotten.

At the time of writing Sally is in London working at a centre for

Sally and Lang Phipps   *Sally on an archaeological dig*

battered wives, where her particular task is to look after the adolescent and often problem sons of the wretched mothers. It seems she is able to make useful contact with the boys whose ages range from seven to seventeen. In an aunt-like way I asked her what the end-product of her work was likely to be. She said she thought it would be useful if she could prove, even to only one or two of them, that it is possible to have a real relationship that does not include either sex or violence. 'If it isn't,' she said, 'these boys are going to be the thugs and murderers of tomorrow.' She is undaunted by the tasks she is faced with; unshocked, uncondemning, clear-headed and brave as a lion.

Lang is now a young giant. When he was about five he wrote me this letter:

Dear Tante
I love you
It is very cold here
Hi ho.
Love L. Phipps.

And a few years later he began writing a detective story. A fragment reached me in London:
'Instead of strangaling her he huged her.'
He may turn into a writer.

37

The day before Reggie left for England I did the second of my three Ed Sullivan programmes. This was memorable for me because Elvis Presley was on the bill. When Reggie took me to the C.B.S. studio, at two o'clock in the afternoon, there were barricades on West 56th Street to hold back the crowds of girls who had been there since early morning. Later we were told that Presley's white Thunderbird car had to be re-sprayed because the girls had broken through and covered it with pink lipstick kisses. My diary says:

Elvis is a pasty-faced plump boy of twenty-one. At rehearsal he wore a navy blue sweater with red stripes round the yoke. His hair isn't long and his side-burns aren't all *that* long either. For the show he wore a Kelly green jacket, grey pants and white buckskin desert boots. When he was introduced to me he said, as he looked away, 'Nice to know you, honey.' I asked him if all the adulation was very trying. He called me ma'am and said: 'I don't want to brag, but I'm kinder used to it now. It's been goin' on a year.' I thought he was pleasant, a bit of a roly-poly boy, but a good singer of his sort of hill-billy songs. We were photographed together. He put his arm round my neck and breathed down my ear-hole.

Ed Sullivan was no ordinary showman. He didn't appear to be either highly educated, cultured or particularly sensitive, but he produced widely contrasted programmes of a quality that captured the nation on Sunday nights for a great many years. The other television companies, jealous of C.B.S.'s success, did everything they knew to woo viewers from the Sullivan Hour, but no one ever held the ratings so consistently as Ed. He had a natural flair and had the courage to risk outlandish contrasts of opera singers, actors and concert artists with clowns, crooners, tumblers and ballet dancers; stand-up Jewish comics and variety turns with stars from the world of sport and athletics. He trusted only his own instinct and could be ruthless in cutting an act at the last moment if he lost confidence in it. This could be heartbreaking. I remember a pair of funny men (or, as it turned out, not-funny-enough men) being sent home only a few minutes before the programme went on the air. Of course they had told all their friends to look in; their agent had broadcast the news of their engagement; and though they must have been given a full fee it was no compensation for not being seen by over a hundred million viewers all across the North American continent. For them it was a tragedy.

Knowing his love of contrasts I should not have been so surprised when he asked me to do a number I wrote with Richard Addinsell, in 1947, about a 'privileged' woman of the upper class:

With Elvis

> The Countess of Cotely!
> Wife of the Eleventh Earl,
> Mother of four fine children,
> Three boys and girl . . .

who, brought up in a protected, blinkered way, had adjusted, usefully, to a very different kind of life. I sang and spoke the piece, dressed to the nines in a tiara with an order ribbon across my white satin gown, standing in a gold frame, as the subject of a 1910 portrait by John S. Sargent.

> When you see her in this flashback it is rather hard to guess
> That she'll be a sort of typist in the W.V.S.
> Speaking worldlily she'll dwindle, she will change her book at Boots,
> And lecture on Make-do-and-Mend to Women's Institutes.

After we had written the number Dick got cold feet about it, because he felt that with Labour newly in power it didn't fit in with the mood of

39

the times. But I admired the way such people had come to terms with the very different situations in which they found themselves, and I didn't drop it, as he wanted me to do, before the revue *Tuppence Coloured* opened in London. I had faith in the piece, and I was always glad I stood out for it; in the end so was Dick. It was the number Oscar Hammerstein liked best when I revived it for the New York production of *Joyce Grenfell Requests the Pleasure*. Ed said it was just the thing for his Sunday night programme as a contrast to Elvis Presley.

For America I changed the lyric, because I didn't think the references to Boots and Women's Institutes and the W.V.S. would mean much, and instead of the original version (as printed in *Stately as a Galleon*), I put in the lines:

When you see her in this flashback it is rather hard to guess
That two world-wide wars will find her quite involved in all the mess . . .
She will get to know the village, and at first it will seem queer
When the bus conductor calls her 'ducks', the grocer calls her 'dear'.

CHAPTER THREE

Touring in North America

IN THE beginning my American and Canadian tours were arranged for
me by the William Morris Agency in New York. I was fortunate to
have a sympathetic manager, Klaus Kolmar – who now has his own
agency – but even he did not quite appreciate the heavy demands of a
two-hour solo programme of songs and monologues; and the itinerary
for the 1956 tour taught me to make sure that never again would I
allow myself to be called upon to travel and play on the same day; nor
cram into a short season so many dates with long journeys between
engagements. Reading my diary for that time is wearing. The pre-
liminaries were always the same. On arrival with my accompanist,
George Bauer, and Constance Alderson who looked after us, we met
the local manager and his staff of lighting and sound men (sometimes
it was the same man). Then we inspected the stage and the piano. Over
every piano wherever I went hovered a question-mark. Was it, as the
contract stipulated, a concert grand in first-class condition? Well
– er – *no*. Often theatre pianos that *looked* like concert grands – they
had the necessary length of strings –were in truth whited sepulchres
with old beaten-up insides and decaying ivories. If it was not too late
we demanded and sometimes got better pianos, but never on Sundays.
My heart went out to my accompanists (Viola, George and William
Blezard) over some of the pianos they had to use. It says much for
their skill that they managed to extract music from the most hopeless
instruments.

George Bauer was my accompanist for all my American and Canadian
tours until he retired to go into business. By that time Bill Blezard and
I were working together in Britain, and Bill was able to get a permit to
go with me to America in time to take over. Connie Alderson, just
starting out to be a stage-manager at the age of twenty-one, was a
graduate from Wellesley, a dark, neat-featured girl, well-read, lively-
minded, with a great capacity for hard work and a fancy, at that time,
for very pointed high spike-heeled shoes that I tried to discourage her

from wearing; partly because they looked so uncomfortable, but also because they left little holes in linoleum and vinyl coverings. For reasons of comfort I have always resisted fashionable shoes unless they were wide and easy. My peasant-type feet cannot cope with points and spike heels; I cannot think when I am teetering.

Connie and George looked after me in a cherishing way. I think they thought I was too trusting, too green; I loved them for their protective care, but hope I convinced them of my own view that trust can beget trust.

The tour began in Atlanta, Georgia. We flew there from New York the night before we opened. It was dark when we arrived, and I was unprepared for the exuberance of the décor awaiting me in my Cherokee Motel room. The only word for it was colourful. The wall-paper hit me first. Great white flowers the size of dinner-plates sprawled in every direction over a shrill yellow background. They were so big that instinctively I stepped back to try and get them into focus. All three beds were turned down ready to receive sleepers, and the blankets were bright green. (This was not the first time I had been given a wide choice of hotel beds. During the war-time tours Viola and I were sent to Damascus and were shown into a vast room with *five* queen-size beds in it.) Colour was not the only noticeable feature of my room in Atlanta. On the long dressing-table-cum-chest-of-drawers there was one of those enormous lamps that are only to be found in American hotels; the lamp-shade was the width of a child's hoop. At the other end of the built-in piece stood a tall, skinny vase holding a bunch of guardsman-scarlet gladioli. In spite of it all I slept well.

I had done advance publicity for shows at home in England, but never with such intensity as in the U.S.A. On the day of that opening concert I appeared on a breakfast-time television programme, taped a radio interview, made three T.V. guest appearances and, separately, talked to two members of the local press. It was the stiffest schedule I had ever been given. It served me well. Before we left the city I had made notes for a sketch about a visiting Englishwoman trying to get a word in edgeways on a commercial radio show, somewhere in the Southern States. I called it 'Time to Waste'. It was a mixture of the Atlanta experience and what I remembered from listening to local radio, years earlier, when I stayed in North Carolina with my mother. The object of these programmes is the plugging, affable but relent-less, of small-ads, sweetened with a little interviewing of 'guests'. It always turned out to be an unequal contest in which the guest lost.

Connie Alderson   *With George Bauer*

Here is an idea of how the sketch went. The accent is rich, ripe North Carolina.

Hi and good mawnin' to you! This is Milly Molly Merrydew [or any other three names suggesting country-fresh gingham wholesomeness] talkin' to you at 8 a.m. in the Top O' the Mawnin' Breakfast Club show – the friendly Breakfast Club show you can't afford to miss.

I've got more fun things in the programme today and we got a very excitin' out-of-town guest all the way from Merrie-Old-England – A warm welcome to you, Mrs Elsie Braddlebury. Mrs Braddlebury is a Lady Mayor, and a mother. Mrs Braddlebury, we don't have Lady Mayors over here – we just have Men Mayors, but we *do* have mothers. Now before you tell us about some of the fun things you do as a Lady Mayor – and a mother – I have to ask you an urgent question: Do you have teen-age problems in England? Before you answer that important question I have to ask you another one: Can you make pie-crust that makes your family say 'Yummy'? I want you to get yourself some Cousin Chrissie's Flick-of-the-Wrist pie crust. It *is* Yummy and you and your family are all goin' to *love* it and say 'Yummy!'

Not being much of an introvert I have never found interviews with the press or on radio and T.V. a hardship. Perhaps the honest truth is that, given the time and a friendly interviewer, I have enjoyed the encounters. I began my professional life as a journalist, so I know a little about being both the questioner and the questioned, and often I am as interested in finding out about the questioner as he or she is about me. I have seldom been misrepresented in an interview, and now that most journalists use a tape-recorder, instead of shorthand, the actual tone of voice and emphasis of the one being interviewed are on record, and the chances are that what is said is reported as he or she said it. But not inevitably. An editor, in any of the media, who wishes to slant an interview in a particular direction can cut and re-assemble the material so that it does not truly reflect the original intention of the person interviewed. By the time the finished product is in print or has gone out on radio or T.V. it is too late to do much about it except rage. Only if the issue is of real importance is it worth trying to have the record put straight. I don't believe I have ever had to do this.

On the whole we had few problems with the local managements who presented us in the various theatres, gymnasiums and halls; exceptions were usually soon resolved either by refusal to accept bloody-minded-ness or by a firm British stand taken and recognised. Montreal landed us with a grudging local promoter who had not provided us with the kind of furniture we had requested. Her Majesty's Theatre was sold out in advance of our arrival, and we supposed he had figured that it didn't matter if the pieces he had collected were gimcrack. Connie sorted him out, and made him produce a pair of presentable chairs and a table to replace the rubbish he had hoped to get away with. He also denied that we had asked for sound-equipment and an electrician, but Connie carried copies of the contract, and he was confounded. All ended well, and though he never apologised, it was evident he knew he had done poorly, for he congratulated me on the show. He also asked when he could book the programme again.

When working, I made it a rule never to accept an engagement after two-thirty in the afternoon. On the day of the concert I went to bed, in a nightdress, with a black chiffon scarf over my eyes and a hot-water-bottle at my toes. I trained myself never to turn over and burrow because that way I went too deeply to sleep; instead I lay on my back, very still, and as I lay there dozing I went through the words of the numbers I would be doing that night. I went in and out of sleep, but I knew just where I had left the lines when I dozed off, and I continued all the afternoon until I had gone through the whole programme. I never cheated. It was my way of preparing for a per-formance. I also believed in a singing warm-up before the show, and so did George; and Bill too. We not only went through the songs in the current programme but sang old songs – Rodgers and Hart, and Hammerstein, Kern and Cole Porter. Bill and I often improvised together as well. When I retired from performing I realised the part of the tour I had least liked was the afternoon rest, the mental run-through, and the packing and unpacking. But I always enjoyed the warm-up.

When I played a season in a theatre (as I did occasionally in America and often in England and Australia) I rarely went out after the show. This was no hardship; I preferred a quiet unwind on my own. I organised something to eat and smuggled it into my hotel room earlier in the day. This was because, although I thought the authorities might prefer me to order food from the premises, I knew from experience how depressing cold meats can become when they have sat about on a plate from the hour when the dining-room staff goes home. And if I relied on room service it took too long to arrive. Anyway I preferred curious mixtures such as ham, cheese, chocolate cake and fruit of my my own selection. I enjoyed a picnic in bed, after a bath, with the radio on. When possible I telephoned home to Reggie, read a book until I was sleepy, and turned off the light about one o'clock. But on concert tours – doing one-nighters in the U.S.A. – George, Connie and I took ourselves after the performance to a coffee-shop and had waffles and other comforts of a sweet nature. Now and then we were taken back to the house of some friendly person involved with putting on the show; this was an opportunity to meet local people, see how they lived and look at their book-shelves. I regretted there wasn't more time to explore the different places where we played, particularly in the colleges and universities from which (until the last tour I did with Bill) we moved on so quickly that we missed getting to know better the students and professors of kindred interests with whom we had made instant contact.

During a stop-over on a free evening in Chicago we found Carol Channing was appearing in cabaret, and she invited George, an old friend and colleague, to bring me to see her show and have supper afterwards. I admire Carol's work. It is original, exaggerated and very much her own unique talent. Everything she does has size and style. We enjoyed her performance to the full, but what I best remember is a moment during the soup course, when she cried 'STARP!', and waved her long arms, fingers outstretched, above her head. She had dropped one of her contact lenses into the bouillon. Someone produced a fine linen handkerchief, and the contents of her soup-bowl were poured through it to reveal the tiny lens. That same night I lost my music-case. The cab driver who brought us from the airport to the hotel where we had reservations drove away before we knew that, because of bad weather, a number of guests had been compelled to stay on, and so our rooms were not available, and the reception office had arranged for us to stay elsewhere. It wasn't until we got to the second hotel that I discovered my case was missing. In it, as well as a spare set of my songs and scripts, were my diary, holy books and letters precious to me. My feeling of loss was great, but I thought to myself there was no reason why honesty shouldn't operate, and I went to sleep. I was woken about two in the morning by the night clerk to ask if I had mislaid any baggage. Up to my room, accompanied by the hotel detective ('ladies must not entertain single men in their bedrooms unchaperoned') came the original driver. He had made five or six trips from the airport since bringing us in, and this was the first chance he'd had to find out where I was and to bring back my case. 'I figured you'd need this,' he said. I didn't fling my arms round his neck in appreciation, but I did thank him enthusiastically and gave him all the ready cash I had in my purse. It had almost been worth losing the bag to get it back from such a kind man.

The smaller the town and university, or college, the friendlier the people. That is a general statement, and at once I think of exceptions proving the rule: great kindness at the huge university at Ann Arbor, Michigan, on the first tour, and later particularly friendly relations at East Lancing and Oklahoma. I had never experienced a 'standing ovation' until the concert at U.C.L.A. in Los Angeles; I didn't recognise it for what it was and, until George explained, I wondered why the audience had risen and some had come down to the front of the stage, applauding.

Our visit to a revivalist university was an eye-opener of a different kind. The establishment was a large and well-endowed foundation in South Carolina. Its rules were strict. Maybe they still are. No smoking, no drinking, no dancing, no movie-going, no jazz. I didn't mind the first two as I have never done either, indeed I dislike the smell of cigarette-smoke, and particularly object to smokers at the hairdresser, where their smoke gets into my clean hair and makes me smell as unpleasant as they do. Smokers tend to think the air belongs to them and they have a right to pollute it.

Connie and George were heavy smokers, but they knew how little I liked the smell of their cigarettes, did their best to cut down in my company, and never smoked in my dressing-room, for which I was grateful. They were much offended that they were not allowed to smoke anywhere on the campus. They were in a fix until one of them remembered that water is supposed to deodorise smells. They went through various contortions with their heads in the shower, puffing their fumes at the falling water and getting soaked in the process.

There were other hazards. On the morning of the concert a woman rang Connie and asked if she might press my stage dresses. Connie explained that my wardrobe had travelled well and did not need any attention. The woman then rang me with the same offer. I thanked her for the kind thought and repeated what Connie had already told her. There was a pause. 'I'm afraid I have to see your gowns,' she said. I again assured her they were uncrushed, and I preferred not to have them pressed. Another pause. 'Your dresses have to be checked to make sure they are not cut too low.' The suspicion that they might be unsuitable was offensive, and I said so. Nevertheless she came to my room to see for herself.

The founder, who had been a well-known revivalist, was now at the repetitive anecdotal stage of his life. I sat next to him at luncheon and as he finished giving his view on smoking, the end of the story reminded him of its beginning, and he told it to me all over again; not once but many times. 'Ah always say if the Good Lawd had intended us to smoke he'd a' put a little chimney in our haids . . .' 'Ah always say if the Good Lawd . . .' George, sitting opposite, began to count the number of times the old man repeated his refrain.

The huge dining-room had to provide two sittings to accommodate the numbers. The young were encouraged to marry early and have lots of children; many of the diners were married students whose young families were being raised in the narrow chilliness of a faith that seemed to me to be singularly divisive, unloving and governessy in a thou-shalt-not way. There was something depressing about the kind of blinkered outlook we met at the university, and not only because it was self-righteous and smug. In spite of the rigid smiles and what seemed to be a contrived public-relationship friendliness, we found the university an uncomfortable place to be in; hell and damnation – and fear of both – seemed very real on the campus. Before curtain-time the students, dressed formally for the occasion, the girls with white gloves and corsages, the boys in dark jackets and buttonholes, paraded arm-in-arm up and down the concrete paths. Perhaps a substitute for dancing together? They filled the purple velvet-draped auditorium (I learned that attendance at my concert was *compulsory*), and before I began listened to light music played on an old movie Wurlitzer organ that rose up out of a hole in the orchestra pit.

I had prepared a programme of straightforward songs and monologues that I hoped would suit the unsophisticated audience. I was sure I couldn't go wrong in including one of my nursery-school sketches, but I had not reckoned on smutty-mindedness, and was unprepared for the reaction of this particular crowd. When I came to the line: 'George – don't do that,' there was no laugh, only a strange silence. The obvious implication of the line is that George, aged about four, is doing something minor but preferably left undone, such as picking his nose. (As I wrote in an earlier chapter I do not know what George is doing but whatever it is, I know it is totally innocent.) The line usually raises an understanding laugh. But not at this strange place. I can only suppose it aroused imagined behaviour so shocking that it could only be greeted by guilty silence. In our turn Connie, George and I were shocked by the suggestiveness they read into some of my material, for it was not there; they invented it. We came away from the place with feelings of sadness that so many decent young people were being indoctrinated by such a strange, forbidding sense of life.

On another tour we went to Canada and opened in Winnipeg in brilliant below-freezing weather. I am a *frileuse* and like to live in warm surroundings, but the overwhelming steam-heat in the Fort Garry Hotel where I was staying sent me rushing to open the double-glazed windows. Briefly. What came in through the crack was malevolent and perishing; I soon closed it, and learned that opening the inner of the two windows lowered the temperature quite enough; it was better to pant than shudder. When I was walking back from the drug store, only two hundred yards away from the hotel, I near as a toucher got a frost-bitten nose. I remembered as a little girl when my family lived in Winnipeg the alarming pleasure of scuffing my shoes along the carpet and then touching the brass bedstead to create sparks. We were there at the time of a disastrous fire, possibly in 1913, and I was held up to a window to see the red sky and leaping flames as whole areas of wooden houses were burnt to the ground.

There were happy reunions with many of the Canadian medical unit I had worked with in the Cliveden hospital during the war. In Winnipeg and in Toronto old friends got together and gave parties for me, and it was as if the intervening years had never been. In Vancouver where I had also lived as a small child, older people who remembered my parents came to my show at the big modern Queen Elizabeth Hall and offered me hospitality enough to last a month. All over Canada I met ex-patients for whom I had shopped, written letters, and in many long-term cases got to know as friends; and after every radio and television interview telephone calls and letters poured in from people who just wanted to say hello, welcome and give my love to London. The strength of the affection so many Canadians felt for their time in Great Britain in the war touched and surprised me; and I was amused at my own feeling of homesickness at the sight of the royal crown on a letter-box.

Back in the United States the Golden Gate bridge in San Francisco startled me by being red. The city, which everyone told me was the most attractive in America, proved to be all I had heard of it. Patronisingly I wrote in my diary: 'Quite unlike other American cities. Full of character and charm.' I felt it might be possible to live and lead an agreeable life in San Francisco without having a lot of money – not true of most places I have seen in the United States. I thought many of the others would be difficult to endure unless one could afford higher-income-bracket surroundings, well away from city centres. But San Francisco is different. It is a city set on hills, with views, air and light, and pleasant architecture. The only thing I didn't like about it was the steepness of the almost perpendicular streets. Cars had to be parked at an angle in case they rolled downhill. Walking down was difficult enough, my toes went to the ends of my shoes, climbing up was worse. I have never had a head for heights, nor the legs either.

My four performances in San Francisco were sponsored by the English-Speaking Union. They had arranged things well and sold the seats successfully. We had a good time. But we also struck an unexpected problem. Because my show was called a 'concert' (even though it took place in a theatre) I was, technically at any rate, not called upon to engage an orchestra. The local Musicians' Union, or perhaps certain members acting on their own, didn't like this, and in a dark alley on his way to work George was threatened by some men who told him that unless we hired musicians to play an overture and a selection during intermission he would find he had broken fingers. The melodrama seemed incredible. I was furious about the threat and wanted to confront the bullies, but serious faces back-stage told me I would be wise to keep well out of it. I can't now remember exactly how the situation was resolved, but I'm sorry to say the threateners won. We had to have a handful of inadequate musicians sawing away for the rest of our time at the Geary Theatre.

I was invited to Stanford University, a few miles up the highway, to talk informally, after luncheon, to a group of students. An earnest young man from the Technical Economics Division (it said so on the card he gave me) came to fetch Connie and me in a tiny little German car in which the two front passengers had to lie full length – or very nearly – while the third, Connie, sat squashed up on to a sort of shelf at the back. As we drove at a speed faster than I like the man told us in detail about his hi-fi equipment (the only music he enjoyed had to have 'emotion and *feel* to it') and about his inability to sit still. We whizzed by a lake on which were bobbing some interesting duck. Please, I said, could we go a little slower so that I could look at them. Did he know what kind of duck they were? He didn't change pace, but said: 'My area of innerest does not include duck.' End of ornithological moment. A kinder woman driver brought us home, but she did not know about duck either. At least it was possible to sit up, all three in the front of her car, and she took the road at a more temperate pace.

The next stop was Hollywood, where I played at the Huntington Hartford Theatre. The audiences were neither as large nor as responsive as they had been in San Francisco, but my diary records that they improved during the six-day run; it is possible that I may have been progressively more entertaining as the week went by. I stayed with Leonard Gershe at his house in Braeridge Drive.

I first met Leonard when he came to London in 1947 as a friend of Dick Addinsell. It was during the pre-London tour of *Tuppence Coloured* (the first revue I did with Laurier Lister). New material was needed for Elisabeth Welch, and Leonard wrote two lyrics that Dick set to music. He has one of the quickest wits I know, sometimes irreverent, always funny. He looks what he is – a New Yorker now turned Californian; slight, dark-haired then, with a springing bounce in his walk. He has a round neat head, still boyish although no longer dark. He has a tender heart, great humour and is affectionate and loyal. In some ways he is a loner, but if you are his friend this is an enduring relationship; you stay welcome.

As a child and all through my adolescence I had been movie-struck. I read movie magazines and knew all that the publicity men of the day wished me to believe about the stars. I could have taken a stiff examination, not only about the pictures but about the players too – what they ate, whom they dated, just how 'real' and 'folksy' they appeared to be. By the time I got to Hollywood the great days of movies were over, and I had lost my passionate interest in them. Television programmes were now being made in the studios and new

Leonard Gershe

names that meant little to me made the headlines. But there were stars who had lasted; and with Leonard I met some of them, and watched others in restaurants. The old stirrings, if in a more detached way, rose up; there was still movie magic around.

Leonard, who is the most generous of friends, brought a party of thirty to my opening, and it included Claudette Colbert, Janet Gaynor and her husband Adrian, who in the early thirties designed all the M.G.M. stars' most glamorous clothes, Clifton Webb, Van Johnson, Ethel Merman, Jean Simmons, Janet Leigh and Tony Curtis. After the performance we all went on to a small restaurant which Leonard had taken over for the evening, a pretty pink room set with pink-clothed round tables lit by fat white candles wreathed in red and pink carnations. Gladys Cooper, an old friend of my mother's and a lively and original woman of great beauty, not only came to the first night – and the party – but brought friends to two more performances later in the week. She was my greatest advocate in the town and advertised me enthusiastically. She was at the theatre the night Igor Stravinsky came to the show and had seen him laugh and applaud. No, I didn't meet him; but knowing he had come – and stayed to the end – gave me intense pleasure.

No host ever gave a guest a better time than Leonard gave me. He moved out of his room into the smaller guest room. This has happened to me with other friends, and it is complimentary, but it makes me feel a little guilty. Leonard cooked delicious meals for me; wouldn't allow me to lift a finger to help in the kitchen; gave me lunch at Romanoff's restaurant, and took me to see the enjoyable horrors of Forest Lawns Cemetery, where there are roads named Tranquillity, Hope, Inspiration and Freedom. He drove me around Beverly Hills and Hollywood in his open white motor-car lined in red and showed me Pickfair, where Mary Pickford still lived, and houses belonging to Fred Astaire, Jack Benny and others. He introduced me to several up-to-date gadgets that I had never seen before. His was the first garage door I met that opened, at the touch of a button in the car, while the driver was still fifty yards from the house, and he had a bed that could be made to rise or fall at the head or feet. The gadget I liked best and now have in my own flat was a sink disposal unit that gobbled up grapefruit skins and other remainders. (N.B. It doesn't do much good to teaspoons if inadvertently they go down the pipe. My hand, though not beautiful, is small enough to retrieve objects that slip through the rubber opening. I have rescued a number of misshapen spoons.)

In 1960 I went back to Hollywood on another concert tour and again stayed with Leonard. He took me to a small party at Judy Garland's house where Tony Curtis and Kay Thompson, the cabaret entertainer, were two of the guests. Judy was living in a rented house with large bare rooms and not much furniture. What chairs, tables and sofas the landlord had left behind were all built low to the ground. Half of us sat on the floor to eat the fried chicken and ice-cream with caramel topping. Judy was going through one of her recurring battles with weight and wore 'a big black net tent embroidered in yellow and gold'. My diary added that her children were 'sweet and natural'.

We played a game called Likes and Dislikes. Everyone present makes a list of five genuine likes and five dislikes. The game only works when it is played honestly. Someone said: 'Don't put "money" as a like because it is too obvious. Write your own special true personal choices.' The completed papers are then thrown into a hat, read aloud by a spokesman, and the players try to guess who wrote which list. It is easier to spot the author than you might suppose. That night the lists were illuminating, touching and funny. I had already warmed to Tony Curtis because he had spoken to me with much affection about his Russian immigrant father who had recently died. 'I miss him very badly.' But I didn't know about his New York, East-Side upbringing and I couldn't guess it was he who put under Likes 'Sitting on fire-escapes at sunset.' (On hot summer nights in the city it is the one place where tenement-dwellers can catch a breeze.)

Kay Thompson's first dislike read: 'Removing adhesive tape from other people,' and mine, instantly recognised by the whole company, was 'The smell of stale tobacco in hotel blankets.' I've forgotten the rest of the likes, but I know Leonard's number one like was 'Wet white lilac' and I had no difficulty in guessing it was his.

Since those days Leonard has written many successful screen and television scripts, but it was his play for the theatre, *Butterflies are Free*, that was his biggest success. It has been translated into many languages, eastern and western, and has played, and still plays, all over the world. He wrote the play after he had seen a boy, blind since birth, talking on television with courage, humour and unselfconsciousness about his life. It gave Leonard the idea of writing a comedy about a blind boy – a tight-rope enterprise that he brought off with sensitivity, *no* sentimentality but plenty of feeling. The play included a splendid character part for the boy's tough, tiresome but endearing New York mother, and Eileen Heckart played it to the hilt. Leonard gave her a line, which turned out to be one of the biggest laughs in the play, that he acknowledged he took from a true story I told him. When *Cat on a Hot Tin Roof* opened on Broadway in 1964 (by today's permissive standards it was as mild as a vicarage garden party) Noël Coward wagged his finger at me and said I *must* go and see it. I was playing eight performances a week at the time, and though I could have managed a matinée I didn't feel much call to see the play. 'You *should* go.' said Noël. 'Such things go on in real life.'

'So does diarrhoea,' I said, 'but I don't fancy paying a lot of dollars to go and watch it.'

Leonard also wrote the 'book' for the movie *Funny Face* that starred Fred Astaire and Audrey Hepburn. It was produced by Roger Edens. Roger was a giant of a Southerner with a deep speaking voice and a way of playing the piano that reminded me of Dick – with knowledge, understanding and his own individual, relaxed but wholly controlled style. As well as composing songs, he produced large-scale musical movies and worked with both Judy Garland and Ethel Merman. He lived in a big house, old by Californian standards, perched on the edge of a cliff at Pacific Palisades. It had an enormous white-walled, white-floored living-room with hand-carved trellis-like white screens that gave the place a feeling of the East. Hollywood-sized sofas were piled high with brilliantly coloured cushions; brightly painted Mexican objects, figures and animals, stood about on tables and in alcoves; the room made a good setting for a party, and I remember it as 'glamorous'.

In London, on his way to Australia for a holiday, Roger came to see us and was charmed by my flower-table – a small eighteenth-century two-tiered circular brass-edged mahogany table on which I like to put flowers arranged by species and colours, but not mixed, in little jugs and pots that I have assembled down the years. Roger was much taken by the tiny white cornucopia, in which I had two rose-buds, as well as by a green Bristol creamer, a stemmed turquoise blue vase with a rolled 'lip' and other small containers. When he came back through London on his way home he brought me a box full of little pots, jars and jugs he had collected for me on his travels. Some are too precious to use for flowers and sit on the dining-room dresser. The rest take their turn on the flower-table.

My later American and Canadian tours, after George had retired to go into business and Connie was married with two small sons, were arranged by Wally Magill. Bill Blezard and Diana Lyddon took over from George and Connie, and the itineraries were planned in a different way.

Diana was an experienced stage-manager. We had worked together on tours in Great Britain, and it was she who was to look after us in my most exciting West End season some years afterwards at the Theatre Royal, Haymarket. She is a country girl at heart, a born gardener, makes her own wine and is one of the most serene people I know. She has red-gold hair, a straight back and trim figure, and a friendliness about her that is invaluable for one who has to deal with stage-crews; crews in halls unaccustomed to lighting cues; and crews abroad who speak a wholly different technical language. One of the most attractive qualities about Diana is her natural expectancy that things will go right; and her patience. She reads a great deal, grows her own vegetables, not just beans and peas but rarer roots and fancy forms of cabbage, some entirely for decorative purposes – pretty purple things with frilled leaves and striped green and white extravagances of the kind admired by Dutch painters of still life. When it was practicable we rented a drive-yourself car, and Diana conducted us through areas of America none of us had ever been to before. We'd get to an airport, find our booked-in-advance car, be pointed in the right direction and off we'd go. Diana liked to drive in her stockinged-feet, and as soon as we were free of the airport she kicked off her shoes the better to feel the pedals.

Wally Magill was an agent who specialised in straight music recitals and lectures. He suggested that most of my performances should be given in universities and colleges where I could combine my concert engagements with giving a so-called 'class', the day before the show,

With Bill Blezard and Diana Lyddon

open to students of the arts – drama, dancing, music and communications: writing, journalism, radio and television. This new plan meant that we stayed at least two, and sometimes three, nights in one place. This was far more agreeable than the old one-night stands. We were able to look around the countryside and even got to know some of the staff and students a little better.

Before I left London I worked on a talk, for the class, written out of my own experience of writing and performing comedy, as well as the few more dramatic pieces that at last I had grown brave enough to include in my repertoire. Years earlier when I had been invited to Oxford by an Experimental Theatre Group to discuss the question of laughter and why it was supposed to be a good thing, I remembered my father, with his passion for proportion in all things physical and spiritual, saying that he believed a sense of humour was only possible where there was a sense of proportion. He said you could not recognise a funny situation until you saw it in perspective. In my talk at Oxford I suggested that comedy was a form of distortion; an unexpected view of the normal, either enlarged or minimised. I tidied this up into a small aphorism: distortion restores proportion. That, I suggested, is why laughter is a good thing; it gives you back your perspective. I used some of these ideas in my new talk.

I found a more open-minded readiness to listen among young students in America than anywhere else. They seemed to be less self-conscious than young audiences at home, whom I found shyer and less ready to contribute, although in the end their appreciation was probably as lively. My songs seemed to be accepted in the same way everywhere I sang them, but the more serious monologues had a quicker response in America. A monologue is possibly the most demanding form of expression there is in the theatre. It is made up entirely of suggestions thrown out in conversation between one visible and other invisible characters. There is no scenery, there are no costumes, no guide-lines – only a hat here, a shawl there or a background indicated in a brief introduction – nothing more. The thing only works according to the measure of attention and recreated ideas it invokes. I had wondered whether my specifically English sketches would travel. I needn't have doubted. Although the references, as in the portrait of the mildly eccentric wife of the vice-chancellor of an Oxbridge University, were decidedly local, the woman (my favourite character) was evidently instantly recognised as 'true', and 'Eng. Lit.' was the one of the most successful sketches I took to America.

During the question period, at the end of my talk, we often discussed ethics, standards and values. This, to me, was by far the most interesting part of the whole exercise. We went down a lot of side-tracks – permissiveness in life, in print, in entertainment. We spoke of censorship. Was I for it? Only as a means of protection for the young. Was I shockable? No, but I was very *offendable*. They asked what was the difference. For me being shocked seems a dead-end reaction; an opting out; a withdrawal. The effect of shock is a limbo state, a kind of paralysis. To be offended involves active responses of rage and compassion; feelings of concern that can work – as distortion does in comedy – to restore a sense of proportion. Shock separates and isolates. For me 'shock' and 'offence' have very different meanings, as different as 'standards' and 'values'. Standards are variable, like fashions; true values – for instance integrity, honour, faithfulness – are spiritual absolutes and do not change. We muck about with such things at our peril.

Another thing we discussed was discipline. My father taught me that discipline is not so much a thou-shalt-*not* as it is a way through to 'thou *canst*'. Music and dance students accepted this without question; but drama and 'creative writing' students felt they must 'express themselves', and that too much self-discipline might block their imaginative impulses. The dancers and musicians pointed out that until you mastered your instrument through the sheer discipline of practising you couldn't express anything. Point taken by the others, if reluctantly.

Violence was something we all agreed we could do without, but there were the usual views that man is an aggressive animal. Capable of nothing else? We batted the subject round a little, and, with justice I think, we blamed T.V. and the press for helping to brutalise us. Even then, in the late 1960s, there were feelings of apprehension and revulsion about the lengths to which films and newsreels were going in a process of making us less sensitive.

I was interested to read what Pauline Kael, the outspoken film critic wrote in the *New Yorker* a few years ago. Reviewing a movie called *A Clockwork Orange*, she said we are gradually becoming conditioned to accept violence, and that some directors 'are saying that everyone is brutal and heroes must be as brutal as the villains or they turn into fools'. She went on to say that

if we don't use our critical freedom we are implicitly saying that no brutality is too much for us – that only squares and people who believe in censorship are concerned with brutality. . . . We become clockwork oranges if we accept this pop culture without asking what is in it. How can people go on talking about the dazzling brilliance of movies and not notice that the directors are sucking up to the the thugs in the audience.

The same applies to the 'dazzling brilliance' of plays and novels. It seems to me you have to be very brave (or insensitive) to accept much of the entertainment now on offer. Looking through keyholes has never appealed to me, and because I find obscenity (words and actions) offensive I have become more selective in what I watch and read.

I have always thought that acceptance of censorship is the coward's way out, but if we believe there is a difference between good and evil we must be sure that the violence used in plays, films and novels is not more evil than the situation it may be trying to expose. I applaud critics who say this. But they are few. The rest seem afraid to commit themselves in case they are accused of moralising; today that is not popular. The need to be accepted turns some critics into cowards.

CHAPTER FOUR

Solo with Bill

WHEN I got back to England in January 1957, after my concert-tour in the United States, I looked forward to trying out a full-length one-woman programme – with William Blezard to play for me – for the first time in a theatre. A three-week tour, of a week in each city, was planned for the autumn. It was to be followed by a month's season at the Lyric Theatre, Hammersmith, in London.

William Blezard, who has played a big part in my solo career, is one of the particular friends with whom I worked and whom I hold in abiding respect and affection. Bill, William, Willy – he answers to them all – had first played for me in *Joyce Grenfell Requests the Pleasure* in 1954. He was always a support on the platform, and if I got into difficulties or forgot my words he skilfully covered my mistakes. His musicianship is considerable and has been the greatest help to me. When we were doing a season in Sydney, Australia, and a cold had reduced the range of my singing, he instantly and apparently without much conscious effort transposed my songs to keys I could manage, and went on changing key according to my needs until I was singing normally again. His patience in rehearsing daily with me before *every* performance, even during long runs, went far beyond the call of duty. I think he felt, as I did, that every performance should be a first time and we tried to give it the freshness of discovery that comes only when hard work has prepared the way. His hand-written music-scripts sit on the page with the precision of a Japanese drawing, clear, articulate and a pleasure to look upon.

It is a sign of sophistication to mix easily in a variety of worlds. Bill is one of the best mixers I know. There is no society in which he would not be at ease and no occasion at which he would not be an addition. He is intuitive, on and off the platform; a great ally, and his humour is the kind I respond to; also – a rare attribute – he can and does laugh at himself.

Physically Bill sometimes seems to be the least co-ordinated of human beings, but this does not prevent him from covering the ground at a great rate in an ungainly but effective manner. Take tennis: he is a left-hander who can bring his right hand into play when it suits him; swerving low he travels at speed, gets to and returns impossible balls. He came in second in a National Cross-Country Race for the R.A.F. in the war. He has, too, a fine way with a bicycle and negotiates the tangle of London traffic as a master.

He is compounded of compressed energy, employed at its best when he is playing the piano; then it is wholly controlled. His familiarity with the keyboard has the naturalness of breathing; this is his element, and he moves in it with confidence, dexterity and grace. But he is not gifted with inanimate objects; what he does to a newspaper, simply by opening it up, is a feat of displacement and crumple. He is also incident-prone. No one relishes adventure more than Bill (once he is the other side of it) or tells about it better or with more relish. A last-minute departure from New Zealand at the finish of one of our tours was typical. He booked on the only aeroplane of the week that went to Fiji (where he planned to break his journey on his way home) and decided to spend his last day with a musician colleague, newly arrived in Auckland. They fell to making music and forgot to watch the clock. Bill came to with a start – the plane was due to fly in an hour; it was already time for him to report and he was on the far side of the city from the airport. His friend told him not to panic. He would drive him there. And he knew a short cut. This was a mistake; it led into a field, and when they got out they joined the dual carriageway on the Airport Road *going in the wrong direction.* Oncoming drivers, horrified by the unexpected car coming at them, signalled with cries and warnings on the horn. The penny dropped, and the friend wrenched his car across the rough grassy divide and turned it in the right direction. They got to the airport as the entrance-gate to his plane was about to close. Bill and his baggage (considerable and including a life-size toy koala bear for his baby daughter) were flung through the door, and he got his seat-belt fastened as the wheels came up and the machine rose from New Zealand.

My one-woman programme, to be called *Joyce Grenfell at Home*, was to be directed by Laurier Lister. I began to work on new material. It turned out to be a productive period; in the next few months I wrote eight new monologues, five short 'pastiche' opening numbers and three full-length songs for which Dick Addinsell composed the music.

With Bill Blezard and a glimpse of Joan

By September I was hard at work learning my words, having singing lessons with Anne Wood and rehearsing the songs with Bill at his house in Barnes.

Bill and I always tape-recorded the songs, old and new, and learned from the play-back just where we needed to do more work. He has perfect pitch, watched my lapses of intonation and helped me – as did

Solo with Bill

Viola and my enjoyable lessons with Anne – to get into better trim. In later years I began to know the *feel* when I was in tune. This was a breakthrough. Although taping helped with songs, it was of no use to me when I was working on new monologues. Listening to myself experimenting was not encouraging. Only when a character was well worked-in from repeated practise, and I could perform it with some authority, did I record it, and then only for purposes of reference.

It was arranged for us to do our final run-through and dress rehearsal at our old stamping-ground, the Fortune Theatre, where three years earlier we had happily played *Joyce Grenfell Requests the Pleasure*, and where Michael Flanders and Donald Swann were then giving their 'after-dinner farrago' *At the Drop of a Hat*. Before they brought their programme to the Fortune Reggie and I had been to see it in the room-sized New Lindsey Theatre off Church Street, Kensington. I wrote in my diary that it was very civilised and 'gay' – in the proper sense of that now debased and misappropriated word – 'and because they were both talented and pleasant people the programme came off well; it was an evening of a very special kind'. After the performance we went back to Mike's studio and discussed whether he and Donald should accept an offer to bring the show into the West End. No, I said, don't. I didn't think either of them was ready for such a move and they had been difficult to hear in the tiny New Lindsey. My inner voices certainly let me down that time. Rightly, they took no notice of my advice, except to instal microphones as soon as possible, and Flanders and Swann became the toast of the town in London, and ultimately all over the English-speaking world. And deserved to.

We opened at the old Olympia Theatre, Dublin, another stage on which we had enjoyed ourselves in 1954. Posters announced the show as A World Première and, come to think of it, so it was. The fact that I was going to give seven solo performances in one week made it seem formidable. But I took some deep breaths, acknowledged that every time was a separate time – a new opportunity – and with that in mind and knowing that I responded to an audience and enjoyed performing I jumped in at the deep end – and found I could swim.

Bill and I were 'managed' by George Desmond and his assistant Vi Coleman; both were very experienced and appeared to enjoy the programme. Many years after I had worked with George, his son Bobby came into our lives, through Athene Seyler. (I always like it when friendships unexpectedly link and widen the ripples of the circle.) Athene had known his father for most of her theatre life and has great help from Bobby who runs a thriving one-man driving service for an appreciative clientele, including us. He demonstrates neighbourliness, consideration and punctuality (hurrah) and the service he provides has the added bonus of good humour. He also has a special feeling for the paintings of Monet and the planting of trees – not only in his own long back garden in South London but wherever he finds a suitable space and can get the necessary planting permission.

In Newcastle, always a place in which I like to be, we had friendly and plentiful audiences. But in Glasgow I started the week badly. I thought I had given a thoroughly poor performance, and must be prepared for a tough press. Sure enough one critic, although he graciously allowed that he had been entertained by certain numbers and went on to quote them, wrote that my range was too small. I must have told this to Reggie, when we had our nightly telephone call after the show, for he sent me a letter telling me to stop fussing about my range; it was what I did within my range that mattered. I wondered; but was glad of his letter and went out and bought him a length of river-coloured greeny-mud tweed that we both thought very handsome. The suit he had made of it lasted for years. But to my utter amazement the rest of the notices were wonderful, particularly the one in *The Scotsman*. It said kind things about my singing; this was always unexpected. I wonder how well a performer is capable of assessing his own performance. So often when I have felt dull and pedestrian, Reggie, or someone else who knows me well enough to speak frankly, has come back-stage and told me I had been in good form. At other times when I have felt particularly in tune, not only vocally but mentally, and free to take liberties —an ad lib perhaps or a new way of timing a line – my special critics have said 'What happened to you tonight? You were a bit off.' Now that I am no longer performing I can see more objectively. I believe that I did better when I was not conscious of myself; not enjoying what I was doing in a *self-indulgent* way. This could lead to the wrong kind of relaxation. All the same I do not think it is possible to give pleasure in performance without feeling some sense of enjoyment – not at being pleased with oneself but at being able to share an experience with the audience. I have noticed in everyday life that I am most contented, at peace and satisfied, when I am totally unaware of myself. If I am registering 'this is me being happy', the happiness – the fulfilled sense of joy – has got away. For me a sense of completion is only possible when I am un-*self*-conscious. This is as true in performance on stage as it is in daily life.

Solo with Bill

The Lyric Theatre, Hammersmith, which like so many other play-houses of character has been pulled down, was an hospitable, dilapidated and friendly house steeped in theatrical history, and as at the Theatre Royal in Bath a faint smell of gas pervaded the back-stage area. At the dress rehearsal I wore for the first time the two new dresses that had been ordered from Victor Stiebel before I went to Dublin. 'Both are exciting – and rather alarming. One is soft peacock, a heavy ribbed silk. It is very grand. The other is black velvet and huge. Weighs a ton. I'm a little scared of them because I like working in lighter silk that allows me to move more freely. Oh I do hope they [Reggie, Virginia, Laurier, Dick and above all Victor] are right. They usually are.' I noted that my dressing room was 'basic, but spacious, with a bed in it. Bliss.'

The opening went off well. The house was warm and I felt free. Just the right sort of detachment – yet I knew what I was doing. 'The two new dresses are lovely and obviously add to the visual aspect of the programme. The black is wonderful and of course Victor was right about it.' I added that the day had been like all the other days before first nights; time to be got through, gently. 'Virginia came and took me out for a little walk in the morning.'

The only blot had been the arrival of a sad, but brave, sensible and un-self-pitying letter from Tommy in New York. His play *Four Winds* had opened and closed on Broadway. The producers originally bought the play because they liked it. Then they began to get nervous about it, made Tommy change important scenes and write in new ones, and by the time the show opened it was no longer his play. I remembered the way the producers had begun to niggle and make changes over *Joyce Grenfell Requests the Pleasure* at the Bijou theatre and I sympathised with him. Out of experience I had been able to take a stand and fight for what I believed in, and I am grateful to say it worked. Tommy, well versed in writing for television, was new to the theatre, and he had hoped his producers knew what they were doing.

At Home, my first solo engagement in a London theatre, played to packed houses. As I wrote at the time, 'It has been a lovely season but I'm glad it is over, and successfully. Bill has been such a help.' The reason I was pleased when it ended was a simple one. Solo performing is a demanding job. I enjoyed being well-stretched, but it was nice when the stretching was over.

CHAPTER FIVE

Australia

When in 1959 William Orr came to London and invited me to do a thirteen-and-a-half weeks' season of my one-woman show in the small Phillip Street Theatre, in Sydney, I was very doubtful about going. Australia seemed a long way away; Reggie would not be able to go with me; and at that time I shared a view common to many of my friends that it was not a country I wanted to visit. The image, fostered by paintings of sparsely inhabited, hot-red desert wastes, peopled mostly by long, thin, raw-boned men in wide-brimmed hats leaning on fences, of tin-roofed shacks, blackened tree-stumps, slot-machines, surfers, beer-drinking as a way of life, and a philistine attitude to culture – 'all the arts are cissy' – did not call to me. Some of these things still exist, and are not of course exclusively Australian. But they don't tell the whole story, and now after eighteen years and five happy visits I love the Australia I have come to know and have begun to understand.

The invitation included Bill Blezard who was eager to go with me, but at that time he was in charge of the music of a successful revue called *Living for Pleasure* for which Richard Addinsell had written the score; and, though it was probably coming to the end of its run, no finishing date had been fixed. After a certain amount of discussion the management agreed to release him and we flew off together at the end of June. As a seat-companion on an aeroplane I found Bill's upheavals and deep burrowings (until he settled in a tolerable position for a maximum of two minutes) fairly disruptive. But he combines this curious physical restlessness with an awareness of other people's sensibilities, and when he saw that sitting beside him was becoming an endurance test he strove to contain his stirrings, and he found a gentler rhythm that gave us both some calm. He is not good at staying long in one position, but on journeys his Churchillian gift for instant catnaps eases the strain. We broke the journey in Bangkok. The oven-heat stunned us and slowed me down, but Bill is adventurous and a natural explorer.

He had no word of Thai, but that did not stop him successfully travelling by tram all over the city.

Our first view of Australia was in Darwin on the afternoon of an autumn day. I remember a low golden light as we walked from the plane. The airport officials, who appeared to be uniformly tall and boyish in their shorts, were friendly and welcoming; what is more they sounded Australian. Displays of shining red apples in a hall looked tempting. My heart rose. I have an inborn readiness for the next event and on the whole expect it to be good. I told Bill I liked Australia. I have continued to do so. So has he.

We were hours late getting to Sydney and didn't arrive until 11.30 p.m., but Bill Orr, his partner Eric Duckworth, and others from the Phillip Street Theatre were waiting for us. Strip-lighting, a tetchy customs man, and too much luggage overwhelmed us a little, but somehow we all arrived at the flat the theatre had leased for me for fifteen weeks. It was on the eighth floor of Macleay Regis at Potts Point. The block is built of plum-red bricks, and the entrance hall has a 1920s cinema-style décor in browns and beiges; if there wasn't a cut-out sunset fanlight somewhere there should have been. After going through a daunting entrance, into a small dark lift, and along a long dark corridor, we came to flat No. 806 which had a view of the harbour that everyone in turn said I must look at. There it was – at least I supposed the vast dark emptiness edged in lights on either side must be the harbour. The lights looked pretty. When the welcoming committee took Bill off to the flat they had arranged for him in nearby Kings Cross, they left me standing in the middle of my luggage. All of a sudden I felt forlorn. I went into the bedroom; no view from there, but a choice of three beds. I chose the one by the window next to the telephone.

Before I went to bed I made a tour of inspection. It was an ugly flat, but it made me laugh when I found in the tiny spare room – where later Mary O'Hara came to stay with me – a canvas seat of an early aeroplane complete with push-button and a space for stowing a life-jacket. The living-room was not over-furnished – two big leather-covered armchairs, shiny and cold, and one giant-sized decidedly easy chair with deep rose-coloured loose linen covers that swore with the scarlet lamp sitting on the wooden bar, and with the chimney breast painted in high-gloss pillar-box red. The chair became a sort of home-from-home for me. I read in it, wrote in it and nodded off in it. Hanging above a gas-fire that I tried to light but failed (it hissed and popped, made blue flames and gave no warmth, so I abandoned it for the time being) was a very small high-hung reproduction of a little-known Renoir picture of people in a café. Some occasional tables stood in unexpected places, and that was all. The kitchen turned out to be a very narrow strip of a room with cupboards along one wall, sink and gas-stove along the other. The bathroom was furnished with an ox-blood-coloured bath, lavatory and hand-basin. Not a waste-paper basket anywhere, but dozens of wire coat-hangers, for which I was grateful. I telephoned a cable to Reggie in London. 'Flat pleasant décor hideous.' It made the operator giggle, and I noted in my diary 'a good start'.

Bill Orr and the others had been right about the outlook. The black space between twinkling necklaces of lights I had seen when I arrived had told me that it was big; but until I stumbled sleepily into the living-room the next morning to make sure it was really there, I had no idea of the beauty of the huge panorama I was to live with for the next fifteen weeks. It was a dazzling New South Wales winter's day. The sun was flashing on blue water dotted with white sails taking the breeze. Through the glass doors of a small balcony, and through the windows of the dining-alcove (up three steps), and from another side-window, was the most enormous, breath-taking view of the harbour – all the breadth and five-mile length of it, from the bridge to the rocky Heads, guarding entry into the more sheltered waters from the open Pacific Ocean. Through a side-window I looked down on the Royal Australian Naval docks, and by craning my neck I could see the top of Sydney Bridge. The main view showed gently rising tiers of houses, in the eastern suburbs to my right, beyond Elizabeth and Rushcutters Bays; and to the left away on the other shore were steeper tiers of houses in the northern suburbs, and the trees of Taronga Park Zoo. (When the wind was in the right quarter the roar of lions was blown across the water, and up to my flat.) Shipping of every kind, size and class sailed the harbour. Pale little crescent beaches curved on both coasts.

The red roofs of undistinguished harbour-side houses looked settled and comforting. I felt steadier and went to see if I could light another uncertain gas supply, this time in the kitchen, to make myself coffee. (Both the kitchen ring and the fire in the living-room were reluctant starters and paused before accepting a match. I leaned away expecting an explosion that I am happy to say never happened.) All the time I was in the flat the view was my ally and comfort. It was exciting in all

A view of the Harbour

weathers; particularly as I once saw it with indigo blue storm-clouds, a vivid rainbow and holy-picture shafts of light. If ever I was tempted to feel homesick or lonely a look out of the window at the harbour and its changing traffic, by day and night, filled any gaps I might have felt. The view became my solace and my joy – justification for the flat.

Before I left London kind people had offered me introductions to their friends in Sydney. I thanked them for their offers but left it vague, because I knew that working in the theatre I was sure to meet people; and unless I am just passing through a city without time for leisurely discoveries I think it is wiser to let friends reveal themselves naturally. If that sounds choosy, it is; but I have found that through introductions you can get involved with people who are not truly on your own wavelength and this can complicate life. I went to Australia with only one introduction (from Joyce Carey) and for that one I was soon grateful; it was to Jim Dickson, husband of Prue Vanbrugh, a dear, kind man, whose advice and help I sought very early in the visit.

In Sydney from the start there were agreeable people to talk to, but it is to Googie Withers that I owe a debt I can never repay for her kindness when I first arrived. She asked me to a luncheon party she was giving to say good-bye to the women friends who had entertained her during the run of the play she was appearing in at the Theatre Royal. She suggested that I should be the guest of honour for the occasion, and in that way meet her Sydney friends. It was an imaginative and hospitable gesture, and, though I do not much like ladies' luncheon parties, I was so grateful for her kind thought that I accepted with pleasure; and in anticipation of a friendly occasion I put on my best hat. It was a hat-wearing time, and Sydney's winter winds demanded some sort of protection. I brought five hats with me to Australia; unthinkable today. That luncheon party turned out to be one of the biggest blessings ever to come my way. I met those whom I continue to count among my dearest friends, and through them others of equal importance came into my life. One of the reasons I love Australia is the quality of friendship I find there; it is deep and of a lasting order, and I prize it beyond rubies.

Googie's party was a splendid launching-pad. As a result of it I found I had entry into a loosely-knit circle of like-minded friends. Nancy Fairfax was there. So were Pat Manning, Helen Blaxland and Dorothy Jenner, an over-life-sized character known to radio listeners all over Australia as Andrea. She has an incautious tongue, is brave (her encouragement and leadership of her fellow prisoners-of-war when Singapore fell was heroic), is vulnerable, funny and was a kind neighbour to me in Macleay Regis. She was a director of the Phillip Street Theatre, and it was she and Pat Manning who made ready my flat, stocked the refrigerator with food and made up the corner bed that I unerringly chose to sleep in. (The other two beds served as useful areas on which to spread letters, painting materials, my camera and binoculars.) Dorothy could wave to me from her flat – three floors down – named me 'Upstairs', and ever since has signed her letters 'Downstairs'. This was at least fifteen years before the T.V. serial of that name.

Pat Manning further endeared herself to me by dropping into the flat with goodies in a basket decorated with a flower from her garden; it was often a gardenia. She also introduced Bill and me to the art of grilling lamb chops over a single copy of the *Sydney Morning Herald* burning in a petrol-can. They cook to my liking (burnt outside and succulent, pink and juicy within) in exactly the time it takes for an average copy to burn through. To the chorus tune of *Bobby Shafto* we sang: '*Nobody* grills like Mrs Manning!'

Pat is one of the old-shoe friends in my life. They don't often occur.

She is slight, pretty, gentle, *soignée* and chic, inclined to underrate herself, good company and a meticulous keeper of houses. She and her husband Neville stayed in our Chelsea flat for some time when we were abroad, and as a 'thank-you-for-having-us', Pat, with my grateful permission, reorganised and brought our linen- and store-cupboards to a state of perfection. (This unaccustomed order did not last as long as I hoped I could maintain it.) In return for our loan of the flat the Mannings let us use their house in Drumalbyn Road as a base during a long tour of Australia that Reggie and I made in 1969. As Leonard had done for me in California, she and Neville moved out of their rooms for us. Pat swore that we had done them a big favour in forcing them to turn out drawers and cupboards that had not been faced for years. We protested in vain, and spent happy, comfortable weeks in rooms overlooking their garden. Pat assured us that the back spare rooms were *just* as good as the front ones. 'Then why don't you let us sleep there?' 'Just because . . .' she said.

Helen Blaxland is very tall, has real presence, charm, and a wide cat-smile that lights up her amusing, handsome face. She pronounces her *r*s with a foreign roll; so does her sister Sheila, and neither knows where this came from, because their non-foreign parents both spoke their *r*s in the usual way. Helen is imaginative, creative and a giver in every sense of the word. Her touch is sure in all she does, from making a posy, packaging a very special present exactly chosen, giving a dinner-party at which she blends agreeably diverse people, decorating a house, working full out for the New South Wales branch of the National Trust (for which she has been deservedly Damed), to writing original, articulate letters in a lively spiky hand. She has humour, perspective, kindliness, and she finds time in her busy life for her friends who are many and varied. A very civilised woman, admired as well as held in affection. Going to the high, thin house set in trees – where she was living when I first met her – with its clear, strong colours, pretty objects, pictures, delicious simple foods and plenty of books – was a special pleasure for me, starved as I was of such things in my friendly but bare and bizarre flat.

Nancy Fairfax is English, and this was an instant link. She is much younger than I am, blonde, with a delicately drawn profile, straight back, direct gaze; and behind a cool appearance is the tenderest of hearts. At first I thought she might be uncompromising and critical, but as I came to know and love her I watched with admiration these tendencies turn to real understanding and generosity. It happened that the day I went to lunch with her, after Googie's party, I had a letter (following a cable) from my brother Tommy in America telling me how his son Wilton had been lost in a boating accident on Lake Michigan. We were alone, and something told me that Nancy was the kind of friend to whom I could talk about it without shyness, for although she is reserved there is great warmth behind that quiet exterior; and, as I soon learned, we share, even if our ways to it differ, the same goal of spiritual discovery. She is the only one of my Sydney friends who regularly writes to me. We share the kind of spontaneous exchanges that require no editing and a minimum of explanation, for we remain in close touch. When distances divide, there is no more rewarding relationship than a letter-writing one. A lot in life is missed by those who don't practise the pleasure of corresponding with an articulate and fond friend.

Vincent, Nancy's husband, is one of those quiet men who at first appear to be reserved and possibly shy. Integrity is not easy to define; it is personified in Vincent. As I got to know him his very individual quality, his earthy humour and humility fused into a whole that is strong, gentle, warm and totally dependable.

He and Nancy are one of the happiest couples I know. Because of this good relationship being in their company is a positive pleasure. There is something sustaining about being with people who like each other.

Before the opening of *Meet Joyce Grenfell* at the Phillip Street Theatre, on 16 July, there was a programme of promotion. The morning after I arrived a 'press conference' (two journalists and a photographer) came to the flat and, dazed by time-changes and my late arrival, I answered the usual questions – 'What do you think of Australia?' 'Which is your favourite film role?' I was photographed looking at the view, wearing my new finely-woven grey hopsack coat and skirt from Victor Stiebel. What I didn't appreciate at the time was the identity of the principal journalist. He was introduced with some emphasis, and I felt I should have recognised his name, Richie Benaud. Had Reggie been there he would have told me I was in the presence of a great Australian cricketer, whose off-season job was journalism.

The Phillip Street Theatre was really not much more than a glorified church hall with about 450 tip-up seats, on two levels. It was housed in a building that had in its basement a library, and above the auditorium there was a film projection room. The dressing-rooms under the stage were simply divided spaces, separated from the library by a

The Fairfaxes: Sally, Nancy, Ruth, Tim, John and Vincent

partition to within one foot of the ceiling – for ventilation purposes I imagine. Conversation from both sides of the partition was audible to both actors and readers. On Fridays we played at 5 p.m. and 8.30 p.m., and I tried to take a nap between performances in my little space; but it was house-cleaning time over the wall in the library, and the cleaners were a chatty lot. One was an ex-chorus boy who sang a good deal; his conversation was gripping and included his plans for the week-end. 'We *might* go to the beach – or we *might* ask in a few friends. Depends on my mood.' During performances extraneous noises penetrated the auditorium from the overhead projection room. Sometimes battle-scenes with aeroplanes screaming and machine-guns peppering – at other times Indians whooping across the plains – made concentration difficult for the audience and for me. Complaints were courteously received, and things improved for a while – but never entirely. The building was pulled down the year after I left Sydney, and I regretted it; the little place wasn't ideally suited for a theatre, but it did have atmosphere.

We had a gala first night and an enthusiastic press. 'Everyone is smiling,' I wrote in my diary next day. But there were dramas back-stage of which I was only gradually aware. I can't now remember all the details, but they concerned ill-judged seating arrangements at the first-night party, when the chairman and the board, who were indeed the theatre's bosses, were not placed at the top table. Meetings were called, and a week later Bill Orr, the theatre's director, was dismissed.

A protest meeting took place, and the staff decided they would not work the show unless he was reinstated. A performance was cancelled, and next day the *Sydney Morning Herald* headline read, 'Comedienne walks out of Phillip Street Theatre', which I had not done. I telephoned Joyce Carey's friend, Jim Dickson, as I thought he was the man to turn to, and I was right. 'I'll be with you in twenty minutes,' he said and took over. He issued a statement to the press making plain that I was in no way involved with what was a purely domestic matter at the theatre. He got the management to cable Reggie in case the story reached London. (It had, but it was clarified in *The Times*.) Bill Orr was chastised, reinstated, the chairman resigned – a storm in a tea-cup. Bill Blezard and I played that night, and kind Jim called by at the end of the evening to see that all was in order, bringing me violets.

It was a pleasing surprise to find that radio programmes and my gramophone records had done a paving-of-the-way for my arrival in Australia. I had not realised my audience already existed. Friendly people filled the little theatre for three months without a single empty seat; they also ate a great deal all through the performances, and that was something I had to learn to endure; but not enjoy. It was noticeable in Part One; after the interval, when chocolates, ices and cold drinks had been sold, it was deafening. It irritated me a good deal, and one evening, in what I hoped was a light-hearted way, I mentioned that where I stood (on the stage) the noise was like scuffling through autumn leaves or the pouring out of dry cereals. There was a silence that might have been pained or just shocked. But not for long. The rustling and chumping soon began again. Somebody must have reported my remarks to the press because a news item appeared saying that Joyce Grenfell (a snooty Pom it implied) did not approve of audiences eating during her show. Nor did I; but I didn't approve of eating during anybody else's show either.

Mary O'Hara, the Irish singer who accompanies herself on a small harp, first came into my life in the mid-1950s when John Gielgud asked me if I would advise a young and very talented Dublin girl, not yet known in Britain, about getting an agent to look after her concert and recording work. He thought she should try and work for intimate audiences, as I was doing in revue. Reggie and I were then living in the old walk-up flat in the King's Road. Mary came to tea with me and sat long at the kitchen table, while she told me about her happy life married to an American poet, Richard Selig, and the concerts she soon hoped

Mary O'Hara

to be giving in England. I was beguiled by her unspoilt beauty and the lilt in her voice; she was the epitome of a fictional Irish colleen – exquisite complexion, starry eyes and all the rest. She had no experience of agents, and the approaches being made to her didn't seem to offer the kind of jobs in the kind of places she felt were right for her programmes.

I've no idea what I advised, but we made friends, and she sent me a copy of one of her first recordings, sung in a clear early morning soprano, very musical and very appealing.

Her marriage to Richard was tragically brief. He died within fifteen months of the wedding. I lost touch with her for a while, but when she arrived in Sydney, to do charity concerts for some Roman Catholic 'good cause', she came to stay with me in my flat. It was a difficult time for her. She was still numbed by sorrow. The reverend fathers who were running her tour were inept at the task; she was at the same time unpublicised and exploited by them. Bill and I went to one of her Sunday concerts and were distressed by the evident lack of presentation and apparent failure to recognise her unique talent. But in spite of this she knocked us sideways – and for the audience of the uncomprehending faithful, and a few knowledgeable concert-goers who had discovered she was in Sydney, the quality of her performance was unmistakable.

Mary was an easy guest; quiet and orderly – the kind that leaves her room and the bathroom tidier than she found it. She was only with me for four days. Breakfast was our meeting time. We had plenty to talk about. I see her now sitting opposite me on a sunny morning, wearing a white polo-necked sweater and holding in her hand a scarlet apple. She was twenty-four years old and a radiant beauty. She said she had something important to tell me. Her life was over. Her marriage had been perfect. The world no longer had any flavour for her. She believed she had a calling and to follow it was the only way she would find peace. She had decided to enter a religious order. Such decisions are personal and private, and I forbore to say what every instinct in me was saying loudly, *Don't*. I did urge her to take time to consider every aspect before she took such an enormous step. She said she had already done so; her mind was made up.

I heard from her occasionally, and then a letter came to say she was taking her first vows – in a Silent Order. I shrank from the picture of Mary silenced. Surely, I imagined, she would at least be allowed to sing in chapel? She gave me her new religious name, and said she might not be able to write to me again. But eventually she wrote to tell me she would be taking her final vows on the day of my birthday. After that there were no more letters but she sent me a birthday card each February. Then a letter came to tell me a friend was bringing me a recording of religious music she had made for the Abbey in which she was a nun; and asking for some information I was able to send her. The friend delivered the record and reported that Mary was well and seemed serene.

I do not know the details about her decision after twelve years to leave the order and return to the world. I do know it was not lightly taken and had occupied her for a very long time. When she left, it was with the understanding of her wise Abbess. It was a right decision for Mary. She came to see me a few weeks after she came out, still bewildered by the world, traffic, noise and crowds. She was too thin and looked as if she had been through a good deal of anguish. But she had begun to feel well again and was picking up the threads of her singing career. She already had engagements booked.

Mary is as tall as I am but three sizes smaller. I had retired from doing my own concerts, but up in the wardrobe I still had some of my stage dresses. They were waisted, with long sleeves, and by pulling in the belts they could be made to fit her. The bright clear colours suited her temporary pallor. It was good to know the dresses, still with plenty of life in them, would again be seen under the lights.

Now Mary is an international star, gives sell-out concerts at the Albert Hall in London and Carnegie Hall in New York; she is often on television and radio, plays at the Palladium and has become a household word all over the world. When Mary was the subject of *This is Your Life* – a television programme of which I do not wholly approve because of its invasion of privacy, but which I cannot resist watching – I was invited to join her family and friends to reminisce about her. It was a successful half-hour of warmth, some laughter and a good deal of emotion. Mary is one of those rare women who look as lovely when they weep as when they smile, and when they do both at the same time, as Mary did that evening, the effect is devastating. Her story reads like a novel. And it is all true. Some day she is going to write it, and it will be well told; for she is not only a talented performer who arranges her scholarly-researched folk songs and sings all sorts of other music – and looks lovely as she does it – but she is also literate.

A few days after my show opened I had a letter asking me whether I was serious when I had said, in an interview, that one of my interests was bird-watching. If so would I care to visit the National Park. It was signed by Alec Chisholm, a very distinguished historian and naturalist. Yes. I did mean it. I explained that any extra-curricular occasions had to take place early in the day because after 2 p.m. I rested to keep fresh for the evening performance. Alec arranged that I should be collected by Elaine Hutcheson from Macleay Regis at 7 a.m. I don't think he was too sure about actresses; he met us at a rendezvous inside National Park.

Alec was a small, fine-featured man with a thatch of thick grey hair that stood on end in a boyish way on the crown of his head – and always did till the time of his death, in 1977 at eighty-six. He was slightly fierce, humorous and very knowledgeable. That first morning he showed me a satin bower-bird's bower full of its blue 'toys', and although that day we heard a lyre-bird (also whip-birds and other wonders) we did not see one. I was thrilled with the bower and, for those interested in such things, I will explain that bower-birds are the only known members of the animal kingdom who create and use something not for display or a courting rite but entirely for their own pleasure. The male satin bower-bird collects principally blue objects to play with, and scatters them around the bower (his theatre). This isn't a nest for putting eggs in. It is a recreation area, a sort of curved, open-topped archway of finely woven twigs; its inner walls painted – by the bird – with charcoal taken from burnt trees. (There are always black charred stumps in Australian forests.) The floor of the theatre is pounded smooth by the dancing of the male. The female bird takes no part in all this. The 'toys' may be blue flowers, blue feathers, a bit of blue ribbon, a plastic spoon, bottle top, glass – anything that is blue. In Queensland spotted bower-birds choose white toys – shells, bones, flowers, etc.

This was the first of many good bird outings with Elaine; and every time Reggie was in Australia she and Alec took us out. My best nature adventure happened on a blustery early spring morning when he arranged for us to go to Ku-Ring-Gai Chase to see a white-cheeked honey-eater. It seems this little bird, ordinarily very shy, becomes brave while it is building its nest, and takes the fluff it needs from any available source – the soft down in koala bears' ears, sheep's wool, hair from human heads and loose strands from woollen jackets and socks. Alec was keen that we should see this happening. Pat and Neville Manning drove us out to the wide open bush territory where he had ordered us to meet him, and a warden led the party to a spot nearby where the little bird was building its nest. Each of us was given a piece of tow and told to stand still, hold it out, and the builder would come and take it for its nest. Sure enough it arrived and took some from everyone, particularly from Pat, who is not the least interested in birds. But it would not come to me, the keen birder. Alec was furious with it. When the party moved off to the cars, I stayed back, obeying a call of nature, and retired behind a bush. The little honey-eater immediately followed me and throughout my visit it removed tufts of

Pat Manning and a white-cheeked honey-eater

wool from the tweed skirt I was wearing. A triumph. Alec was pleased, but less so later when we had our lunch at a picnic table, watched by kookaburras. 'Beware,' he said 'they are great thieves.' As he spoke a big brute of a bird swooped down and swiped the entire piece of chicken-wing he had been about to bite into.

A montage of special pleasures remembered from my first Australian visit includes a box full of Western Australian wild flowers sent me by Cynthia Robinson, a school friend who married a farming botanist, ornithologist and naturalist. They were unlike any flowers I had ever seen – kangaroo-paw, apparently made of bright red and green felt, blue orchids that looked like patent leather, and other delights. And I met a man at a party who asked me if I liked orchids and before I could say 'not much' promised to send me some. They arrived, a dozen sprays of them grown in his garden. On that scale I managed to enjoy them; but they never seem quite real – I prefer a daisy. And shirley poppies. I bought them from flower-stalls run by women, like the 'flower-girls' who once had basket stands in Piccadilly; and for about five shillings I could buy a fat fistful of tightly-shut grey-fuzzed shells that fell open, and off, in the warmth of my room, and allowed crumpled buds of yellow, white, pink, orange and red to unfold into flowers. Also in the montage: white butterfly yachts in dozens below my windows, on Saturdays and Sundays there could be hundreds; Granny Smith apples, the first I had seen, crisp, juicy and clean to the bite; milk paid

77

for by metal tokens bought from the milkman at the beginning of the week and left in a little milk box outside the front door. (And I had never before met an incinerator-chute down which I could throw the rubbish. It all went down to a fire at the bottom, but bottles and tins had to be left tidily in the cupboard that housed the chute).

I regret that while playing there I never mastered a rock-firm Australian accent. I could say a line here and there in what I think was the right way, but I never felt secure enough to speak Australian on stage. I was always able to hear the accent I wanted to reproduce, but it stayed in my head and came out wrong when I spoke. I discussed the problem with a Sydney taxi-driver – in Australia it is good manners when you are travelling alone to sit in front with the driver who is usually full of conversation – and was told by him: 'It seasy; all you have to do is downt owpen yer maouth – and lean on somethin'.'

I wrote a sketch, 'Telephone Call', set in Sydney, for Bettina Welch to use in her own country, and she successfully performed it on stage and television. But at home and in America – for my own use – I transposed the scene to England, and that is how I recorded it for the gramophone. Now when I am no longer performing monologues I believe I have at last acquired an approximate Australian accent. But I am not as fluent in it as I am in 'Sarth Effrican'; that strange distortion of English comes to me without difficulty; I am sorry it is not more familiar to British audiences, for I would love to have used it on the stage.

Bill Blezard and I enjoyed ourselves at the Phillip Street Theatre. Audiences were warm and soon so were the spring days. The impact of Australia came to us both in a mixture of delight and disapproval. I cannot now remember Bill's precise complaints, which he told me about when we were on our own; but I was depressed by the emphasis on over-elaborate hats and dressing up that I met, not among friends, but at duty luncheons and charity functions. I was depressed by the litter abandoned in the countryside. We never went for a drive or walked in the bush near the roadside without coming upon bursting sofas, old bedsteads, refrigerators and, later, television sets. There was always a trimming of beer and Coca-Cola cans, plastic bottles and bags. (Oh yes, we have our own supply of litter in Britain, but not on such a scale or so generally distributed; and Australia is a big country.) We both were depressed by the quality of most newspapers – this was before *The Australian* began publication – and by the segregation at parties of men and women. But the kindness, the friendliness, the flowers and trees (to my surprise wattle turned out to be our mimosa and came in a variety of sizes and colours), the birds, the sun and the harbour, all came under the heading of delights.

For me Sydney has the most naturally attractive setting of any city in the world. San Francisco and Hong Kong may be contenders for the prize, but I put Sydney well ahead of both. I realise I am fortunate in having friends whose houses have clear views of the harbour, but Sydney is a steep and hilly city, and if you don't have a waterfront aspect it is still possible to find a room with a view over the roof-tops. Vantage points occur all over the suburbs. The place is full of surprises. Houses are built in unexpected places, against cliffs in gulleys where trees are preserved. A short dead-end street ends in a tiny yellow beach. You can find small plots of bush surviving among clusters of houses clinging to ledges, where intrepid architects and engineers have hung them. One such house in Vaucluse is approached down a driveway planted with low-lying flowers and small species of strawberries (like lengths of embroidered ribbon) between the cemented wheel-lines. The driveway is entirely supported by steel girders rising from the deep gulley underneath, and the house, built against the gulley wall, looks on to the tops of trees and bushes. A sensational house and an architectural achievement. To live in I prefer something less dramatic and greenery-enclosed, but to visit it was exciting and pretty.

Both Bill and I lived for letters from home. He devoured the blue flimsies that came from Joan, and kept them crumpled up in his pocket. He shared with me accounts of his two-year-old son Paul's developments and sayings. (His daughter Pooky was born later.) Before he left London, Bill and Joan took Paul to a church where the ritual was high – with incense and genuflecting. He stood between them in the pew and was much taken by the way a priest went down on one knee as he approached the altar; Paul accompanied his knee-bends with a clear, piping voice: 'Up *down* – Up *down* . . .'

Bill spent much of his time composing on the theatre piano, and towards the end of the run we wrote a farewell song – 'Thanks for having us, Phillip Street.' Not a dry eye in the house. We both felt a real sadness at the ending of a good, long visit, and both promised ourselves and the management to return in two or three years' time.

Reggie had arranged to come and join me at the end of my theatre season, and we were to have a holiday. We hoped to see something of the countryside. I asked Nancy and Vincent if they could suggest hotels where we might stay. They said: 'You can't stay in country hotels in Australia. There aren't any.' This was very nearly true at that time. They arranged for us to go to Queensland to stay with Vincent's cousin Joan, and her husband Barney Joyce, who breed Santa Gertrudis cattle on their station at Eidsvold; and Nancy got in touch with Sylvia and Bob Ritchie down in Victoria, who kindly invited us to spend a week with them at Delatite, near Mansfield.

Reggie's arrival in Sydney, early in October before the show finished, coincided with a spell of cold wet weather and gales. The harbour stayed the colour of dirty dishwater for six days; then at last the sun came out and revealed it in all its sparkling blue wonder of which I had told him in my letters. My friends made him welcome at once; Jim Dickson took him to the races; Nancy and Vincent invited him to dine; Elaine Hutcheson drove him out to the country for a day of bird-watching. He also helped me cope with packing up my stage stuff, with my taxes and an exit permit. Helped? He did everything for me.

Before we went to stay with Nancy's and Vincent's friends and relations, we had a few restoring days, after the wind-up in Sydney, at a small resort off the Queensland coast. 'Downstairs' (Dorothy Jenner) had suggested Hayman Island, and got in touch with the manager of the hotel there and told him we wanted to be as quiet as possible. I added that we would like a 'lodge' (it was a cottage hotel) well away from the main building, please, and safely out of range of bar noises, and of one of my least favourite modern menaces – piped-in music. This intrusion of privacy is bad enough in America, where surely it originated; but now the meaningless background wall-paper sounds have proliferated all over Britain too. At that date it seemed more difficult to avoid in Australia than anywhere else I had been. So strongly did I feel about it that I wrote a lyric, soon after my 1959 visit to Australia, that Dick Addinsell set to a march-tune.

It remains a deeply felt plea:

> Bring back the silence,
> The silence we once knew,
> Before unending music was unendingly piped through
> To restaurant and office,
> Railway station and to store,
> Bring back the silence, we beg
> And we implore.
> It pours into the Ladies' Room through cleverly hidden vents,

It pours along the corridor and into the Gents
(They tell me).
Bring back the silence to stairway, lift and hall,
For we who care for music do not care for it at all . . .

Hayman Island was a successful mixture of simplicity and sophisticated creature-comforts. For those who wanted diversion there was sailing, tennis, dancing and social life. For those of us who only wanted quiet it was easily available. As we hoped, our lodge was the one farthest away from the main building, and it had good beds, pleasant, uncluttered décor, space and its own verandah, with white wicker-work chairs and a table. We were looked after by a young cheerful sun-tanned staff in informal dress – shorts for the men, brief cotton frocks for the girls and sandals for everyone. The clear pale turquoise sea was less than a hundred yards from our verandah. Reggie and I loafed, read, meandered slowly, exploring the tracks that went around and across the island. None of the other guests appeared to walk, and we never met anyone else on our travels. But we saw white cockatoos with lemon-yellow crests, a beach curlew, whimbrel and great white-breasted sea-eagles, crying their sad cries. One evening at sunset we came face to face with a pheasant (it seemed a long way from Norfolk), and on that same walk three sinister black fins like conning-towers appeared out of a flaming red sea. Shark! We came away after five days, rested and ready for what turned out to be a rough ride in a bucketing motor launch over bumpy waves to the mainland. Our visit to Eidsvold Station, three hundred miles north-west of Brisbane, began the following day.

I had no idea what a cattle station in Queensland would be like, but because of early impressions, inspired by those paintings of bare Australia, I imagined it might be set in harsh, flat, treeless and sand-coloured country with an infinite horizon. I visualised great herds of cattle putting up dust clouds, in the middle of which would be a house of some kind. I know there are such places, but Eidsvold Station is not one of them.

It was a hot, rainy dawn as we drove to Brisbane Airport, heavy and unpromising, but jacaranda trees were coming into their bluebell-blue blossom, and pelicans bobbed on the river. As the plane rose, lush green countryside, red soil and more rivers appeared below us. The sun came out, and sugar-cane fields showed a green more vivid than the meadows. It was a summer's day when we landed on the little airfield at Monto. In 1959 the population was one thousand seven hundred and sixty. Joan Joyce was there to meet us, standing by her station-wagon, with her head tied up in a cotton scarf printed with the Eidsvold brand mark, a J set in an inverted half-circle.

On the whole I find first impressions are reliable; that you can recognise someone's essence and identity before you know much about their character. Joan had an almost non-committal casualness, as if she had known us for ever. I guessed she was a person of perception and feeling although in spite of the immediate friendliness, she did not then reveal much of her true self. I was right. She is what my Nanny used to call 'deep'. I liked the way she threw off amusing and amused comments that had to be caught on the wing. Nothing was underlined. We three, she, Reggie and I, were soon at ease with each other. At the top of a hill a few miles out of Monto she stopped the car and said this was where we would have our picnic. The view went on for miles, the silence was heartening.

At Eidsvold Station Barney Joyce came down the steps from the grey-painted house to welcome us. He reminded me of the young Douglas Fairbanks senior of my youth. He had the same elegant, fine hair-line moustache. He is Irish, stocky, smiling; a swashbuckler and a romantic – with flair, panache and charm. He wears his cattleman's wide-brimmed hat with a dash and a difference. His clothes are unconventional, collected by him wherever he goes – Texas, Hawaii, Sydney, London. He had bright pink shirts before they were fashionable, and wears splendid waistcoats made of skin or brocade, and yellow linen safari-suits. His style suits him exactly. He is a cattle-man of distinction, well-known in Queensland where his bull-sales at Eidsvold are renowned for being 'occasions'; in 1977 he put on an exhibition of Australian painting as an accompaniment to selling bulls. A born showman.

On our first visit to Eidsvold Barney and Joan were still living in the old rambling homestead. High hedges of bougainvillea in all pinks, purples, reds and whites rioted on one half of the front lawn and along the drive. A verandah ran round three sides of the house, and the part facing west was shaded by grape-vines. It was early spring, with heavy dews and cold dawns before the sun rose high enough to warm the day. A grey thrush nested in a tree just outside the rooms where Reggie and I slept, and woke us daily with its sweet shrill piping notes. We breakfasted on the back verandah while bee-eaters, locally known as rainbow-birds, sat on the wires and made sudden swoops on the insects and bees in Joan's flower-beds. I wore a shawl over my

Barney and
Joan Joyce

dressing-gown, and had been glad of a hot-water-bottle the night before.

The old house where Joan and Barney lived until Gilford Bell built them a new one nearby is a typical Queensland construction on stilts. Part of the large area under the building served as a useful place for storing trunks, stores, an extra ice-box and household goods. The other part made an open-air living-room. A thickly growing creeping plant climbed up some of the support pillars; it was a more robust and far more prolific kind of jasmine than I've seen at home, starred with little white flowers of delicious scent that filled the night air with fragrance. It was there that Joan and I sat and sewed and learned more about each other's lives and interests and ideas.

It was in this garden room, on the second night of our visit, that Joan gave a small buffet dinner for us to meet some young farming neighbours. Del and Robin Hart drove over, with their baby son Cameron lying in a basket at the back of the car, and David McCord, at that time a bachelor, who appeared to be at least seven foot tall, came alone carrying a suitcase. I saw him arrive and supposed he was going to stay the night. After drinks upstairs in the breeze-way open room hung with pictures by Nolan and Pugh and other Australian painters that Reggie and I were beginning to recognise, we went below for food. When we had eaten I noticed that Robin and David had disappeared; I supposed they were talking farming somewhere else, but suddenly I was aware of suppressed whispers, and with a bound they came in, out of the darkness of the garden into the bright lights, dressed as two Ronald Searle St Trinian's schoolgirls in gym-slips, wrinkled black stockings and battered school hats. They sang, unaccompanied, a song made up by David. The surprise was total; particularly mine. It was the friendliest of tributes, and much appreciated. We made them do it all over again, and then I was invited to contribute, and the evening turned into an entertainment. I did some monologues and songs. It was as well none of those present was too disturbed by the slippings in and out of key that I am sure I do when unsupported by an accompaniment – for I don't have perfect pitch (but nor did they). Bravely I sang on, hoping.

Ada, an elderly aboriginal woman much loved by the Joyces, who had lived most of her life on the station and was now retired to her own rooms behind the house, was with us that evening. She bowed in her chair with groans of laughter and was a most rewarding audience. When the party was over we moved into the garden to see off the Harts and David McCord. A full moon was up in an inky blue sky and the grass was heavy with cool dew. Cameron Hart, aged one, had slept undisturbed throughout all our gaieties.

Until this visit I had never dared wear trousers, because I know that I am not flat-bottomed or long-lined enough to look well in them. But because we were going for picnics in the bush Barney lent me an old pair of his trews, and I got the feel of the things. Since then I have never been without trousers in my wardrobe. Indeed I now wear them most of the time. Recently Reggie counted the pairs hanging in my cupboard and they far outnumbered his. I looked decidedly curious in Barney's, for he is not as tall as I am, and he wears his low on the hip. (I still look pretty funny in trousers, even those that are made to fit me, but I no longer mind; I try to wear very long tunics and jackets to cover my hips. I have settled for eccentricity, and very comfortable it is too.)

It is a pity that neither Reggie nor I ride, because Joan is a great rider, and she and Barney hold that to see the Queensland bush and its birds properly you should view them from the back of a horse. Nevertheless, from on foot we saw a great many birds new to us, and Joan let us take their car to a distant creek where red bottle bush was in flower, and there in the strong evening light, at about five in the afternoon, we added more and more birds to our growing list. Barney's old trousers got a lot of wear.

Leaving Eidsvold after our perfect holiday of good weather in new and fascinating country, and above all with kind new friends who already had become part of our lives, was a wrench. We took a local train, joined the sleeping-car train at a junction, and went on to Brisbane. I remember three things about that journey. In the local train we moved slowly through bush-land, much of it gently burning, but so familiar is the sight to Australians that no one except Reggie and I looked up to see whole tree-trunks smouldering in orange fires, and spiralling blue-grey smoke and occasional little tongues of flame leaping when a breeze fanned the embers. All the way to the junction we saw kangaroos, and one jumped companionably beside us, keeping up with the slow train. The third memory is of a paperstall entirely stacked with cartoon magazines – adult stories-in-pictures for non-readers.

Next day we flew down to Melbourne and spent three nights at our favourite Australian hotel, the Windsor, before going to stay with the unknown Ritchies at Delatite, about a hundred and twenty miles away. The Windsor is far more dignified, traditional and spaciously comfortable than any hotel left in London, and in those days it was staffed by dear and welcoming porters and chambermaids who looked after us like old family friends. The very first time we stayed there I noticed that the drip-dry shirts I had washed for Reggie were not hanging where I had left them in the shower. I asked Myrtle the chambermaid if she knew where they could be. 'Yes,' she said. 'They didn't look nice enough rough-dried, so I've just taken them along to the pressing-room to give them a little touch of the iron.' How is that for service?

The high spot of that first visit to Melbourne was a grey, cool morning spent in Sherbrooke Forest where we were taken to look for a lyre-bird, an elusive creature of myth and mystery – and a dozen different voices. It is the Mike Yarwood of the bird world and a magnificent performer, not easy to see; and I know many Australian birders who have never seen one. It is a species of pheasant, a not very interesting-looking dark brown bird. When the male displays its lyre-shaped tail, in the way a peacock displays its fan, it becomes exotic and almost beautiful. Unlike the peacock, whose voice is hideous, the lyre-bird, in all its variations, sings gloriously. Our guide was an expert birder. He knew exactly where the lyre-bird was likely to be found, and within five minutes of leaving his car we saw *four*, including an old bird, well known to him, which stepped up on to a fallen log within eight feet of where we were standing, and gave us a virtuoso performance for ten minutes. It sang in its own loud sweet shout of a song, embroidering the air with melodies; it laughed as a kookaburra, rang as a bell-bird rings, imitated several other local birds and ended by giving us an instantly recognisable blackbird's song. The Australian blackbird sings pleasantly but not quite as mellifluously as ours does at home. Here it is the most confident of performers; there it sounds slightly apologetic.

Sylvia Ritchie telephoned and told us that her eldest son Geoffrey would collect us from the Windsor, and that she had arranged for him to take us to Healesville Reserve on the way to Delatite. Here is another nature note: at Healesville we looked up at a gum tree, over a hundred feet high, and saw koala bears, doped to the eyes as they always are, due to a diet of gum leaves which are high in soporific properties; or so we believe. We were taken by the warden (sometimes it pays to have a face made familiar by the movies and television) and allowed to see, and feel, a duck-billed platypus. What can the Almighty have been thinking of when he designed this curious beast – an egg-laying, aquatic, furred mammal? He was satiny to the touch, and I admired his webbed feet, apparently shod in the same fine leather from which my grandmother's French gloves were made. He was taken out of his straw-filled box, and I was given the dubious honour of holding him. His heart thudded under my hand, but the look in his eye was impersonal. The warden pointed out his defensive weapons, a pair of nasty-looking sharp spurs at the back of his webbed feet. We drove on through country unlike any we had yet seen in Australia, the trees bigger, the land greener, and more open than the parts of New South Wales and Queensland we had already been to. Some of it reminded us of Cumberland, but on a gigantic scale.

Pictures of pleasant places are set in my mind's eye, and I do not know whether the view I now have of Delatite comes from my first sight of it or from some other visit. As we drove up the avenue, through a dark tunnel of giant conifers with branches sweeping to the ground, we could see ahead of us the house, bathed in sunlight. It is one of those period Australian country houses which I had read about and admired in early prints. It sits in a frilling of low, thick-set bushes – rosemary and lavender perhaps – a broad-faced, single-storey building, cream-stone-coloured, with a pale grey roof below which a second roof, like an extra skirt, overhangs the verandah supported by ornate white-painted, iron lacework arches. The arches caught my eye and caused me to exclaim with pleasure; surely iron lace is one of the most successful Victorian inventions.

We arrived late in the afternoon, and the sun, far down the sky, lit the house, like footlights in a theatre, with a romantic and becoming

Delatite

glow. The double front door, flanked by a pair of tall windows on either side – a design as simple and pleasing as a child's drawing, apart from the exuberance of the iron lace – stood wide open. At first the house appeared to be small and compact, but inside all is spacious and high-ceilinged, and there are out-buildings and additions that make it a house of some size.

Sylvia was smaller than I had imagined, and shyer. Her thick bobbed hair, that fell into her eyes, was dark brown. When she smiled her face lit up like a young girl's. It still does. Until we came to know her better it was not easy to discover how entertaining, informed and well-read she is, for she is modest and has an inadequate opinion of her own value. But all who know her are fully aware of her sterling worth, as well as of her talents for cooking and the growing of flowers. To sum up her quality in my favourite word: she is good. Sylvia, like Alec Chisholm in Sydney, was not used to actresses, and after we had come to know each other she admitted that when Nancy had asked her if she would invite Reggie and me to stay, she had not known quite what to expect. Was I more alarming than she had feared? No, she said, because I didn't seem like an actress. I suggested this might be because I had never felt like anything but someone on to whom entertaining had been unexpectedly thrust. The actresses I knew were human beings first – or most of them were; but perhaps if one wasn't familiar with stage people one might, thanks to the press, the movies and romantic novels, expect to find them striking attitudes and appearing larger than life. Come to think of it there are one or two who never seem quite complete until they are on stage speaking lines, and there are still a few actresses and actors who strike attitudes and appear to be larger than life; but fewer than there used to be. Economics makes sisters and brothers of us all, with the possible exception of pop stars.

Sylvia took us out into her garden on that cool, clear early summer evening. The pear tree in the middle of the lawn was still frothing with green-white blossom; lilacs, guelder roses and rhododendrons were in flower, and the most prolific pale mauve wistaria cascaded from the arches of the verandah where we sat, after a walk between box hedges along flagged paths sniffing the delicious scents of roses. That non-sense I had always heard about flowers only smelling properly in Britain had long been exploded by the delicious rose-smells I met in Africa and in Australia.

Bob Ritchie came back in his Land-Rover from doing some jobs on the property, and joined us. He wore a blue shirt exactly the same colour as his eyes; a thick-set man of attractive country looks. He walked with a heavy limp, the result of being wounded in New Guinea during the last war. Both he and Sylvia, who are our contemporaries, belong to the generation of Australians who still feel strong links with England. Bob's years at Cambridge in the 1920s had been a time to remember with pleasure. All the three Ritchie sons came to England for a time after they had left school, and their memories, too, were good ones. But no longer, I think, among the general public are there the ties that once bound Australia and Britain so closely together. Geographically America and the Far East are more immediate, and understandably those are the directions in which Australians now look. All the same it is often London that first beckons to travelling young Aussies when they set out to see the world. David Ritchie, the youngest son, now lives in England.

Geoffrey Ritchie, who farmed with his father (he and his brother Robert have taken over the property) was about to build his own house on a site with enormous views of paddocks and far hills, a mile or two from Delatite. At that time he was living with his parents while his wife Kay was in Melbourne expecting their first child. He is a quiet young man, like his mother in looks, and with the same shy manner.

The baby he and Kay were expecting was a son, and by the time we got back to Delatite in 1963 Simon was a beguiling small boy of four with pale salmon-pink gold hair and an irresistible friendliness. For some reason he took a shine to me and decided I was Reggie's mother. At that age one's mother is the ideal, so I was flattered.

'Shall we go and see your mother?' he asked Reggie.

'She's writing letters in bed. Better not disturb her.'

'I'd *like* to go and see your mother,' he said and firmly led Reggie to my bedroom. He had just mastered hopping on one leg. 'Would you like to see me hop?' 'Yes, I would.' Pause while he remembered how to do it and then with a look of concentration he set off, his fair hair rising and falling with each hop. He got to the end of the room. 'Would you like to see me hop again?' 'Er – yes – I'd love to.' There was no end to this game; he was willing, given an audience, to hop for ever. I found a way of drawing his attention to some other ploy and dragging Reggie by the hand he went off to pursue it.

Reggie and I went to the sheds with Bob to watch the visiting shearers, who are contracted yearly to visit the property at this season, exercise their skill in stripping, at high speed, the fat fleeces from sheep held between their knees. I found it an exciting but disquieting sight – a shed buzzing with electric cutters wielded by tough young men hell-bent on beating each other's record. We were assured that the sheep didn't mind being flung on to their backs, gripped firmly and clipped all over, sometimes with little nicks that drew tiny spirts of blood; but it didn't look much fun for them. I believe the job is paid according to the number of fleeces clipped. The day before we arrived one young bruiser, all muscles, curls and surly face, had achieved a record total of two hundred and eight fleeces.

Now that all the Delatite visits have begun to merge, I can't remember exactly what happened in which year. One morning Bob drove us in his Land-Rover to the paddocks to look at his herd of Herefords. As we got there a pair of colossal bulls began a battle. They stood glaring at each other, moved backwards at a stately pace and then, wham! – they charged each other, square head on square head, grunting. The sound of the impact was hideous. The sheer mindless ferocity of the encounter of two solid bulks of flesh and bone prompted by animal instincts of rage turned me away. Bob had immediately dispatched a man to fetch the dog capable of separating the beasts (some kind of bull-dog trained to hang on to the upper lip of a fighter until he stops fighting), but the battle stopped as quickly as it had begun, and the creatures lost their fury and began to eat grass.

As a nice contrast, Sylvia showed us, in a low, thickly-leaved bush

Sylvia Ritchie birding at dawn

by the front door, the smallest nest I have ever seen. It was made by a grey-fantail and was the size of an egg-cup. In it were three tiny eggs. I believe it was our enthusiasm for birds that fired Sylvia's newly-awakened interest. She had begun to watch birds, encouraged by Claude Austin, a considerable authority in Australian ornithological circles, but had rarely had anyone on the spot to share in her discoveries, and there we were, for a week anyway, binoculars ever at the ready round our necks (we never went out without them) and a bird book to hand. Sylvia outstripped our knowledge years ago and has become an expert.

I must confess, however, that I had to get used to her performance at the wheel of a car. I know I am a tiresome passenger because, having been a driver myself, I am acutely aware of the road and all who travel it, as well as the niceties of being in the correct lane and the right use of the indicators. Also I am not fond of speed. I believe I tend to push myself back against my seat as a sort of unspoken plea to go slower. Reggie says I draw in my breath a good deal, too. On a later visit to Delatite it was Sylvia who collected us from the Windsor. She is one of those intrepid drivers who, when they speak to the passenger sitting beside them, looks him in the eye. I don't think this is a good idea. We set off briskly and moved erratically, I thought, out of the way of trams; in some cases only *just* out of the way. As we travelled through the Melbourne suburbs I closed my eyes, not daring to look. When I couldn't resist peeking I kept my gaze firmly on the way ahead hoping this might influence Sylvia to do the same. It wasn't so bad when we got out into the country, but we didn't always seem to be on our side of the road when we turned corners. Needless to say we arrived unscathed. I must have been braver than usual because, until I told her later of my doubts, she had been unaware of them and was distressed to think she had been the cause of my unease. Why hadn't I said something? Next time I must speak up. And ever since then if her driving has seemed to me to be on the daring side I have spoken up. She has never shown any signs of resentment; that is evidence of an angelic nature. People do not like to have their driving criticised. At his mother-in-law, Gladys Cooper's, memorial service Robert Morley told us that there were only two subjects about which her family was never allowed to find fault. One was her making of marmalade – known, of course, as Cooper's – the other her driving. We gathered this was of the spectacular, con-versational kind, with hands-off-the-wheel gestures. Much as I admired and was devoted to Gladys, I am grateful that I was never called upon to ride in a car of which she was the driver. I never saw Sylvia take her hands off the wheel.

Jim and Margaret Darling came to spend a night when we were at

Delatite. He had retired from being a most successful Headmaster of Geelong Grammar School and was then Chairman of the Australian Broadcasting Company. With Sylvia and Bob we sat up late that evening and discussed conscience and integrity. We talked about Lord Reith, Malcolm Muggeridge and Sybil and Lewis Casson (friends of the Darlings and ours), all of them people of convinced beliefs; some wiser than others in what they said in public. The Cassons, as I saw it, were the only two under discussion who clearly demonstrated by the way they lived the Love I recognise as the only true power.

At breakfast the next morning we sat on at the round dining-room table in the window talking about *Honest to God*, a book that at that time was causing controversy and some distress among orthodox Christians. Jim thought that the author, John Robinson, had over-simplified the concept of God. He seemed, said Jim, to think we could almost do *without* God. As I had read the book and saw it in a different light I was amazed by Jim's view of what the Bishop had written. The whole point, it seemed to me, was summed up in the quotation he gave from Dietrich Bonhoeffer's writings: 'God as the very ground of my being.' I thought Jim suspected simplicity; he seemed to want his religion to be complicated. This was the very opposite of the way I felt, but, in spite of the difference of our approach to the discussion, I believe we both enjoyed stretching our minds, and from time to time whenever we meet we have continued to do so. Jim and Margaret come into our lives at infrequent intervals, but from my point of view every meeting has been a good one. Sometimes talking to those one respects, but who see from another position, is useful exercise, and I find it helps me to rethink more clearly instead of repeating old familiar arguments.

CHAPTER SIX

And New Zealand

I MADE three extensive tours of Australia in 1963, 1966 and 1969, and during those years I played in Adelaide, Brisbane, Canberra, Hobart, Launceston, Melbourne, Perth and Sydney. Reggie was with me a good deal of the time and also when I toured New Zealand and played in Auckland, Christchurch and Wellington.

My second tour began with an engagement in Perth, where Reggie and I arrived from Hong Kong and were met at some unearthly hour by Simon Wincer, our new manager from Sydney. He was about twenty-two, tall and attractive with a sense of humour and auburn hair. He was also unflappable and very good at his job. He delivered us safely to the splendidly Edwardian Esplanade Hotel, where, even as late as 1966, the parlour-maids in the dining-room still wore starched aprons and caps. Simon was a happy addition to the company. He appeared to be amused by both Bill and me and watched the performances from the prompt corner with appreciative attention. By this time Bill had begun to branch out in his solo 'spot', and for the first time gave in public the parlour performance he had hitherto only given in private. This was his virtuoso display of piano-playing from unexpected positions. First he got into the lotus position, seated below the keyboard, and with his hands on a level with his nose, he played Chopin's Minute Waltz. Then (and this was the more spectacular act) he played a boogie-woogie piece from the horizontal, flat on his back; this time his hands were high above his head, hidden from his view by the jutting keyboard. He and Simon got on well, and Simon, years younger than either of us, became the father-figure of the troupe, looking after our welfare and managing our performances with care, craftsmanship and good humour.

It was on this tour that Reggie recommended to Bill the foam shaving-cream he had begun to use. Bill bought himself a can of the compressed stuff. Next day Simon, who was in the same digs, heard wild cries coming from the bathroom, where Bill, never in control of inanimate objects other than pianos, had pressed the button and

*Bill's party
piece*

released a flood of sudsy foam from a container that would not turn off. Bill and the bathroom were white with sweet-scented fluff. Simon helped to restore some order.

I also remember the picture of Bill and Simon on a farm in Western Australia where we all went one Sunday, both of them astonished by the wonder of cows and sheep, as if neither had ever before seen such animals. I mentioned this. 'Not *close to*,' they said; they were as fascinated as if the beasts had been lions and tigers.

Simon managed a second tour for us in 1969 and then came to London to work at the B.B.C. and I.T.V. as a trainee studio-manager. He returned home two years later and was soon directing television programmes. Now, as a freelance, he is a successful director of T.V. films, and is also writing scripts. He married a beautiful Melbourne girl, Christine, and they live with their three small children a few miles out of the city.

It was always winter-into-spring when I toured out there, and I remember with shivers the uniform cold and draughts back-stage everywhere we went. I also have iced memories of a bathroom, opening out of a frigid bedroom in the old South Australia Hotel in Adelaide,

*Simon and Christine
Wincer at their wedding*

where the louvred windows, geared to long hot summers, were permanently fixed at 'open'. Through slanted slats teasing winds had easy entry. A hot bath at the end of a working evening was a luxury I looked forward to, but didn't get at the old South Australia. As I paid more for that bedroom and igloo of a bathroom than I had ever paid in any other hotel in my life – with the exception of a night at the Savoy Hotel in London during our honeymoon, where at least we had a panoramic view of the Thames as well as a warm bathroom for the enormous price of £5! – I felt a sense of grievance. No sympathy from the reception desk clerk either when I asked, please, would it be possible to close those windy louvres. I was obviously looked upon as a pampered Pom who couldn't take a little cold weather. The coldest theatre was in New Zealand and, although I can't remember precisely where it was, I know that to go to the lavatory called for resolution, dire need and an overcoat before I could face the long glazed-brick corridor, down which blew a wind brisk enough to disarrange my hair. Winters in New Zealand were even nippier than in Australia. As I was frequently told: it is closer to the South Pole.

In Wellington we were warm as toast. Reggie's youngest half-sister

Laura, and her husband Bernard Fergusson were in residence both times we went to New Zealand. He was Governor-General, a job that his father, and *both* his grandfathers, had held before him. They invited us, and Bill, to stay at Government House, and we much enjoyed our visits. Bernard and Laura were a huge success in New Zealand, and the years they spent there were, I think, the time of their lives. Life at Government House was a rare experience for us, and we were fascinated by the variety of V.I.P.s who came to meals. One was a large smiling Polynesian dignitary, dressed in a neat wrap-around skirt that made him look like a cross between Bud Flanagan in drag and a hospital matron on her day off. He was agreeable and chatty; but a maharajah, with three almost entirely silent Indian ladies wearing cosy cardigans over their gauze saris, was not easy to talk to. He had on his flexible fingers a number of beautiful antique rings and for a short time these made a talking point. I tried several possible openings and in a pause he told me he was very, very, *very* keen on modern music. 'I know Benjamin Britten,' he said. 'So do I,' I said with pleasure, expecting the conversation to flower, but it came to a dead stop. At his end of the table, Bernard, who is not easily defeated, was having a thin time with two of the silent ladies. He ploughed on, remembering the names of Indians he had once met, and it was only when the Maharajah next to me overheard a familiar name and said: 'Yes – yes – I know who you mean,' that the conversation didn't entirely peter out. My admiration for Bernard and Laura, and all those who in the line of duty have to deal so often with unresponsive guests, sometimes with very little English, is great. Bernard is a naturally sociable man and makes more contact than most of us. His conventional military appearance is misleading; he is not only brave, but also poetic, romantic and an imaginative writer. *The Trumpet in the Hall* is one of the most delightful books of memories.

In New Zealand I was to speak as guest of honour of some women's organisation at the time when being a bird-watcher was still considered eccentric by those who weren't used to the idea. Botany was respectable, flower-finding plausible, but watching birds was too peculiar. There were a number of fancy-hatted women present. The President introduced me and, as if she were revealing a shameful secret, said: 'And I *believe* Miss Grenfell is a *bird-watcher*!' Cue for titters. I smiled bravely. 'Later when I get her in *private* I am going to ask her just what it is that a bird-watcher does!' Laughter. I couldn't wait for privacy. After thanking her for her kind welcome I said I'd like to relieve her

The Fergussons: Laura, Geordie and Bernard

anxiety right away. 'Bird-watchers,' I said, 'watch birds because they are interesting; because they are often beautiful: and because they are part of life.' This outspoken revelation caused embarrassment. Down went the eyes and everyone appeared to be counting the buttons on their blouses. To speak so freely in public, at ten-thirty in the morning, about life was as startling as if I had said a rude word or my knickers had fallen off. It took a little while before the audience trusted me not to go further than good manners allowed.

I can't pretend that my motive had been in any way altruistic. I was irked by what looked to me like lack of imagination, and my governessy reaction was self-indulgent. Nevertheless it broke through a barrier of reserve, and when it was time for questions they came thick and fast and some were even concerned with the watching of birds – and the celebration of wonder. New Zealand, like Australia, was very welcoming to us, and we both enjoyed our times there.

Being a bird-watcher is always a good way of making friends and seeing the countryside; this was particularly true in the Southern Hemisphere. In New Zealand we were shown local birds by both Dick Sibson and Graham Turbott, who together wrote *A Field Guide to the Birds of New Zealand*. We were handed on from new friend to new friend. Everywhere we went some kindly birder took us out. When Reggie was on an official tour with Bernard and Laura, I went to Piha Beach, near Auckland, where the cliffs are charcoal grey and black sands sparkle in the sun. I found myself crawling on my stomach into a dark, low-ceilinged cave to see, by the light of a torch, a tiny blue fairy penguin and its newly-hatched sparrow-sized chick. Both of them were furious with me for disturbing their quiet, and made small angry noises and threatening moves. Reggie had seen them on another occasion; while I was playing in Melbourne, Sylvia Ritchie took him to Port Phillip Bay to watch flocks of the little creatures come in on the evening tide to return to their nests in the sandy banks above the beach. It was dark when the magic moment arrived, but because it was the breeding season and the event is a famous tourist attraction, floodlights were trained onto the breaking surf at the water's edge. When the attractive little twelve-inch birds arrived, they jumped or were hurled out of the waves, reeled a little, shook themselves, ignored the lights and the crowds, and headed like a swarm of miniature waiters up the beach, doing their flat-footed comedy walk to their holes.

As I do at home in Britain I remember the cities I worked in as a performer by the calibre of their audiences. But why one place seems to produce quicker wits than the next is a mystery. So is the fact that the house on Monday may be brilliant – it often was – on Tuesday dim, good for subtlety on Wednesday, and so on. There was a time when Glasgow was a livelier theatre city than Edinburgh, and the reason was supposed to be because Glasgow was a port, more crowded, cosmopolitan and tougher than stately Edinburgh. In the last tours of my performing life I found both cities equally responsive and quick in the uptake. But one thing that never did change as I toured Britain was the necessity of slowing-up my speech whenever I went north of Birmingham. This was because my own southern tongue and the occasional Cockney accents I used in sketches were, in spite of television and radio, foreign to native Northerners. I had no such problem in Australia, Canada or New Zealand, where so many of the population originally came from Britain, and where even those great emigrants, the Scots, have had to become familiar with all forms of English as she is spoken.

Even so audiences in Australia do vary from state to state. No doubt the pace of life has something to do with it; the rat-race sharpens reflexes, and the larger and more pressurised the city the livelier and quicker-witted is the theatre audience. It follows that Sydney has the speediest uptake for satire and subtlety; or so I found it. Everywhere else I went the tempo had to be slightly adjusted. I discovered, as I had done with mixed audiences in hospitals and small units during the war, that if I started slowly with my clearest articulation, I could – when the house had grown used to the sounds I made – gently increase the tempo, so that by the time I got to Part Two of my programme I was up to my usual London/Sydney rate.

Canberra, essentially an international city, is another place where I had no need to adjust tempos. Its theatre is very modern – or was when I first played in it in 1966. It had a black interior, a shallow rake, and comfortably spaced seats upholstered in a plastic material that looked like white leather. I am grateful to say I had full houses during my brief seasons there (I returned three years later), for I was told that actors in plays that had not drawn large audiences found it discouraging to see through the gloom, the other side of the lights, empty seats that looked like white teeth in a giant black mouth.

Terry Vaughan was in command of the theatre, and when he took us to the airport for our flight back to Sydney the plane was late, and we sat in the sun reminiscing about old jokes and mutual television and radio friends at home in London. Diffidently he asked me if I liked riddles and puns. Yes. This was his own invention, and a splendid one it is:

Question: How do you tell a drunken Italian in an air raid that bombs are falling?

Answer: Hi, tiddly Eyetie – pom-pom.

Tasmania surprised us. We knew it was a beautiful island but it proved to be attractive too, and I loved the Regency look of some of the older houses. We were unprepared for the sophistication of the audiences that came to see us in Hobart and Launceston. Hobart has the oldest and prettiest theatre in the Commonwealth of Australia – a miniature 'grand' house. Bill's piano was dated 1880 and looked more impressive than it sounded. I believe the seats up in the circle were uncushioned, but that did not deter the crowds, and I am proud to boast that we had to put on an extra performance during our little season in the island's capital. In Launceston, a small town and not at all a 'show-biz' kind of community, we had the best general audience of any, including Sydney, that we played to in all our visits down-under.

But of all the cities in the Southern Hemisphere where Bill and I performed, Sydney remains our favourite. Perhaps it is because it was the first place where we worked that the congenial three-month engagement in one theatre still has a bright shine on it. We had time to settle in; it was then that I met friends who have remained so important to me; and what with the sun, the camellias, the cosy feeling of the funny little Phillip Street Theatre, the kindness of the management and stage staff and of Olga who dressed me, and the enduring loyalty of an audience that came again and again to see us – all of it adds up to make Sydney Number One in our chart. When I went back four years later I rang the overseas operator to put in a telephone call to Reggie in London. She took my name and number and said: 'Welcome home. I'm the one who handled your overseas calls when you were here before.' Small – and happy – world department. That little incident is another of the many reasons why I have special feelings for Australia – and Sydney in particular.

I seem to have managed to be in Sydney always at the time when rhododendrons, laburnums and violets were out in suburban gardens in what we in England would think of as an all-seasons mixture of flowers. (One travelling year Reggie and I experienced five springs one after another – in England, in London and up north in Cumberland; in America, down south in North Carolina and up north in Connecticut, and finally out on Long Island staying with Tommy and Mary when their cherry and pear trees put on a display of such frothing exuberance that we found ourselves, daily, standing and staring and singing praises.) 'Nothing can touch an English spring' is a patriotic boast and very nearly true. It is – as Kathleen Raine's poem celebrates it – a 'slow spring' and gives you time to watch its development. But spring anywhere is exciting. In Adelaide the city grows climbing geraniums of all colours up the standards of the telephone poles in its streets. In Sydney it comes with a burst of shrubs, and a glory of warm sunshine; and in the harbour the little white sails, that have kept up steady numbers all through the winter, proliferate and, come the spring, hatch out extravagantly.

In my 1963 and 1966 visits to Sydney I took a flat in a new block built right on the edge of the water on the tip of Darling Point. ('Surely,' wrote Leonard Gershe from Beverly Hills, 'it should be "Darling, don't point".') It was found for us by Bettina Welch, who had been my neighbour in Macleay Regis in 1959. Bettina is one of the world's most kindly helpers as well as being a good actress and a pretty woman. The flat belonged to her brother-in-law who travelled a good deal and was often away from home. From the big living-room where I sat opposite French windows leading on to a balcony directly over the water, there was an uninterrupted view of the harbour, almost as breath-taking as the view I'd had from the eighth floor at Macleay Street. It was from there, as I sat to have my breakfast and early supper from a tray after the show, that I watched the ferry-boats go by. They plied across the harbour, from suburbs on both shores, to bring workers to and from the business section of the city. An enchanting sight. Sometimes, before going to bed, I childishly stood up in my dressing-gown and waved across the darkness to the last ferry of the night on its way to Manly. It was never close enough for me to see if anyone waved back.

On the last night of my final appearance in Sydney, at the old Theatre Royal, I sang a farewell song Bill and I had written out of sentiment and affection for the ferry-boats:

> When I think of Sydney
> It isn't the Bridge I see.
> Kings Cross? Opera House?
> They don't speak to me.
>
> When I'm far away
> It's the Ferry-boats of Sydney
> That I long to see.
> I can do without those new buildings on the sky-line,
> Skyscrapers are not my line,
> It's the Ferry-boats I am mad about.
> They ride on the water – toys painted bright –
> They glide across the Harbour from morning to night
> To Taronga Park for the Zoo,
> Mosman and Kirribilli,
> In darkness they look like harmonicas at sea,
> Windows full of light.
> It's the Ferry-boats of Sydney mean Sydney to me.

The 'harmonica' line pleased me because it was exact, and every time I saw the boats it accurately confirmed the image.

When I am asked why I have fond feelings for Australia the answer is that I love the strangeness, the difference and vastness of much of the landscape I have seen; I love the midwinter sun that blessed us so often, particularly in New South Wales. The fact that audiences made me feel welcome with their opening round of applause before I made my first entrance, and gave me a feeling of belonging, also has something to do with it. But first and foremost it is because of the friends we made there.

If I were to draw an Australian friend-tree, on the lines of a family tree, it would start with Nancy and Vincent and grow up with many flowering branches, most of which trace back to the Fairfaxes.

They introduced us to their friends who in turn introduced us to *their* friends and so the tree has grown. The many branches are all of value to us – some of them – Clive and Yrsa Fitts, Beatrice Morrison and the Arrighis – haven't yet come into this book.

Clive has just retired from being an eminent heart-specialist. We first met on a bright late winter Sunday (my day off from the show I was playing in Melbourne) when he drove me fifty miles down the coast to Shoreham to meet Yrsa. He and I talked about everything under the sun. He is literate, excellent company, humble, with charming looks – another bow-tie man. He has a way of twitching the end of his nose like a rabbit when he speaks. We liked the same kind of books, and some time later he sent Reggie and me Eric Newby's *Short Walk in the Hindu Kush*. We matched this with Helene Hanff's *84 Charing Cross Road*; a fair exchange of two attractive books.

84 Charing Cross Road is an affectionate book of letters, funny and touching, written between the author in New York and the manager of a secondhand bookshop in London during the uncomfortable years just after the war, and continuing into the late 1960s. Friendship with the staff at Number 84 develops all through the book. It is a story that, if you need such a thing, restores faith in human nature; if you already know that there is more of man's humanity to man than Burns suggests it is a confirmation. I have yet to meet anyone who has read it who hasn't felt the better for it.

The Fittses came to London the summer that Helene Hanff's book was published in England. Reggie learned that she would be signing copies in Hatchard's bookshop during the week when we were taking Clive and Yrsa to see Peter Brook's circus setting of *A Midsummer Night's Dream* at the Aldwych. I wrote a note to the unknown Miss Hanff telling her that we loved (no exaggeration) her book, so did our Australian friends, and we would be delighted if she would join us all for dinner and the play. The answer was yes. It was a successful evening. None of us much liked the look of the production – the harshly-lit stark white cube in which the play was seen – nor all of the gimmicky clowning that went on, and yet the poetry seemed clear. The four confused lovers, sometimes so difficult to be amused at, were funny, and we enjoyed the *Dream* more than ever before.

Beatrice Morrison is a friend *via* Sylvia *via* Nancy, and lives on top of a wooded hill on a bluff above a bending river the colour of French *café au lait* – greyer than ours – in a cream-painted, single-storeyed house, called Killeavy, in a leafy garden. From her bed she can look down into trees that somehow grow on the cliff, and in spring she sometimes gets a direct view *into* birds' nests below her. The place, fast being encroached upon by the sprawl of outer Melbourne, is an oasis of greenery and flowers – wild orchids still grow in the grass – and birds.

In books I read as a child there were sometimes descriptions of a loved country aunt with rosy apple-cheeks and kindly wisdom, who was unchangeable, reliable and someone to whom one could turn for support and restoring confidence. That is a rough sketch of Beatrice. She is also a charmer of character and quality, has a beguiling young smile, a splendid enthusiasm for life itself, and a formidable intelligence. Beatrice and Sylvia have known each other since they were in their teens and are two of an exemplary kind.

When the first volume of *The Lyttelton Hart-Davis Letters* was published in 1978, we sent copies to Australia and knew without any doubt that Beatrice and Sylvia (and we hoped all to whom we sent copies) would get the same satisfying delight from reading it that we had. We were dead on target. Letters of appreciation and enthusiasm came winging back to London. Reading letters about the book, from Beatrice and Sylvia in particular, was almost as good as reading the exchanges between George Lyttelton and Rupert Hart-Davis.

'I know,' wrote Joan Joyce from Eidsvold, 'you will like my Arrighi cousins.' And we did. 'They are going to live in London for a time.' Eleanore (Nellie) and her two daughters, Luciana, then twenty, and Niké, just turned eighteen, arrived, found a flat, bought a small white beetle-shaped car and settled in. A few weeks later they knocked on our door. All three Arrighis looked like Botticelli girls, lithe, graceful and fine-boned, with long necks and enigmatic smiles. Their voices were reed-like, their laughter infectious, and the impact they made on Reggie and me was immediate. Through Luci and Niké we had an insight into a young and inventive world unfamiliar to us. We have a number of very likeable nieces and nephews – twenty of them, and forty great-nieces and great-nephews – but none of them quite as original and creative as these two Australian-Italians, whose father, until his death, had been the Italian consul in Sydney. Nellie was included in their expanding circle of new friends; and we had a warm place on the outer edge.

During their stay in London the decorative Arrighi sisters often came with their mama to see us in Elm Park Gardens; and each time they appeared in a new disguise. For instance they went through a twenties phase when both girls used dark lipsticks, and Niké frizzed her hair and took on a Betty Boop manner. That mood passed, and one day Reggie met her on a Number 14 bus dressed in a gingery-tweed Norfolk jacket and knickerbocker suit, with a small Homburg hat on her head and on her feet mountain-climbing boots. Reggie brought her home to show me. Niké knew her costume was as comic as we did, and revelled in the raised eyebrows and double-takes that her outlandish appearance had invoked. Perhaps this reads as if she had set out to shock; she hadn't. She was out to amuse herself and incidentally anyone else who appreciated the joke.

Another evening when Luci and Niké called to see us on their way to a party it was more difficult to pin-point the exact period of their costumes. Niké was still vaguely in her twenties phase, weighed down by necklaces, and I seem to remember a heavily-beaded satin shift, probably found at a thrift shop. Luci, with her brown hair brushed back off her high, smooth forehead, had on a dateless black dress to the ground, and around her elegant neck, a large white Elizabethan ruff made of stiffened pleated net. We assumed they were going to a fancy dress party. No, they said, just out to dinner; where, as Luci told us afterwards, she hadn't been able to eat anything because the ruff choked her. The girls seemed able to transform themselves from pink-cheeked rustic characters to pale sophisticates in a matter of hours. Their visits always provided us with visual surprises and, although some of their get-ups were not to our eyes as becoming as others, Luci and Niké never looked less than their own entirely original and endearing selves.

Both the girls draw well. Luci went to the B.B.C.'s Television Art Department, and, among other things, she designed three T.V. films for Ken Russell, won an Arts Council travelling scholarship to America, and returned to design sets for the feature film *Women in Love*, also for Russell. Niké, to earn money for her training at R.A.D.A., went to Paris and modelled for the house of Balenciaga.

When Niké first went off to Paris on her own both Nellie and Luci were concerned about her for she was pretty as paint and looked about fifteen. But she assured them she was quite capable of looking after herself. She took an apartment – it was a maid's room with only a tiny hand-basin in it – at the very top of a seven-storey building; she figured that none of her would-be gentlemen callers were likely to make the distance to her eyrie. She solved her no-bath problem by

Reggie and the Arrighis: Eleanore, Luciana and Niké

using the luxurious bathroom of a piano-player admirer in a nearby apartment house. As long as she heard music she knew all was well. As soon as it stopped she cried out: 'Oh, do please play that heavenly Mozart again.' It always worked.

Luci, for a change of pace, also went to Paris and modelled for Yves St Laurent, while Niké was still with Balenciaga. After her sabbatical, Luci returned to London and designed Schlesinger's *Sunday, Bloody Sunday*. The last picture she worked on in Britain was *Watership Down*.

After R.A.D.A. Niké became an actress and worked in all the media. It was while she was playing a nun in a movie that she left the studio, one Friday afternoon, still wearing her habit for the journey to Italy, where she hoped to stay with her mother for the holiday week-end. It was a period of go-slow strikes at the airport, and Heathrow was crowded with frustrated travellers standing in long queues. Getting away was doubtful; the week-end on the continent looked less and less likely. But not to Miss N. Arrighi. Smiling demurely she joined a queue – a youthful reverend sister who melted all hearts, and was at once pushed forward to the very front of the long waiting line – and got away on the first plane to Italy that left the tarmac. At Rome airport Nellie awaited her by the gate; bird-like cries of 'yoo-hoo' seemed to be coming at her from the unlikely quarter of a bouncing nun, who ran toward her at speed, squealing happily. If Niké's intention this time was to cause amazement, it succeeded.

Luci married Rupert Chetwynd and took on his ready-made family of five children from a previous marriage. Her own children, Aaron and Alalia (Lally) were born in London – two very individual characters with the looks and charm of their parents. I am Lally's 'courtesy' godmother (no church vows) and I take much interest in this budding artist – heaven knows in which direction she will go, but it will certainly be a creative one. Today the Chetwynds are based in Sydney – full circle for Luci – and Rupert wings his high-powered way circumnavigating the globe to carry out his international business commitments. Luci wrote to say that her dream is to live in a really romantic caravan plus wool-shed – Aaron is designing it for her. She is already playing a large part in the quickly progressing Australian film industry.

Nellie fell ill and Niké gave up her acting life to look after her mother until she died. At Nellie's funeral an old family friend said to her: 'Now dear, go out to Australia and find yourself a nice Italian.' As it happened she did go to Australia to stay with her aunt, began drawing again and successfully exhibited and sold her pictures. At that time they were strange, skilful but to my eye disturbing and sinister works. The few I saw did not reflect the character I thought I knew. But like her varied hair-styles and fancy dresses her drawings, which still sell, have changed, and I am told they would no longer frighten me. In Hong Kong on her way back to Europe she met her Italian, Paolo Borghese; they married, still live there and now have a small daughter.

Both the Arrighi sisters write us entertaining letters, illustrated with their economic and evocative line drawings. We keep in close touch. When last seen they still looked like Botticelli girls.

CHAPTER SEVEN

The Haymarket, Festivals and Small Theatres

APART from my season at the Lyric, Hammersmith, I only played three other times in London: at the Scala for a week of charity performances called *For Seven Good Reasons*, at the Queen's and, for me the most important of all, at the Theatre Royal, Haymarket.

The Theatre Royal is probably the prettiest, the most romantic and the most distinguished London theatre still standing and in full operation. It had a rule, recently cancelled, whereby only the name of the play – not the name of author or star – was allowed to be advertised on the side of the portico in the Haymarket. Ruth Draper was the first person to have her name up in lights because 'Ruth Draper' was the name of her entertainment. I believe I was the second, when my programme was called 'Joyce Grenfell'. Ruth commissioned Tom Van Oss to paint a small oil of the front of the house to record this particular claim to fame; Reggie arranged for photographs to be taken to prove my name had been up there too. Playing in that theatre gave me a sense of being part of theatrical tradition. All the great actors and actresses had worked there. But I wasn't an actress; I was neither flesh, fish nor fowl, difficult to pigeonhole. The name *diseuse* wasn't right; monologuist-singer was hideous. (At the B.B.C., although I never played the halls, my contracts came through the Variety Department.) There is no special name for whatever was my calling. To be allowed to tread the boards of an historical house like the Haymarket filled me with a sense of awe and, damn it, privilege. I enjoyed every moment of my three weeks' stay; the audiences poured in, and, speaking for myself, a good time was had. My only regret is that I didn't use the star dressing-room. This lovely spacious room is inconveniently situated on the third floor, and there are a great many steep steps to climb before you reach it. My quick changes, while Bill did his piano spots in each half of the programme, did not allow me time to go up so high and down again without losing my breath. I have always settled for comfort and convenience before grandeur, and happily

The Haymarket: my name in lights

used the Number Two dressing-room at stage-level. It was also easier for my visitors. All the same the Number One at the Theatre Royal is a pearl among dressing-rooms, and I am sorry I never occupied it.

In England, in between concert-tours, there were films, television and radio jobs, and a good deal of my spare time was taken up in writing new material for future programmes. I have never liked doing two things at once – playing in a film by day and working in a theatre by night – and I found it impossible to write and perform in the same period. First things first is a good rule, and I gave full attention to whatever claimed priority, not for reason of virtue but because I found it made sense. I also took part in the Aldeburgh and King's Lynn Festivals, and regularly went to both.

I have never lost the childhood pleasure of a first sight of the sea, and at Aldeburgh the first sight of the sea comes into view over the roof-tops, as you turn the corner by the parish church and descend the sudden and unexpected little hill that goes down to beach level. In Suffolk the East Anglian skies seem higher than elsewhere and because the sea is the North Sea it is more likely to be beige-grey than green-blue; but whatever colour it happens to be, for me it is the most romantic and somehow a more friendly sea than any other around our coasts. From the second-floor front bedroom that Reggie and I usually stay in at the Wentworth Hotel, we look out at it and on to the fisher-men's huts where fresh catches of crab, cod, plaice and sole are hauled up in metal bins from the little motor boats that take the men out to the fishing-grounds. We are usually in Aldeburgh for the Music Festival in June, and dawn breaks early at that time of year. On fishing days we are awakened by the sound of boats being pushed down over the shingle beach to the water, followed by the putt-putt of their engines starting up. Ordinarily I do not like being awakened by engines of any sort, but because it is part of the holiday pattern, there is something reassuring about those busy noises.

For Reggie and me Aldeburgh means a combination of special pleasures – people, music, sea, wild flowers, birds and Herbert Axell. Since his recent retirement he and his wife Joan live in a pink-washed Suffolk cottage a few miles up the coast road at Westleton, but when we first knew them, a long time ago, Bert was warden and the imagina-tive creator of the Royal Society for the Protection of Birds' reserve at Minsmere. Then they lived in a bungalow on the very edge of the marsh in close contact with all that went on in that wonderful birdy place. In his foreword to Herbert Axell's book *Minsmere, Portrait of a Bird Reserve*, Prince Philip wrote, 'We [the British] certainly lead the world in the conservation of wild-life. Minsmere, under the guidance of the author of this book, has made a quite exceptional contribution

With Herbert Axell

to the development of new techniques in the management of bird reserves.' We were witness to these developments and every year we had happy times with Bert exploring the site, and sitting in new and old hides observing birds we might never have spotted by ourselves. It was on a heavenly June day, as we walked along a narrow gravel track between head-high reeds on the marsh, that he pointed to a pair of marsh harriers, rare British birds that regularly nest at Minsmere. We put up our field-glasses just in time to see the male bird fling its catch of a field-mouse to the female who caught it in her talons as she flew below him. Sensational. Bert has added considerably to our birding life. He is a large man with a large heart and a handsome boyish face. He looks particularly splendid in a dark-blue knitted cap, jacketed in layers against the East Anglian winds, and hung about with a camera, telescope and his binoculars.

When I first went to Aldeburgh the Festival was still a small, family-like affair. Viola Tunnard had just become involved in it, and suggested that I should join her for a few days and go to some of the concerts. She took a room for me in the house where she lodged with other musician friends, and at once I was caught up in the atmosphere

At Minsmere 'the grass is as high
as an elephant's eye'

and interest in what was going on. The following year I took Reggie to Aldeburgh, and we have been there in June ever since.

In those days most of the performances took place, within walking distance of hotels and lodgings where visitors stayed, either in the undistinguished Jubilee Hall that sits with its back to the sea and its front opposite a builder's workshop in a narrow side-street, or in the parish church, or a mile or two away (just walkable) in the Working Men's Club at Thorpeness. For bigger orchestral concerts two beautiful churches, one at Blythburgh and the other at Orford, were called into use. At that time there was a sense of containment, the patrons came to know each other well by sight, and it was not unusual to come upon Benjamin Britten and Peter Pears, who with Imogen Holst founded the festival, carrying chairs, unloading music-stands and generally giving a practical hand in arranging the hall. A certain amount of informality and improvisation still prevailed.

It is difficult not to regret that when small and personal enterprises succeed, they tend to grow, spread and become much bigger; and then they need more and more organisation. The remarkable thing about the Aldeburgh Festival is that, although it is now internationally famous and operates on the grand scale, with its main venue five miles away at the Maltings Concert Hall in Snape, it has kept its special flavour; it is still an informal, country-seaside event – not at all towny – a genuine festive celebration. The same friendly feeling persists, and the same friendly faces appear, year by year, among those who act as ushers, or work in the Festival office, or come to the programmes. Most of the original patrons are now white-headed, but looking down from the high back rows of the auditorium (as I did in this year of writing) I saw below me a pleasing punctuation of darker heads among the snowy ones. In spite of the huge rise in the price of tickets young people are still coming to the concerts.

Thanks to the imaginative idea of the Prince and Princess of Hesse who established a fund that enables students who are interested in music to come for a week to attend rehearsals, performances and meet the artists – in return for which they help with some office work and in the general running of events – there is a guaranteed quota of young people at all the concerts. It is now the Hesse students who move the chairs around and help to clear the platform. They come from all over Britain, the United States and Germany, and every year seem livelier, more attractive, and more exhilarated about their good fortune at being part of such a festival. For years Reggie and I have met them at parties, given in their honour by Ben and Peter at the Red House. They wear a Hesse Student badge, so it is easy to spot them, and we talk to them whenever we have the opportunity. Their enthusiasm is refreshing. It is, as they have frequently told us, the time of their life.

When Ben was alive they had the privilege of watching him at work; he not only accompanied Peter and other soloists, but when he was well enough he also conducted. Peter carries on the tradition of student parties and contributes his great knowledge and musical understanding that the young can draw on in the same way; and now that Slava Rostropovich has become a valued part of the Aldeburgh scene he also adds his own particular magic. When you are young it is good to have heroes. I still have mine.

The keynote of the Festival is its quality. Benjamin Britten established the standard of excellence – he knew no other – and this is carried on by Peter Pears and Slava Rostropovich. Performers invited to take part continue to aim (as they have always done at Aldeburgh) at doing better than their best. This is as true of the great names as it is for those who are starting their careers.

When Ben invited me to give one of my programmes, as part of the Festival, it was the accolade of my professional life. Like the students I too had respect and admiration for him. The demanding standard he

With Benjamin Britten and Peter Pears the day I sang my tribute

expected made me, like others before me, want to produce the best of which I felt capable. I worked harder, practised longer, honed and polished my programme, and as I now realise, instead of trusting to the work already done, I fussed on, concerned about the impression I hoped to make, so that when the night of the concert arrived I felt stale and uninventive. But I was asked to come and be part of the Festival again, and that time I had more sense and less egotism and made a better job of it. It was the year of the Festival's twentieth anniversary, and Bill and I wrote a song in praise of Ben and Peter with a recitative aria, full of puns on Ben's name – *bene, beneficial, benefactor, benefit, beneficent,* and even *Big Ben*. I didn't dare sing the piece 'cold' in the performance without showing it first to the subjects of its praise, and on the day of the concert Bill and I went up to the Red House and sang it to them. Twice. I think they were pleased by our little tribute. Ben gave me an affectionate hug and said he had been much moved. Peter was equally responsive. This made me feel a lot less apprehensive about performing the piece in public that night. Again it was encored.

For some reason I had to go up to London that year in the middle of the Festival, and while I was there Bill and I made a gramophone record of the song, and I took back with me a copy for Ben and Peter. Finding the front door of the Red House open I left the package, with a covering note, on the hall table. There was complete silence after this, and of course Bill and I wondered and didn't know quite what to think. It wasn't until at least five years later that the little package was discovered, still unopened, at the back of a cupboard in the front hall. Ben's letter after it was found made up for all my wonderings.

Both of my Festival concerts took place in the Jubilee Hall, for which I have a fond feeling. It is the size I enjoy – the front row is within easy touching distance of the stage and there is no need to use a microphone. The only times I played in the Maltings were when, during another Festival, I took part in a recital of poetry and music with Max Adrian and George Malcolm, and, on a separate occasion, gave a performance of my one-woman programme in aid of some local good cause. I love the look of the Maltings, its space and the bare rose-brick walls, and I enjoyed standing on its big stage, but although it is a responsive hall for singing I didn't find it an easy house to speak in. I had to use a mike and didn't feel as free as I had in the little old Jubilee. Given the choice I always preferred working in intimate surroundings.

It was good to be part of the Festival in King's Lynn too. This medieval Norfolk town is now divided into shopping precincts and has other modern amenities, but the low ancient buildings, churches and the splendid open space of the big Tuesday Market remain as they have always been. Most of the week the market is a municipal car park, on other days it reverts to its original purpose and becomes an open-air market. As a visitor I prefer it in this guise; I like walking down the lanes between stalls piled high with fruit, flowers, vegetables and wares of every kind. It is the stuff that grows that calls to me. Early in the day the scents are fresh; proper country-garden smells. Another pleasure is the sound of strong local accents; they still persist in Norfolk, and long may they last.

The churches of St Margaret and St Nicholas are both used for concerts. St Nicholas has one of those carved wooden ceilings, that I have seen only in East Anglia, where painted angels, their wings spread wide, range the length of the nave. There is another such ceiling in the church at Blythburgh, and it, too, is a beauty. At St Nicholas I once spent a happy hour lying full-length along a pew at the back of the church listening to Sir John Barbirolli rehearsing an orchestra in some Haydn, and gazing up at the heavenly fly-past as I listened. I don't know how I happened to be there, but I lay low and, like Brer Fox, I said nuthin'; I remember it as one of the better ways of listening to Haydn. It was having the best of all possible worlds in sight and sound, even though the pew's unyielding knife-board narrowness didn't make for much bodily comfort. Fairly early in our festival-going life Reggie and I learned never to go to a concert in a church without taking with us our foam-filled cushions, always kept at the ready in the boot of the car.

Over the years I appeared at Festivals in King's Lynn, at various times with Bill doing our programmes; and once with Joseph Cooper and others of the regular team of *Face the Music* in a stage version of the quiz. I also took part in a poetry recital with John Betjeman, when Viola and Martin Penny joined us to play piano duets. The quiz was mounted at the modern Polytechnic, but all the other engagements took place in the ancient Guildhall of St George, a few paces from the Tuesday Market, a sympathetic and historic building, red-carpeted and warm.

When John Betjeman and I compiled a poetry programme we did it partly by telephone and partly by letter, but, for me, best of all in sessions at Elm Park Gardens. He used to arrive carrying an old-fashioned flat straw bag of the kind meant for fish. In it was a fat bulging of poetry books. In summer I see him wearing a panama – or was it a boater? – but that may be a trick of memory connected with his appearance in television films. In winter I know he favoured a well-worked-in soft felt hat, so limp that its brim undulated in the manner of the small boys' felt hats of the 1920s. We spent whole afternoons reading poetry to each other. 'Oh, do you know this – Kipling – it's absolutely *marvellous*.' One of John's most endearing attributes is his enthusiasm and generosity of heart. He read me 'The Mary Gloster' in his own modest understated but vivid way – not relishing his own performance of which I'm sure he was unself-conscious – but bringing out all the drama of the sad and bitter story. I sat on the edge of the sofa, totally held by his reading of the piece.

We called one of our programmes 'Innocence and the World'. John said I should begin it by reading Blake's 'Infant Joy', a poem that is the epitome of innocence, and practically impossible to read simply enough. I was very unsure about doing it. Its few distilled lines are the most difficult I have ever had to speak aloud. Wordsworth's 'Lucy' isn't much easier. It is almost as impossible to read others of his simpler poems too. In the same programme we chose a group to suggest the feeling of Pre-Raphaelite painting. We had a feast with Meredith's 'Love in the Valley', selecting passages that graphically describe spring and wild flowers and the feelings of young love. John's knowledge of poetry is immense, and he introduced me to much I had never even heard about – Gibson's 'Flannan Isle', and a dark and powerful piece by an actual Pre-Raphaelite, William Morris, called 'The Haystack in the Floods', a spine-chiller about Joan of Arc, whom Morris, in his medieval mood, called Jehane. David Cecil heard it and said kind things about the way I read the piece. Very supporting, for although I much enjoyed taking part in poetry recitals I wasn't sure I was very good at it. I think I got better as I did more, but I always found giving poetry recitals more difficult than doing my own shows.

I am constantly writing about the quality of zest, but it is so very much a part of John that I have to bring it in yet again. I love his poems and, while I relish the funny ones, it is the more penetrating and serious writings that I like best. His memorial poem to his Oxford friend Basil Dufferin, and the better known 'In a Bath Teashop' are two of his poems that never fail to move me.

In the end all concert-tours are roughly the same. At home, town-halls were the biggest houses, outside of theatres, that I played in. Bill and I, with Diana Lyddon to stage-manage for us, worked in a number of such halls. They tended to be rather bleak places with feeble lighting equipment, no stage curtains and echoing acoustics. The background to the platform was often an organ with the inevitable rise of pipes above it. We took with us a ten-by-fourteen-foot beige rug, and focussed the available lighting on the small working area it marked out. At one time we also carried a pair of tall, folding pale grey screens that were meant to enclose the platform and reduce it to the size of a little set. But the screens were never tall enough to hide the organ-pipes, and their paleness looked chilly, so we abandoned them. This was a relief to Diana who drove the rented van that carried our extra lighting and sound equipment, my stage dresses, props and the furniture – a rocking chair, an oval-backed Victorian dining-room chair, a small decorative table to dress the stage, and a folding card-table to stand behind the piano, on which she put my glass of water, props and a copy of the running order to remind me what numbers I was doing that night. We slightly varied the programme from place to place to include special requests or items which Bill and I thought likely to please particular audiences. The seats of the two chairs, which are now in my work-room, were upholstered in bright geranium-pink velveteen. They added a useful touch of colour to those non-committal municipal halls.

In one of the North of England town-halls (it may have been Sheffield) there are, or were, a pair of large cream-coloured plaster lions flanking the steps that lead up from dressing-rooms below to the centre of the platform. I did not fancy having the lions crouching behind my back all through the programme, so, for once, the screens came into their own and we used them to hide the beasts. But this meant that to make my entrance I had to climb up the stairs and over the lions, all in the dark. I managed perfectly for my first entrance and made the return journey safely when I left the stage while Bill played. But when I came back again, on tiptoe, during the closing minutes of Bill's spot, I not only fell up the stairs but also over the lions, and neither of these movements was silent. Bill looked anxiously from the wings, where he had gone after his calls, and he and Diana mouthed, '*Are you all right?*' I nodded bravely, and was a good deal more careful in Part Two.

It was at Tunbridge Wells that Bill arrived at the Assembly Rooms, where later we were giving a performance, to find that although he had brought with him his trousers, a clean shirt and black tie he had for-gotten to pack his dinner jacket. He looked at his watch, it was 5.15 p.m.; he decided there was just time to get to Burton's. Waiting to cross at the lights he asked a man the way. As he ran in the right direction it began to dawn on him that all the shops were shut. Early-closing day! He walked back towards the Assembly Rooms and again met the man who had told him where to go. He poured out his troubles. His new friend hailed the nearest passer-by by name and explained Bill's predicament. The second man was immediately sympathetic: 'Try on this jacket I'm wearing. If it fits I'll go home and fetch my own dinner jacket and you can wear it for the show.' He turned out to be the manager of the Rooms and exactly the same size as Bill.

The main differences between touring at home and what I had known in North America were the great distances travelled there and the size of the auditoriums. Nowhere in Britain was I ever faced with a house of 4,500 seats (3,600 of them filled) as I was during my first tour as a soloist, at the University of Michigan. It was also, apart from small music club appearances in England, the first time I had played outside a theatre. When I saw the Hill Auditorium at Ann Arbor I trembled. It was vast. My walk to stage centre at the beginning of the show seemed to go on forever, and at the end of the performance, after I had come off-stage, I decided that unless I took to a Groucho Marx-like slope-crouch-run, to get me back for my call, I would never make it before the applause died down. The funny run was a success and the audience called me back twice more. For these calls I improvised other unlikely walks and got plenty of exercise. That night I had a good microphone (or as good as was then possible) and knew from the beginning that I was getting through to the big audience, but I feared that my face must look like a featureless blob. From that experience I learned a valuable lesson: that as long as an audience can hear clearly it can, in a sense, see too. Inflections of speech can be made to convey the lift of an eyebrow or the suggestion of a smile. They signal the same message. I was able to prove that if the sound is good an audience will believe it sees more than it does. But large houses call for broader treatment, pace has to be slowed up, and in huge halls some subtlety inevitably has to be lost.

For a long time I used foot-microphones even on the smaller English stages. Though some were better than others all restricted my movements, because they stood just in front of the footlights and their limited range compelled me to work within a prescribed area. Then the great day arrived when someone told me about a brand-new Rolls-Royce class of body-mike, the size of a fat lipstick, that functioned as a walkie-talkie. Freedom was mine. I could move about the stage wherever I liked. I wore the little metal cartridge in my boned brassière, and the battery, encased in a cigarette-pack-sized container, went under my girdle, below my stomach. Until I learned to wrap it in cotton wool it felt decidedly cold when first I put it on. The mike was linked to the battery by a short wire concealed under both my bra and my pantie-girdle; another aerial wire waved freely under my skirt. To use it I had to have a Post Office licence that allowed me to broadcast on a special wave-band from the body-mike to the amplifying system in the theatre. When Reggie got it for me he was warned that, as it operated for quite a distance both inside and outside the building, I had better remember to turn it off whenever I left the stage; and I always did.

I wore it for the first time at Chichester in Sussex, where I was playing in the unfamiliar and exposed 'round'. I have never been more grateful for a good microphone than I was that night. In the Chichester

Theatre there is no comforting proscenium arch. The audience, instead of being seated only in front of the performer, is also placed on either side of the long thrust stage. It was always my instinct to get close to the audience and in a way this was easier in the round, but unless I worked at the very back of the stage (thus defeating the purpose of the thrust) half the audience couldn't see my face. Doing my kind of sketches under these conditions was difficult. The invisible characters I talked to had to be positioned, and that was the direction in which I had to address them. For instance, in a two-character monologue called 'Life and Literature', I, as a green young girl, sat on a low stool gazing up at the face of an unseen, worldly and famous author. I couldn't move the author about the stage or the point of the piece – a quiet encounter in a dark corner at a literary party – would be lost. At Chichester, to make sure that all of the audience could, at some time, catch at least a glimpse of my face I had to add to the rapt gaze of the innocent young thing exaggerated writhing movements of shyness – swivelling around on the stool and looking over my shoulder – for the benefit of the people sitting in the side seats; some of them were actually behind me. Reggie was there that night, and when he came out of the theatre and overheard someone say; 'It goes to show that if you articulate and project your voice as Joyce Grenfell does you don't have to use a microphone,' we knew we had got the right instrument.

In 1963 I took it to Australia and, at the rehearsal on the day of my first appearance in Perth, I showed it with pride to the friendly Polish new-Australian in charge of electrics. He linked up the theatre loudspeakers to my equipment, and I started to test the acoustics from the stage. Reggie and Bill, sitting in the auditorium, were signalling that I was coming through loud and clear when I was drowned out by an Australian voice directing a radio-cab to go and pick up a Mr Pentworthy from Maraboorie Avenue and take him to the Art Gallery. I was on the same wavelength as a local taxi-hire firm. There was no way of overcoming this difficulty, and for the rest of the tour I had to make do with the usual limiting foot-mike; adequate but primitive after the wonders of my lovely little lipstick. The risk of getting on to the fire brigade or the police made it impossible to use it anywhere outside Great Britain.

For choice I preferred to play in theatres where I didn't have to give seven performances a week and where amplification wasn't necessary. That was one of the reasons I didn't play more often in London. I loved the luxury of playing in a small auditorium. It was not such a paying proposition for the promoters (or the performers), but for me there were the great compensations of intimacy, and of not having to use a microphone. In a small house I found it possible to reduce the size of my performance to its original concept – without, I hope and think, losing projection or a sense of occasion. No matter how small, a theatre can never be the same as a room, but Rosehill Theatre in Cumberland is the perfect compromise. It is not too cramped, nor is it embarrassingly snug, with artists so close to the audience that they don't know where to look. It is exactly the right size for a 'chamber' performance, and I enjoyed being there both as player and as a member of the audience.

Rosehill Theatre was originally a large stone barn in the grounds of the charming four-square Georgian house lived in by the dynamic, sadly lamented, Sir Nicholas Sekers. It is near the industrial town of Whitehaven, where the silk industry he established, when he came from Hungary, still flourishes. Oliver Messel designed its interior and turned it into a jewel-box of a place with foyers and an auditorium with two hundred and twenty-eight seats. He used muted colours for the outer rooms, but for the auditorium he chose red walls, red seats, red carpets and a red velvet curtain, with plenty of gilt and glitter in the chandelier-like wall lights. The stage equipment is complete with a good lighting-board and a Steinway piano kept in concert condition. The acoustics are a joy.

In Miki's time (for some reason his name was reduced to Miki and not, as might have been expected, to Niki) he persuaded the world's top musicians to come to Rosehill. It was his idea to establish a theatre-concert hall in an area where very little entertainment was available; a distressed industrial area, sparsely populated and in need of a centre where the highest quality was guaranteed. He persuaded hard-headed businessmen in the north-west, from Manchester to Carlisle, to join him in creating a fund to subsidise the venture.

In a short time, because of his enthusiasm and drive, Rosehill was established. Such were the rewards of Miki's welcome that musicians invited to come and play – and you had to be invited – were willing to come for fees a good deal lower than they could command else-where. And they got so much pleasure playing in that little theatre to audiences hungry for real quality, that they came again and again. Miki invited only those he considered worthy of Rosehill; among the names of those who played there are Janet Baker, Benjamin Britten,

Miki Sekers

Clifford Curzon, Kirsten Flagstad, Yehudi Menuhin, Peter Pears, Sviatoslav Richter and Slava Rostropovich. There is a story about a well-known European singer who wanted to be able to add Rosehill to her list of 'appearances' at the Metropolitan, La Scala, Glyndebourne, Salzburg, etc., etc., – but never made it. It is possible that her choice, when on Roy Plomley's radio programme *Desert Island Discs*, of taking eight of her own recordings to solace her on the island may have had something to do with it.

Miki's wife Agi made the artists welcome to their house filled with flowers and the modern paintings they had collected together. Supper parties after concerts I gave (or attended) were good times; I remember the delicious home-made dishes spread out in the pretty dining-room for the artists and a favoured few of the audience, some of whom had driven as much as a hundred miles to be there.

I have a vivid picture in my mind of a day Miki and Agi arrived in the dining-room of the Wentworth Hotel during the Aldeburgh Festival. I think it was the first time that Rostropovich came to the Festival and he was lunching with the pianist Richter and his wife at the far end of the dining-room, opposite to where Reggie and I were sitting. I noticed that they seemed rather a quiet trio; nobody said much, their heads were down as they spooned in their food. Rostropovich looked up and saw the Sekerses. He sprang from his chair – there is no other word for it – crying out something, in Russian I suppose. Miki saw his approach, took off towards him, and the two men went into a bear-hug dance and revolved, making un-English noises of mutual happiness at their encounter. It was a meeting of human dynamos, energy-packed with zest, and it infused into the room a direct charge of excitement and good humour.

At Wavendon there is another theatre where I have enjoyed playing. John Dankworth and his wife Cleo Laine created it out of the stables behind their Victorian Gothic rectory in Buckinghamshire. It has no fancy pretensions to beauty – no red velvet, no period charm, no footlights. It is a functional auditorium, equipped, I believe, with every known electronic device. I have seen it hung about with wires and leads, in an alarming-looking way. When I played there I went through my performance in blessed freedom, because of the size of the hall, from mechanical aids. It is a good and friendly place to work.

John is a composer, arranger, conductor, and player of clarinet, saxophone and piano; Cleo, for my money, is the best, most intelligent

Cleo Laine

and most interesting singer of modern 'ballads', 'standards' and jazz *in the world*. Together they have set up the Wavendon All-Music Plan. This includes concerts of 'straight' music and jazz workshops, and recitals by artists (as well as themselves) of the calibre of Julian Bream, Richard Rodney Bennett, Leon Goossens, Stephane Grappelli, John Williams, and big names from the Ronnie Scott circuit. When Leon Goossens had his eightieth birthday the Dankworths put on a celebration in his honour with tributes in person and on tape from many of his musician friends. Janet Craxton, a Goossens pupil, was one of them. She played part of a clarinet sonata dedicated to Leon by her husband Alan Richardson. John and Cleo invited me to be the compère on this affectionate occasion.

The Dankworths believe, and so do I, that all music, when it is good of its kind, is music. At Wavendon festivals you can listen to a string quartet one night, modern jazz the next; a *Lieder* recital; a programme by Cleo and John, perhaps with his settings of Shakespeare songs; and performances by Richard Rodney Bennett; and 'standards' newly arranged by Richard or John or both. Not for them the élitist attitude still prevailing in Britain, but now slowly beginning to disappear, that would divide 'straight' from all other kinds of music with the possible exception of a little authentic 'folk'. Folk has always been respectable. This division has now gone from most of the American musical scenes. There, quite lately, I saw, on a television programme, three world-renowned opera singers sing their own solo arias, and later come on stage together disguised in matching, glittering gowns as the Supremes, and with evident enjoyment sing the kind of pop number for which that trio is famous. In Britain such an occurrence is still a rarity. But Yehudi Menuhin broke down barriers when he was recorded improvising on a jazzy piece with Stephane Grappelli; and André Previn, with his compositions and performances, crosses all frontiers in England, just as Leonard Bernstein does in the United States. Hope rises.

A third pleasing small 'house' is the Georgian Theatre in Richmond, Yorkshire, restored to its original design by a group of local enthusiasts led by Nancy Crathorne, wife of the former Minister of Agriculture Tom Dugdale, the first Lord Crathorne. (At an Agricultural Show in the neighbourhood Tom ran into a fellow Yorkshireman who was world-famous as a judge of poultry. He introduced Nancy: 'I think you know my wife.' The poultry man came closer and gave Nancy a long look. 'Noa,' he said, 'if you'd a bin a fowl I'd a known yer, but I never can recall the human face.') Nancy discovered bolts of ancient, heavy, dark bottle-green wool cloth, the kind from which old uniforms were made and used it to cover the seats and to make stage curtains. She brought back to life the nearly derelict building that had been used first as a granary and then for furniture storage.

The tiny theatre is still arranged as it was in the eighteenth century with the balcony set square instead of curved as it is in later theatres. This means that the side seats – arranged as small boxes – face each other and not the stage. Sitting thus, or on the narrow bench-like seats in the stalls, makes attendance something of an endurance test for the long-legged and long-backed, but the place has kept its period atmosphere.

CHAPTER EIGHT

Movies

IN MY first book of memories I said very little about the part films played in my career. I am afraid I looked on them as a side-line to what I thought of as my real job – writing and performing my own material on stage, radio and television. This was ungrateful, for making movies provided me with a way of reaching a new and different public, and to my film appearance I owe a far wider audience than a lifetime of working in theatres and concert halls could have given me.

In some ways I found that filming was the most challenging of the media. It seemed restricting, and I didn't find it easy having to speak lines composed by someone else. Much film dialogue appeared to be written to be read not heard; when spoken it didn't come trippingly off the tongue. The only kind of dialogue that worked for me had to sound as if it had just been thought of, and give the illusion of never having been written down. Now and then I was allowed to suggest new lines and, immodest as it is to say so, they usually turned out to work better, and produced the laughs I had failed to get with the original script. I preferred giving live performances on a stage, but enjoyed the communal aspect of working with a group of people all concerned with the job in hand. Actors are not invariably overburdened with the team spirit, but I was fortunate in working with agreeable people who kept their egos in check. For the few weeks we were all involved in making a picture we became a unit. Gradually I sorted out the nicely distinguished contributions made by the producer, director, the camera crew and continuity girl. It was rather like being at school with the producer and director as head and vice-head, backed-up by a number of prefects all with special duties. I found it interesting to meet the backstage boys, designers who made the blueprints for the sets, the 'chippies' and masons, prop-men and 'sparks' who brought it all together. I found that giving full attention to the film was a luxury, and restful. The time spent in the studio lifted the responsibility of doing domestic chores at home. Or it did for me, for I had the kindly aid of Mrs Gabe, our dear housekeeper, who took over all the shopping and cooking whenever I was working. Her loving kindness and imaginative help are frequently recorded in my diaries, with a gratitude I continue to feel.

I didn't begin my film career as the galumphing schoolgirl character that I got stuck with later. The early parts I played were straightforward young women of no particular idiosyncrasy. For the record: the first film I appeared in was a wartime propaganda documentary 'short' directed by Carol Reed. Celia Johnson was the star, and the piece showed her as a young mother writing a letter to her two children evacuated to America. In it she described life at home in England under the bombing. I was the American woman who had adopted the little evacuees, and it was my voice that read aloud to them their mother's letter as scenes were shown of her queueing with her ration book, putting out incendiary bombs, digging-for-victory, making-do and mending clothes, saving paper and through it all being understatedly stiff-upper-lipped and cheerful. The 'short' was made for showing in the United States, partly I think to thank Americans for Bundles for Britain and partly to let them see how we were making our war effort. While we filmed Celia stayed with me at Parr's Cottage and we drove together to the old Gaumont Studios in Shepherd's Bush, now a part of the B.B.C., where the make-up man had a canary in his room almost exactly the same colour as the heavy chrome foundation he put on our faces. For those black-and-white movies we also wore an almost black lipstick. Off-screen we looked very unappetising. For some reason we had to be kept unnaturally neat, and the wardrobe girl and 'make-up' hovered around us between every take, to make sure there were no wisps and our collars were exactly in place. Very unlike life.

Maurice Elvey directed another propaganda film in which, if you looked carefully, I was *just* visible. *The Lamp Still Burns* was a full-length picture faintly disguised as a romance, but really intended to persuade girls to become nurses. Rosamund John played the heroine, her hair fiercely rolled up in tight page-boy style. My brief appearance showed me as a lecturer telling the nursing recruits about blood transfusions; a role that didn't give me a great deal of scope in which to develop character.

Anthony Asquith, called by his friends Puffin, invited me to play a slightly larger part in yet another propaganda movie, *This Demi-Paradise*, in which I was cast for the first time as a sort of ex-deb ninny.

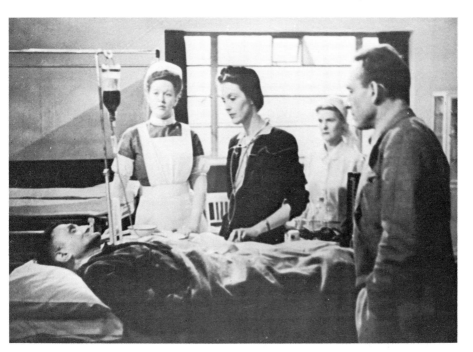

In The Lamp Still Burns

I played others of this type in *While the Sun Shines* and *Run for Your Money*. The idea behind *This Demi-Paradise* was to show how Anglo-U.S.S.R. co-operation was working. Laurence Olivier played the Red Comrade visiting Britain on a goodwill mission; Margaret Rutherford was an eccentric Lady Bountiful, boss of the village where much of the action took place; and the pretty young love interest was Penelope Dudley-Ward.

Margaret Rutherford's comedy performances are justifiably famous – her Madame Arcati in Noël Coward's *Blithe Spirit* is the definitive one – but until I heard her read poetry I had not realised the range of her talent. I believe she always meant to be a straight actress, but her face was made for comedy, and she was given few opportunities of playing anything else. To hear her read poetry was a revelation. She had none of your beautiful-voices-for-beautiful-verses mannerisms, no special poetry voice, no pretentious or over-understanding delivery. She read with naturalism and power, and was as successful with quiet reflective pieces as she was with full-blooded dramatic poems. It isn't always easy to dissociate a familiar face from a familiar voice, but when Margaret read you heard only the poem. She had a quiet, humble dignity that came through, too.

I remember two things in particular about making this picture: wearing a very chic hat and a slightly too small dress originally made for Valerie Hobson to wear in another film; and an interminable day re-taking a complicated crowd sequence. A vast set representing the village, with a sloping street up the middle, was built in one of the biggest stages in Denham Studios. Down this street I had to bicycle, and I must have done the journey twenty times. It was a difficult scene to shoot because it involved various villagers, an on-coming car, Larry walking up the street and me on my bike (as the jolly ninny) coming down it, all having to move on separate cues. The idea was to try not to run into each other. I found it hard to keep to my allotted route, stay on the bike without wobbling as in passing I waved at Larry, and time my three-word line so that the mikes could pick it up: 'Hello!' I said, 'Back again!'

I can't remember when *Poet's Pub*, taken from Eric Linklater's satirical novel about rustic revelry in suburbia, was made, but I know I welcomed the chance of playing a part I could get my teeth into, and enjoyed parting my hair in the middle and winding up my pigtails into 'ear-phones' for the Liberty-cotton-print-frocked, arty-crafty, folk-dance enthusiast. I wore my own flat red sandals to leap about in. Whether this, the first of the galumphers I played in films, preceded my invention of a similiar character for the 'How' radio series that Stephen Potter and I wrote, or whether it was Linklater's eager, nature-loving eccentric that inspired 'Fern Brixton' is lost in time. They were certainly twins in their tastes – neither was overburdened with humour; both were gauche, earnest and eager. I led the country dancing in one scene, and in my joyous gladdery I bounced so high off the ground that I rose out of camera frame and was asked, to quote George Robey, to 'kindly temper my hilarity with a modicum of reserve', and keep my head down.

And then came the plummiest of all the parts I was ever offered – Miss Gossage in *The Happiest Days of Your Life*. This was my introduction to Sidney Gilliat and Frank Launder and the start of several happy experiences playing for them variations on the theme of the games mistress. Miss Gossage was the queen of all the galumphers; repressed and upright, she was a more essentially overgrown English maiden-lady than the folk-dancer in *Poet's Pub*, and I had a good time playing her. *The Happiest Days* told the story of a girls' school (Headmistress Margaret Rutherford) evacuated, in error, to join a boys' school (Headmaster Alastair Sim). The big confrontation scene, in

Gossage in The Happiest Days of Your Life

which the pupils of both schools staged a pillow-fight to the last feather, stays uncomfortably vivid. This was because the pillows were laden with rather more feathers than usual – not only of regulation size but also of an infinitesimal kind – that went up the nose, into the mouth, ears, eyes, hair, down the neck, into one's shoes and any-where else it is possible for a feather to go. The arc-lights were par-ticularly hot that day, and the dear little boys and girls didn't *act* at pillow-fighting, they pillow-fought with gleeful delight; and I, by order of the director, was one of the principal targets. We battled for at least one whole day, and I am not sure there wasn't more the next day. When I got home I brought with me a great many feathers.

These clung to carpets, wafted into curtains, floated on to food and made their presence felt for days. In spite of baths and changes of clothing I was haunted by feathers long after the sequence was safely over.

Playing Miss Gossage was for me 'a-doin' what comes naturally'. I had always observed mannerisms, and in my time – overgrown at fourteen, eager to be good at games and lamentably ungifted – I had been a bit of a galumpher. I remembered how it felt to move awkwardly, and without thinking it out I gave Miss Gossage a bouncy immature way of walking, too juvenile for her years. I also remembered an endearing awkwardness in the way a child, caught in the act of doing something it shouldn't, moves from the exact spot of its misdemeanour as if to distract attention from the deed and the place. In a scene with Margaret Rutherford I walked up a broad staircase, she as the Head in front, with Gossage in her wake. Gossage paused to write her name in the deep dust on top of the banisters. The Head caught her at it and ticked her off. In playing the scene I made an instinctive move, one shoulder up and my head slightly jerking to one side, proclaiming shame at being discovered. When I saw the sequence in the finished film I was amused by the movements I had made. Without any deliberate intention on my part they seemed to tell a good deal about poor buttoned-up Gossage. One or two critics wrote in appreciation of this tiny moment, and to this day I meet people who remember it. I can't pretend it was a cleverly worked-out bit of business; it was purely instinctive. 'A-doin' what comes naturally.'

I can't remember whether writing in the dust was the director's idea or mine. I think it was probably mine, based on an incident at my own school when I was about fourteen. I had written on the bottom step of the main stairs in the hall: 'This step has not been dusted.' The school was assembled and in a voice hushed with hurt feeling and pretended shock our Headmistress told of this wickedness and asked the girl who had perpetrated it to stand up. Up I stood, amazed at the fuss, and was roundly scolded for my lack of thought and unkind impertinence. I was made to go and apologise to the maid responsible for the non-dusting, and very unfair I knew it to be.

It was always pleasant working with Frank and Sidney; they were civilised and amused human beings, as well as good makers of comedy, and they created round them an atmosphere of goodwill and friendliness. Their four St Trinian films, based on the drawings by Ronald Searle of macabre schoolgirls, were called *The Belles of St Trinians*,

Blue Murder at St Trinians, The Pure Hell of St Trinians and the only one I did not appear in, as I had decided it was time to superannuate Ruby Gates the Policewoman, *The Great Train Robbery*. All these films are still to be seen on television, usually at odd times, either early in the morning or very late at night. In *Blue Murder* I played on the recorder to woo Cecil Parker. We were, for some forgotten reason, marooned on a desert island. Try as I did, and I practised for days, I could not extract more than a whimper of notes out of the instrument, and when we finally shot the scene my musical performance was so inadequate that next day it got huge laughs. I was delighted with the sounds – or absence of sounds – I made, but, sadly, the scene ended up on the cutting-room floor for the good reason that the sequence had no bearing on the rest of the picture, and it had to go.

In the Boulting Brothers' film *Here Comes the Bride* I was again called upon to make music, this time, as one of two aunts. The other was Athene Seyler, a treasured friend since I was a girl. In the film I had to play the organ for the arrival of the bride. There was no copy of Lohengrin's 'Wedding March' available and I had to have a go at playing it by ear. Athene said she got such giggles at my version that she mewed like a kitten. Looking at rushes (the showing of film made the day before) we decided we both looked pretty funny – she, a sort of sponge and I a reflection in a spoon.

Irene Handl was also in the film, as the dressmaker who came to fit the wedding-dress. At lunch-time she told us about the delicately 'refained' landlady with whom she stayed in Brighton: 'You know Miss Handl, ai know mai father was a gentleman because whenever he had – er – anything to do with mai mother, he always thenked her and said: "That was *mowst* enjoyable."'

Athene and I travelled together to and from the studio. One day we sang hymns all the way down to Shepperton. She said she loved watching choir-boys singing so roundly that they made themselves yawn: '*Holy, Holy, Hooowly.*' Another time we sat in the car between takes and heard an arch lady singing a folk song with a refrain that we both thought sounded like '*Hi-diddly-bum-cum-peedle*'.

Funny sounds make me laugh more than funny sights, particularly when the funny sounds are made by not very talented amateur musicians. (I include myself in this group.) But only in small doses, and only on gramophone records, have I been amused by the agonising off-key singing of Flora Foster Jenkins, an elderly American, foolhardy, you might suppose who hired Carnegie Hall in New York in order to render – that is the only possible word to use for what she did – a full-length programme of operatic arias in a voice that hardly ever got near the right note. She filled the place. People came from far and wide, not for music but for amazement; it is alleged that she knew this and was not deterred by it. All she wanted was to render.

Dick, Arthur Macrae, a witty writer and companionable man, and I went with Winifred to a matinée of a programme of Asian music and dancing. Winifred said we mustn't miss it; it was rare and exciting. The house that afternoon was thin, and so, for our uneducated taste, was the entertainment. It was also very long, slow to the point of inertia, and on a stage apparently lit by glow-worms. Hard to bear. Winifred found it beautiful, and she may well have been right. She sat up very straight on the edge of her seat in rapt attention. Somehow her total absorption in what the rest of us found a non-event, together with the very occasional, widely spaced and unfamiliar sounds that came from a sad-looking man playing a single-stringed instrument, gave us church-giggles. So did the small sounds made by tentative touches on a light-weight gong and a few shakes of what sounded like sleigh-bells contributed by two seated figures in the furthest shadows. If we had known something of the musical language, the sounds might have made some sense to us, but the unfamiliar sliding about of the musical line, and the paucity and infrequency of notes, struck us as strange and comic. Of course, we knew it was unpardonably rude to laugh at other people's art and earnestness; arrogant too. And we did try to control our church-giggles, but tiny explosions from Arthur, and small mewings (like Athene's) from Dick, were too much for me; and we all had a bad time trying to behave.

I am glad to have been spared what must have been a pretty testing performance for the audience at a concert in Delhi. Somebody sent me a review of it and I quote it in full: 'Kumari M. V. Seetharatua (Osmania) attempted Paridhana in Bilahari on the veena. One string was out of tune throughout, and a raga mazika thana, in a strange combination of Simmendramadhyaman, Mohanan and Sri Ragam did not improve matters. I would suggest that participants should also be tested in their ability to tune their respective instruments.'

Solemnity with which one is not in tune, or by an individual taking himself, his art or his thought more seriously than seems warranted, has always struck me as legitimately funny. A fair target. I hope I am not unkind or superior about this. It isn't that the one who laughs is on a higher plane looking down, but rather in another place, seeing from a different point of view. The fact that one isn't supposed to laugh makes laughter inevitable and, somehow, all the more enjoyable; but it goes without saying that such laughter must be private and internal. Life would be a lot duller if there were a law against private mockery. It is what comedy is about, and it need not be cruel. In fact if it is cruel it becomes destructive and ceases to be funny.

Cameo parts in films can be very rewarding. The brief scene at the hotel reception desk in *Genevieve* was filmed in one morning. The idea of playing the woolly-brained but amicable receptionist of this establishment of very limited amenities appealed to me. For the sequence, I wore my hair in the same plaited ear-phone style I had used in *Poet's Pub*, added dangling black ear-rings, and spoke with my jaw jutting out more than it does when I am being natural. In answer to Dinah Sheridan's and John Gregson's enquiries about hot water for a bath I said: 'Not just *now*.'

'*No* hot water?'

'Oh yes – there *is* hot water – between 2.30 and 3.15 p.m.'

I was obviously concerned by their great need for baths and got permission from Cornelius, the director, to add a line to the script. As I lurched towards the tired travellers, my ear-rings swinging, and craned my neck to follow their retreating figures as they went upstairs to a bedroom next to the church tower in which the clock was soon to strike so loudly that it scared the living daylights out of them, I said: 'I think they must be Americans.'

Only once in my film career was I supposed to look glamorous. This was when I played a duchess in *The Million-Pound Note*, called in America *Man with a Million*, based on an O. Henry short story and directed by Ronald Neame. Maggie Furse designed beautiful period dresses which I wore over restricting period corsets that did a lot for my figure. The film was shot in colour, and the star was Gregory Peck. He was even better looking off the screen, and larger. It was summer, and we did location scenes in a big garden near Denham Studios. Between takes Greg got out of his grey frock-coat and I saw it was not the tailor's padding that gave him such broad shoulders. They were his own. Added to his good looks (he reminded me of those splendid young men Uncle Dana Gibson drew in his cartoons for the *Life* magazine of his day) he was as unspoilt and friendly as I had hoped he might be.

My ma was over here on a visit and came down to watch the filming.

With Gregory Peck and Hartley Power in The Million-Pound Note

She was as pleased as a young girl to be introduced to the leading man. It so happened that Greg's father was there, too, and the two parents sat side by side in deck-chairs sharing pride in their offspring. (There was never a more sentimental mother than mine. For a time she kept under her pillow a letter from Tommy written when he was a small boy at private school. She never read it; she just took it out, kissed it good-night and put it back again. Then one day she opened it. It wasn't from Tommy – it was a bill from Peter Jones. My mother thought this as funny as we did.)

I only made one picture in Hollywood. This was offered to me while I was staying at Eidsvold, in Australia, after a three-month season of my one-woman show. A cable came from Aubrey Blackburn, my London agent: 'Would you consider re-routing return to play two goodish scenes as Julie Andrews's crazy, tweedy mother in M.G.M. film approximately two weeks Hollywood around November 11 can air mail script but if no please confirm.' I think he expected me to say no, but this time he was wrong. My reply said 'Answer yes if you consider part right. Send script Sydney.'

The film was *The Americanisation of Emily* written by Paddy Chayefsky and directed by Arthur Hiller. It was a bitter story about the irresponsible and self-indulgent behaviour of some top United States naval brass stationed in London during the war; an exaggerated exposé of a small band of easy-livers who took advantage of their privileged position, disregarded rules about food and liquor rationing, and were infinitely supplied with nylon stockings. They had themselves a high old time – there was plenty of willing local talent to play along with them – while most of their compatriots (and ours) were pursuing the war. The picture offended a number of people on both sides of the ocean. Julie Andrews was cast as the young English A.T.S. driver, seconded to the U.S. Navy. She had lost her husband and a brother and friends in the fighting, and falls for the handsome American officer (James Garner) whose creed is live now and let tomorrow take care of itself. I played her mother, Mrs Barham, who is also numbed by the losses she has suffered and refuses, but not on any metaphysical grounds, to 'accept the reality of death'. Instead, and this was the 'crazy' referred to in Aubrey's cable, she pretends with euphoric Pollyanna cheerfulness that her son has not been killed. Jim Garner takes Mrs Barham to task and makes her face 'reality'. We had a tense scene together in which he had to break down my dottiness and reduce me to tears. Restored to sanity by this treatment Mrs Barham thanks him for his kindness. Ho-hum. This scene, a long one, was the first dramatic one I had ever played, and it certainly stretched me. I was grateful for the opportunity of trying to do something different from all those ninnies and galumphers. But I did wish I had been able to believe in the character I was asked to play.

Once again kind Leonard let me stay with him in contentment and comfort for my two and a half weeks in California. My diary records my first visit to M.G.M. studios.

11 November. When I got there three youngish men in sweaters and sneakers armed with cameras, flash-bulbs and autograph pads were standing at the gate. My cab driver told me they wanted my autograph; I denied this, they couldn't possibly know who I was. 'Oh, Miss Grenfell,' they chorused, 'We *do!*' I found it hard to believe but it was encouraging. Talked to Paddy Chayefsky about the part. He is small, bearded, erudite with an immense vocabulary. V. nice to me. Had seen my T.V. programmes in England and couldn't believe it when they told him they had got me for the picture. 'Perfect,' he said. All of which makes the job more and more hazardous.

But also comforting.

That evening Leonard took me to a party and there I met Reggie's first favourite film star, Norma Shearer, 'in a sage green velvet sheath with orange beads. She now lives only for dancing and ski-ing. She must be 65.' No comment. I noticed that in all the houses I went to with Leonard the rooms were decorated with artificial flowers; cheerful and brightly coloured, but I didn't like them then, and I don't now. Another fashionable period touch: posters by Toulouse-Lautrec and stone heads of Buddha everywhere we went. After a visit to a gift shop, full of useless but amusing objects, I decided in a superior way there was more money spent in California on such things than any-where else in the world.

When I went to work a day or two later I was asked to look at the set and check it for accuracy. From the script, Mrs Barham and Emily appeared to come from an educated upper-middle-class background, but the set showed a cliché view of an out-of-date working-class front-room in a terraced house, cluttered with lace doilies and statuettes (from a fairground?). The mantelpiece had a plush runner across it, and there was an aspidistra and many photographs of some rum-looking relations. A sort of Balham, circa 1925, more suitable for Noël Coward's *This Happy Breed* than for a hard-hitting comment on life in the 1940s. The set didn't in any way match the vowel-sounds Julie Andrews used; nor mine. I wondered whether I should speak up. I had been asked to pass the set as authentic, and I couldn't. I am naturally bossy, but it seemed early days for me to tell my unknown fellow-workers that they'd got it all wrong. But I did, and was warmly thanked for my frankness. There wasn't a great deal of time; we were shooting that morning, but all the doilies, the plush runner and most of the statuettes and photographs were cleared away, and we were left with wall-paper, chair covers and carpet of forgettable autumnal colours that blurred into an acceptable background. Just.

13 November Lunch with Paddy Chayefsky, Julie and Jim Garner. P.C. is full of talk, much of it enjoyable but so fluent and so fast that I lose the thread as we go, but the bits I hang on to are provocative and of interest. He is full of wild ideas and *some* are reasonable. He is very 'ebulgent' [A word I invented for a Brooklyn Jewish sales-girl I put into a monologue called 'Counter-wise']. Arthur Hiller knows what he wants and is patient.

Nice. I kept thinking how thrilled I should have been forty years ago to find myself in Hollywood and lunching at M.G.M.

14 November We've done most of the big scene and I have run the gamut from dotty to tears. It wasn't easy. I'm not at all sure I was any good. I nearly made myself cry, but had to have eye-drops to produce tears. I find I have to stay very quiet on the set [between takes] when I'm doing a serious scene or I lose the feeling. It was all rather wearing.

15 November I went to rushes of yesterday's scenes. I look pretty rough, but the playing is better than I dared hope. Saw coloured T.V. tonight for the first time; too difficult to tune-in but the ads were lovely! A preponderance of shocking pinks and livid lime greens and it seemed impossible to find the right colour for faces. Today the wardrobe girl, talking of long dresses, said: 'They make me feel so gracious, so *femme*.'

22 November [The day President Kennedy was assassinated]. I was in the bedroom packing. Leonard came in to talk. The telephone rang. Clifton Webb said his maid had just heard the news on the radio. We switched on at once. We sat in shocked silence. Cold all over and shaky.

The unthinkable had happened.

To date my last appearance in a film was in *The Yellow Rolls-Royce*, a three-episode story linked by the vintage car. Some of the exteriors were made at Cliveden. I played in the third episode as Ingrid Bergman's Virginian lady travelling-companion. Yet another ninny with only one line of note. It passed by so swiftly that only the most devoted fan could have registered it. Ingrid said to me with some curiosity: 'Why are those Arabs looking at you like that?' Coming from the straight-backed and cautious travelling-companion my reply, drawled in a Southern accent, had its element of surprise: 'Lust.'

CHAPTER NINE

Fringe Benefits

IN THE last twenty-five years a number of what I like to call 'fringe benefits' have come into my life – none of them directly connected with my career. I hold no degrees and am not an authority on any subject, with the possible exception of my own work as a writer-entertainer, and these jobs are, I suppose, the result of having a face made recognisable by public appearances. Three of these fringe benefits are not jobs at all; they came to me as pleasing surprises. I was made an Honorary Fellow of Manchester Polytechnic and, later, of Lucy Cavendish College, Cambridge. The third is the least likely; I am an Honorary Kentucky Colonel. Don't ask me why, unless it is because I spent a happy four days staying in Louisville, where I spoke on behalf of the English-Speaking Union, and the giver of such things was my chairman for the evening. I have a signed and sealed certificate to prove my claim and it hangs for all to see, framed, outside the door to the bathroom.

The fringe benefits that involve the giving of interest and time are varied, and have, in their different ways, been demanding. As with all that has happened to me, I learned how by doing. The first was membership of the Pilkington Committee.

THE PILKINGTON COMMITTEE

In the summer of 1960 I received an invitation, in a large best-quality white envelope, from the Postmaster General asking me to serve on a committee being set up under the chairmanship of Sir Harry Pilkington 'to consider the future of the broadcasting services in the United Kingdom . . . to advise on the services which in future should be provided by the B.B.C. and the I.T.A. . . .'. There was more, but these were the main points. Reggie and I were having breakfast when I read the letter. I handed it to him. 'They must have made a mistake – they

Coffee-break for the committee: Elwyn Davies, Betty Whitley, Harry Pilkington, myself, Denis Lawrence and Edmund Hudson

can't mean me.' Reggie said, of course they did; and what is more it would be the most interesting job I was ever likely to be offered. 'You'd love it,' he said. I read the letter again. Perhaps it would be quite interesting; but I wasn't very confident about the contribution I could make to such an enterprise. All I knew about broadcasting, I said, came from writing for radio, being a radio critic, listening a great deal because I enjoyed it, and occasionally appearing on television. 'That is more than most other people can say. You'd better accept.' I wrote to the P.M.G. and thanked him for asking me; I'd be very pleased to serve.

In my diary for 4 August I wrote: 'At six o'clock I went to Selwyn House to meet Sir Harry Pilkington. He's like an overgrown schoolboy with a *good* face; wrinkles around his eyes like my pa. He's obviously full of energy, wit and brain. He also bicycles everywhere, wet or fine, and grows prize-winning roses up at St Helens in Lancashire, where he lives. At that time he was a widower, but was courting and, during the years of the committee, he married Mavis, his present wife and looked happier every time I saw him. That first meeting at the London flat in Selwyn House, where he stayed during the week, was a social occasion arranged for the committee members 'to get to know each other by sight'. I recorded that I felt inadequate, 'my mind doesn't seem to click the way theirs do. I'm quicker in some ways but not as informed as they appear to be about the workings of committees. We seem to be a very diverse crew, which is good.'

I was glad to find Peter Hall of the company. Being in the same profession I thought we probably spoke the same language. He and I shared a taxi after the meeting, three solid hours of it, and agreed it was going to be interesting as well as hard work. He told me that it was to the B.B.C. Third Programme, to which he began to listen as a young boy, that he owed his tastes and standards. It was sad that he had to resign from the committee because he found his work with the Royal Shakespeare Company at Stratford-on-Avon so demanding that he could not get away to attend our meetings in London.

From the beginning Harry made it clear to us that he was only interested in delivering a unanimous report. We must be of one mind; he would not allow any dissenting minority reports. He asked us to arrange to spend our luncheon times together, as valuable results came from informal exhanges out of office hours.

We were indeed a mixed lot; that was the purpose of our selection. There was no one on the committee, including our two permanent civil servant secretaries (G.P.O.), for whom I didn't feel respect, some admiration and, in several cases, affection. Here are their names, together with the jobs they were doing at the time of the committee; and brief first impressions made before I knew any of my fellow-members, recorded on 20 September.

Harold Collison: General Secretary of the National Union of Agricultural Workers. A prominent member of the Council of the T.U.C. Agriculture was his special interest. 'Dear, bumble-bee voice. A spine of steel. Good, too.' (By which I meant he was a 'whole' man.)

Elwyn Davies: Permanent Secretary to the Welsh Department of the Library of Wales. 'Fiery.'

Richard Hoggart: Senior Lecturer in English, Leicester University. Author of *The Uses of Literacy*. 'Lively, compassionate, useful for the work.'

Edmund Hudson: President of the Fertilisers Manufacturers Association. 'Lives in Edinburgh. Nice.'

Francis Newark: Professor of Jurisprudence at Belfast University in Northern Ireland. (He joined committee later, so no assessment in diary.)

John Shields: Newly-retired Headmaster of Peter Symonds School, Winchester. 'Friendly.'

Reggie Smith-Rose: Director of Radio Research at the Department

of Scientific and Industrial Research. 'Helpful – non-aggressive.'
Betty Whitley: Journalist, social worker. Wife of the Rector of St
   Giles Church in Edinburgh. 'Deep.'
Billy Wright: Footballer. 'Warm – sensible.'
Denis Lawrence and Stella Fisher were the Committee Secretary and
   Assistant Secretary. 'Like look of both.'

I was not sure why I was on the committee; I represented no special
interest or area, but perhaps I was there as Regular Listener. I was certainly a passionate believer in the power for good I felt radio and television were capable of disseminating.

We met in full committee seventy-eight times. Some of these meetings were week-end occasions spent out of London. In addition there
were sub-committee meetings. Between times a great deal of homework had to be read. Fat foolscap-sized envelopes thudded through
our letter-box in Elm Park Gardens, and papers piled up all over the
flat. Reggie had been right about the interest of the job. It was eye-
opening in ways I hadn't imagined. We took evidence, written and
oral, from a number of sources. There cannot be many organisations
connected even faintly with broadcasting communication that were
not included. Both the B.B.C. and the I.T.A. sent representatives from
all departments and advisory bodies, those based in London and the
regions. The arts, educational and religious bodies – mainstream and
minority religions; technical interests, film interests, political, medical
and trade union interests; associations of viewers and of listeners,
workers in youth clubs, and of course advertising interests – all were
represented. We saw many distinguished individuals, all of whom had
something to say; some more interesting than others. And then there
were the commercial companies.

I must declare my aversion to the kind of vested interest that comes
disguised – or tries to disguise itself – as disinterested public benefac-
tion. We saw several groups, noble lords among them, who looked us
straight in the eye and said smugly that all they wanted was to give the
public what it wanted; they were not, they said, so presumptuous as to
give them what other people (us? the B.B.C.?) thought they ought to
want. It was probably Richard Hoggart who suggested that it was
fairly presumptuous to treat viewers as if they were incapable of
appreciating something more demanding than pre-digested pap. And
how did the companies know what viewers wanted if they were not
given a choice?

Our committee rooms were in Cornwall House, on the south side of Waterloo Bridge. On committee days I parked my car at the far end of the Festival Hall car-park, and walked under one of the arches to get to the office. I discovered that because of the arch's beautiful echo it was possible to sing an arpeggio and immediately hear back a chord. Every time I went to a meeting I paused there with pleasure, and sang out in full voice; and as there was no one to stop me, or wonder at my goings-on, I sometimes stood there for a full three minutes belting out. Very satisfying! In the office we were each given a locker with a key, a clean towel and a square piece of white soap with E.R. on it. It felt like being back at school, in more ways than one.

The days when we interviewed witnesses were long, and to amuse myself (and to keep my attention from wandering) I started to make small drawings of those who came before us. I drew on my lap – or behind a pile of papers and a carafe of water – and hoped it wasn't obvious to my subject that I was having a go at his face. I hadn't done any concentrated drawing since as a child I had covered any available paper; but I found that with practice I was beginning to get likenesses. At first I drew in pencil but then I discovered that the discipline of working with a Biro was more effective. The longer I kept at it the fewer lines I needed to use, and with increasing confidence my slight talent improved. Sometimes the drawings were caricatures; mostly they were attempts at straight portraits. I enjoyed the day when my eye and hand responded well. Bishop Cockin was one of our witnesses, and his pleasing face was interesting to work on. After the committee finished sitting he wrote to me (about a charitable concern, I think) and said he had been intrigued to watch me looking up and down as I drew behind a barricade of books and papers, and wondered if my likeness of him had turned out satisfactorily. By that time I had collected all the drawings, dated and identified them, and stuck them into a couple of notebooks, otherwise I might have sent him his likeness. Looking at my collection of faces, and the women in hats (some Welsh ladies, in particular, wore very purposeful hats), is a reminder of a time in which I learned a lot about human nature. Occasionally I still come across a face in the street that seems familiar, and yet I can't place it. Then I realise I have made a drawing of it, and that is why I know it so well.

I wonder whether it was very disconcerting for the witnesses to be so closely scrutinised. At the time I was too interested in what I was doing – I was also listening to what was being said and chipping in when I had anything to offer – to notice any discomfort I may have caused. If it did upset them, and it isn't too late, I make apology for my unwinking gaze and head-bobbing.

Before we started to hear witnesses the committee had to learn about the whole vast complexity of broadcasting; how everything was organised and financed by both channels. We went to the B.B.C.'s Kingswood Warren experimental establishment and were shown the difference between line systems. I struggled to grasp the technical details; I can't say I understood all we were taught, but I figured others in the group made sense of it, and I could trust their judgement when it came to making recommendations for the introduction of new techniques. I told Harry I wasn't any good at figures and scientific facts, and he said that wasn't what I was on the committee for. He didn't clarify this cryptic remark. I think and hope I may have been of more use in assessing testimony than in struggling to master the intricacies of line-definition, standards and frequencies. We were given – this was a big moment – a demonstration of coloured T.V. I thought it was 'wonderfully good, makes the whole difference, but both Sir H. and Mrs Whitley [this was before we were on first-name terms] thought it bad and dull.' I decided they had no visual taste!

After a day spent at the Rediffusion Studios, in Wembley, we discussed the question of pre-recording programmes. Some of the committee had the illusion that there was something a little bit shady about it, that it was an easy way out for the T.V. company, and saved money. I assured them that it wasn't and didn't, but added that I thought something *was* lost unless viewers were shown an actual performance. I wonder how I could have thought anything so foolish; for, of course, every recording *is* a live performance – filmed. I always treat a recording as the real thing, and I don't believe it alters my performance at all. I suppose it is possible that, unconsciously, I am aware that if I fall flat on my face during a taping the moment can be deleted and I can start again; but knowing the expense of a retake, I always treat a recording in exactly the same way as I do a live show. Studio audiences do help to make a recording into an occasion, and I am grateful to them, but (as I wrote elsewhere) my material was conceived to be overheard by one person at a time, and when I was still performing, I preferred to play sketches on radio or T.V. without a studio audience. The dual pull between the invisible viewer at home and the public in the studio poses a question: who is one playing to? I tried to think first of the viewer – after all television programmes are designed

Harold Cottrom

Edmund Hudson   Aug 30 1961

Betty Whitely

Richard Hoggart

Sir Kenneth Clark

Bishop F. A. Cockin.

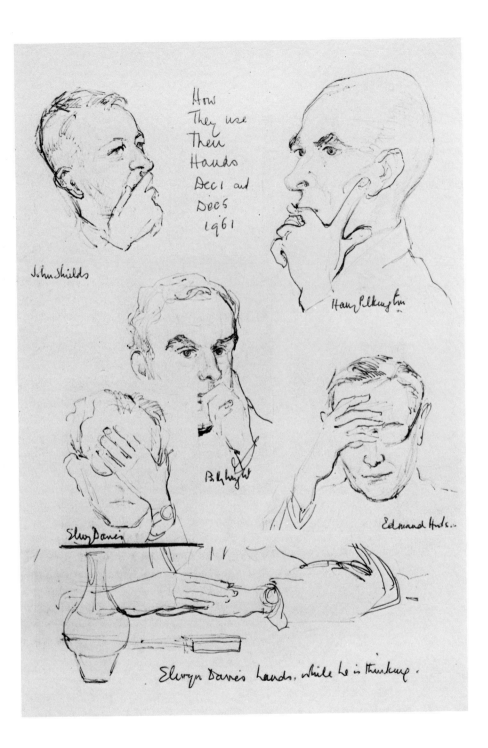

How
They use
Their
Hands
Dec 1 and
Dec 5
1961

John Shields

Harry Pilkington

Billy Wright

Elwyn Davies

Edmund Hunt

Elwyn Davies hands, while he is thinking.

145

primarily for him – and trying to accommodate both the live spectator and the viewer at home tends to diffuse the relationship of performer and audience.

The committee's investigations took us to Scotland and Wales, and a sub-committee paid a visit to the United States and Canada, Northern Ireland and the Isle of Man. In my innocence I was surprised by the rather prickly nationalist feeling we met, some of it in ecclesiastic circles. Much later back in London a point came up about unity, and I remember Betty Whitley turning a little pink, sitting up straighter than usual and saying in her pretty Scots voice: 'That, if I may say so, is a Pisky fiddle!' She was very likely right; denominations have a tendency to try and score off each other. I liked her for speaking up, and I relished her use of words. 'Pisky' for Episcopalian, or Church of England, was familiar to me, because I had often heard the expression in America, but it came as an amusing surprise to the rest of the committee. As my Welsh mentor Tom Jones had done, Betty put her native land a good way ahead of the rest of Great Britain. I am very proud to be English, but like most of us in this island I am a mongrel, and I find nationalism an un-grown-up way of thinking. The world is a small place, and dividing it up into little blocks may be cosy, but the time has come for us to realise that we don't have to wave our special flag to express our individuality or retain our particular qualities. I agree that 'small is beautiful' and I prefer to live as we do in our own little bailiwick, but in world terms we have to think bigger than that. After all the ideal is to be of one mind and this must mean universal understanding. I can't say it is very apparent as yet but there are signs of a growing awareness of it, as a necessity. We began to take oral evidence:

Gruelling day at Cornwall House. Lord Reith in the p.m. He is a giant all right – physically, mentally; aggressive and arrogant. And has charm. Looks years younger than he is. Vigorous. Not aware of the change of time. His splendid suggestion of 'allowing' Harrods, to sponsor an hour on B.B.C. (T.V.) but of *course* not to advertise beyond the bald announcement 'Harrods presents' showed how out of touch he was ... He said it was wicked and wrong to allow the Religious Advisory Council to look after both the B.B.C. *and* I.T.A. .... When asked what he thought was the purpose of the Religious Advisory Council he said it must be for furthering the ideas of the B.B.C. – *not* the I.T.A. Someone murmured it might be for concerning itself with God, but he dismissed that. It was a fascinating interview, but no use to the committee – except to see an exhibition of superb self-satisfaction. Attractive man but not loving.

Fringe Benefits

13 April. Sir H. thinks all witnesses should feel uneasy with us and we are instructed not to reveal our own feelings. I find this hard as I am given to bursts of approval, smiles and undoubted grunts . . . Sir H. was presented with a tandem bicycle today as a wedding present from some city group or another.

[Next day]: I drew Sir —— repeatedly and every time I looked up I caught his eye. He isn't easy but I did a goodish one. Tried Mrs Whitley but she is very elusive. It is a very pretty face particularly when happy.

Saw direct pictures from Moscow via Eurovision. First time it has been done. Watched spaceman Gagarin arrive back in Moscow, kissed by Khruschev. Red Square thought to have had 200,000 people in it.

20 April. [Meeting in Cardiff.] We had a gay dinner . . . Richard's collar kept coming undone and his tie slipped, but I refrained from telling him. *Sometimes* I'm not bossy.

In June 1961 Harry had to go into hospital for some treatment and we missed his wise, lightly-guiding hand. In our telegram to him the Committee said: 'Unanimously send wishes be good obey the matron.' During his absence we were well led by Francis Newark and Edmund Hudson.

I had come to know the members 'out of school' when they dined with us at Elm Park Gardens, usually after long days of meetings. I particularly enjoyed talking to Richard Hoggart. He confessed that he cherished feelings about 'class'. I wrote in my diary: 'I told him, given time, I'd cure him. At least he didn't pretend about this.' I remember we spoke about class voices, and I told him of my own dislike of what I thought of as an upper-crust Pont Street voice – the kind that stands out in a crowd, in a bus or a restaurant. Richard said it had taken him years to be able to get past the barrier of such a sound, because he equated it with superiority, authority, domination, expectancy of obedience, and arrogance. Before he joined us he had served on another committee with a woman he came both to like and admire and to whom he had admitted that hearing her speak (before he knew her as an individual), had raised all those images in his mind. We agreed it was foolish to allow the sound of voices to get between ourselves and other people. Of all the unproductive resentments, including racial and religious prejudices, I think class is the most idiotic. I recognise that 'class', as a divisive weapon, is handy for those who believe in 'divide and rule', but as one who believes in unity as the better way I dislike it and know it is evil. Inverted snobbery is almost as bad as the other old-fashioned kind. I wonder why I am irritated by the tone of voice of

147

upper-crust Pont Streeters; the answer may be that the sound implies insensitivity and an air of complacency. Another form of I'm-all-right-Jack? It is also ugly. I must admit that, if I listen, I realise that one or two of my friends have the kind of voice I deplore, but, because I love them and know they are neither arrogant nor superior, I am no longer bothered by the way they sound – all of which shows the folly of being fooled by the outward and audible.

Accents and voices have been my stock-in-trade, and I relish the variety, particularly of local accents, found in these islands. When I was young there was a 'refained' urban accent that has almost entirely disappeared. It came from a veneer of elegance being superimposed on a foundation of uncertain vowel sounds. 'Thank you, I'd like some more tea' came out as 'Thenk yew, aid lake sum moor tee.' This was an 'upping' accent. Today 'downing' is more fashionable. Some upper-middle and middle-class young deny their backgrounds and pretend they come from the working-classes. Their accent is of no-man's land, and their speech, on purpose slovenly, is larded with 'I mean', 'you know' and 'kind of'; 'harv' for 'have' and 'hut' for 'hat'. The reason for this camouflage may be suspect; is it to suck up to the masses just in case the tumbrils arrive? All the same, movement between classes is far freer than it was when I grew up; the passport upward is ability – which is good news. Judging by the interest in watching sport and pro-grammes like 'Mastermind' (both have followings of millions), there is general admiration for excellence. Perhaps some day a government (of any party) will have the vision to cherish and not resent the excellent among us and, instead of punishing enterprise, creativity and effort by crippling taxation, will encourage developments that in the end bene-fit the community. It cannot be the aim of governments to drive away excellence; but that is the inevitable result of their present policies.

At the interviews witnesses gave us glimpses of viewers' and listeners' problems ranging from poor reception in mountainous places to inter-ference from foreign transmitters. We also heard from the Association of Small Shopkeepers of unexpected difficulties. A man with a local grocery store complained about the wide variety of goods advertised on television. As soon as he had got in the latest cat-food and break-fast cereal, the T.V. showed yet *another* new brand, and his customers, caught by the tempting ads, asked for only those goodies they had seen on their screens the night before. He said he couldn't keep up, nor was he able to dispose of one lot of stock before another was demanded.

He begged for pity; asked us to put ourselves in his position. Please, could the committee make the advertisers stick to one brand for a while longer, and thus give grocers a fair chance.

I am all for small locally-owned shops and the personal service that goes with them, and I remember with pleasure going as a child to our village grocer in the King's Road, Chelsea. There was always a delicious nose-tickling smell of spices, mixed with freshly-ground coffee, bacon and biscuits. Sugar came out of a sack – or was it a barrel? – and was scooped into soft, thick, blue paper bags with a giant trowel, the ends of the bag were neatly folded; and the whole package tied with fine string pulled from a ball on a wooden peg. There aren't many such shops left in London, but up in Cumberland, where we go in spring, one of the delights of shopping is still finding family grocers' stores where the same good smells are to be sniffed. Like most people I welcome the convenience and economy of supermarkets, but the pennies saved hardly compensate for queueing to pay at the check-out, the loathsome smell of artificial floral air-sprays, and the faint whiff given off by acres of plastic devices and packaging. I wonder whether when today's children are grown up they will look back, as they shop for their tiny complete meal-in-a-capsule T.V. dinner of the future, and remember with nostalgia the strip-lighting, jumbo cartons and the colourless lumps of pre-parcelled meat in the food chests, at the shopping-centre supermarkets of their youth. Maybe they will even long for the sickly pink smell of such places. What is yet to come may be even worse.

The committee continued to meet all through the summer of 1961. When Harry came out of hospital we went north, for a week-end conference, to his house at St Helens. My impressions of the members had changed since I had made a list of them the year before, after our first full meeting. I didn't make a complete new assessment, but on 9 July I wrote a few notes: 'Elwyn: romantic. John: another schoolboy, Sixth Form. Richard (a Yorkshireman) sometimes looks like a saint-in-torture. Edmund stirs calmly.' It amused me to observe their mannerisms of speech, how they put their questions, and their various styles of deliberation. I now called them all by their first names. For the St Helens meeting some of us stayed in Liverpool and travelled out to Windle Hall by a bus-like train, sitting up in front, almost with the driver. The wild flowers came at us, instead of being passed by as in an ordinary train. Back in London for the autumn we continued to see witnesses. I was gloomy about the quality of the testimony given to us, in particular by the Independent Television Authority; and yet the more we heard of its difficulties, and what we came to realise was the inadequate power it had been given, the more we sympathised. The programme companies often claimed they wanted to produce more high-quality television, but weren't very convincing when they added 'but not at peak viewing hours'.

My diary reports:

We saw members of the Royal Society and the British Association for the Advancement of Science. They made a pleasant change. Their brows were in fact high. I did some drawings and couldn't believe there could be so much cranium as I had drawn. There was. [I went on to record how much I admired the concentration and grasp of the other members of the Committee.] I make little darts at subjects, sometimes relevantly, but am not good at thinking through. A sort of useful feminine lack of logic can get to a central point without processes. Not always, but now and then. [I do not approve of self-justification.]

6 September. [A busy day hearing those concerned with Toll T.V. and T.V. for public showing. They turned out to be non-starters, and we weren't surprised.] The quality of witnesses varies widely and it is safe to say that the middle-men of the television industry – i.e. non-creators who merely organise and collect – are a non-flowering lot.

20 September. Saw the Roman Catholic Archbishop Heenan of Liverpool. He began by saying he didn't see why Jews weren't allowed some of the time on the air allotted to religious broadcasting. Made a lot of liberal remarks. Very attractive, Irish. Small pink boyish face and huge working-man's hands. He wants a chance to preach and teach doctrine on the air. [The recommendation was not made.] It was the first anniversary of the Pilkington Committee. I found a card saying 'Have fun now you are one', and put it at Harry's place in the Conference Room together with three tins of boiled sweets for us all to share. It was also Elwyn's birthday. A lot of singing went on. We toasted ourselves and Elwyn – in boiled sweets.

30 September. [Week-end conference at Gilbert Murray Hall, Oadby, Leicester.] Harry wore a thick-knit string-coloured sweater over short-sleeved shirt. No tie. Leaped through the window [during coffee-break] without his sweater into cold wind. I became mum and made him go back to get it. I think he was glad. Behaves as if common-sense rules didn't apply to *him*! We discussed prizes in cash or kind for Quiz Shows on I.T.V. Harry summed up the Committee's views: The prizes should be trivial but the programmes shouldn't.

To this day the quizzes are trivial and prizes pricey.

All through the first five months of 1962 the committee worked at drafting its report. Harry and I were the only members who lived within five miles of the office; as well as the house in Lancashire he had the use of a company flat in St James's where he stayed mid-week. The others came from Scotland, Wales, the Home Counties and outer suburbs. This meant journeys, and for three of them overnight trips by train, or very early starts by aeroplane.

2 May. We went through five chapters very thoroughly; chewed over sentences, weighed words. We met from 9.30 a.m. to 5.15 p.m. that day and when I left for home two sub-committees, made up of members who had already put in a full day's work, began their sittings that would last well into the night. Only one member of the Committee skipped meetings to pursue his own interests; most of the others made considerable personal sacrifices to get there as often as possible. I was full of admiration for them. (I was my own boss and able to arrange my jobs between committee dates.)

The members had decided to give Harry, as a present to remember us by, a desk ruler made up of my drawings of us all. I selected drawings done at different times, and Edmund Hudson arranged to have them mounted between two lengths of perspex. On 20 May we discussed the kind of questions we might get at the press conference in June when the report was published. Because some of our recommendations involved radical replanning of the Independent Television Authority we knew they were likely to be controversial, and we prepared ourselves for criticism and resistance from the television companies.

In Chapter Three of the Report we tried to analyse the purposes of broadcasting. The charters of both authorities, the B.B.C. and the I.T.A., accepted that they included the dissemination of information, education and entertainment. After two years of close study we were more critical of the I.T.A. than of the B.B.C., because we felt that its aim, 'to give the public what it wants', was a misleading phrase. 'It is in fact patronising and arrogant in that it claims to know what the public is, but defines it as no more than the mass audience . . . What the public wants and what it has the right to get is the freedom to choose from the widest possible range of programmes. Anything less than that is a deprivation.'

In view of our assessment I suppose it should not have surprised me when there was roar of rage against the Report from some of the newspapers. I had forgotten how heavily many of them had invested in commercial television.

The Report came out on 27 June. We met early at Cornwall House and gave Harry his present: 'Desk ruler a great success.' Then came the press conference. 'A tough morning. Room full of journalists. We sat at a long table behind mikes. Harry was nervous, but his speech was very good and said all that needed to be said on our behalf.' But the force of hostility and resentment directed at us surprised me. I was not used to seeing the naked face of threatened power – and greed. Of course the *Mirror* was enraged (we had expected this), but so were the *Express* and *Mail*. I got the idea that none of them had understood the Report – if indeed they had read it! An unpleasant hour. Resentment and a sort of dumb incomprehension were depressing.

Reggie, together with wives of some of the Committee Members, joined us for luncheon. 'A relief that at last the egg is out. We all listened to the news on I.T.V. Very fair and well done. But a quote from Peter Cadbury said that the place for the Report was the waste-paper basket.' He had looked furious all through the conference. That night we were bidden to dine with the Postmaster General at the Savoy.

After a delicious dinner Mr Bevins spoke and said he didn't think our recommendations would be acceptable to the Government [Tory]. Harry said they would do well to ponder the report for it was a serious and deeply reasoned argument. It needed a courageous Government to face up to its implications.

28 June, the next day, 8.5 a.m.: 'Harry rang: "It's Ephesians 6 verse 12." That is the verse that talks about spiritual wickedness in high places. I reminded him that the next verse recommends "having done all, to stand". We had certainly done all we could to present an honest, thoughtful report and we could stand by it.' 'Of course,' he said.

Papers true to form. *Mirror* and *Sketch* screaming their rage. *Daily Mail* loud. *Daily Telegraph* surprisingly violent. *Times* good on the whole. Harry says it is as well to get the noisy reception now, before people read the Report. The Oakseys [Lord Oaksey was the judge at the Nuremberg Trials] were here tonight in full agreement with all we've said. Disinterested, thoughtful people must be impressed by a cogent well-argued paper. Bernard Levin reviewed what the press said about the Report, and was good.

Sunday, 1 July. The press, generally, was not hostile; indeed the *Sunday Times*, the *Observer* and *Sunday Telegraph* conceded that we had stated the truth. The *Sunday Times* thinks the Government will do something about networking [one of our recommendations]. The *Observer* finds us right but smug and 'moral' – as if 'moral' is now a dirty word like 'peace'.

Fringe Benefits

As its humblest member and the one with the fewest qualifications I can say the Pilkington Committee did its job conscientiously, honestly and with good will. Some of us had to be convinced over certain issues, but in the end we were happily agreed and, as Harry had demanded, we produced a unanimous report. In 1977 another committee, under Lord Annan, offered its conclusions about broadcasting. Its findings do not appear to have been much more welcome than ours were, and another government has postponed deciding about the future both of radio and television. Re-reading the Pilkington Report I still believe our chapter on the Purposes of Broadcasting stands as the definitive statement on the subject. I am proud to have been a member of the committee that produced it.

Reggie had as usual been right. Serving for those two years was enormously interesting; it stretched my mind. To meet and work with a dedicated, entertaining and agreeable group of people of integrity was both educational and a pleasure.

FACE THE MUSIC

The scene is a B.B.C. studio in Manchester, a few years back during a recording of the television programme, *Face the Music*. I was a member of the panel that evening, and it was my turn to answer the question put to me by the chairman, Joseph Cooper.

'I'm going to play the opening note – just one note – of a piano piece. Can you tell me the name of the piece and of the composer?'

He played a single note *somewhere* above middle C. I do not have perfect pitch, but off the top of my head without any hesitation I said: 'It is called *La Fille aux Cheveux de Lin*, and it is by Debussy.'

An ace! I felt as if I'd won at Wimbledon, and I can still feel the glow. This did not often happen to me when I took part in *Face the Music*.

For those who do not know the programme, it is a general knowledge quiz about music in which Joe puts questions to a team of three players who are not professional musicians – they all earn their living in other ways – but whose interest in and love of music has led them to listen and enjoy it enough to have acquired some familiarity with music of all kinds. In each programme there is a guest who is a professional musician – a performer, conductor, lecturer, composer, professor or a musicologist. To give an idea of the variety of guests who have appeared in the programme up to the time at which I am writing here are a few of their names: Isobel Baillie, Clifford Curzon, Colin Davis, Norman del Mar, George Malcolm, Yehudi Menuhin, Nina Milkina, Gerald Moore, David Munrow, Peter Pears, André Previn, Marisa Robles, Evelyn Rothwell, Georg Solti and Eva Turner.

The genesis of *Face the Music* goes back to 1954, when the original idea for a musical quiz was suggested to Walter Todds, then a radio talks producer. At that time he had worked on many programmes with Joseph Cooper. Joe was, and still is, not only a pianist but also knowledgeable about music, and a man of intelligence and humour. The two of them evolved a programme named *Call the Tune*. Walter's original suggestion for a title was *Face the Music*, but those in authority preferred *Call the Tune*. Thus the more appropriate name was ready and waiting when it was needed for television.

In the pilot programme of *Call the Tune*, made to see if the idea worked, Walter tried out two discussion spots, and remembers asking the team whether it was right to jazz up the classics. History does not relate the replies, but I have to admit that I rather like hearing Bach with a *slight* swing beat, although I don't care for the swooping strings in song arrangements based on pieces by Chopin, Tchaikovsky or Beethoven. I am not offended by the treatment of Borodin's music in *Kismet*; the tunes are strong enough to be indestructible, and it isn't a bad thing for them to be heard by a new audience.

Anona Winn was one of the early team members. I joined two years later, when my fellow-players were Stephen Potter and Paul Dehn. To Paul I owe a discovery, he shared with me, that continues to give surprise and pleasure to whomsoever I pass it on. He found that with very slight repunctuation Shakespeare's sonnet XVIII makes perfect sense when read from the last line upwards. It is as beautiful that way, and there is something particularly tender about ending the sonnet on its opening line 'Shall I compare thee to a summer's day?' Paul told me that there are other Shakespeare sonnets that can be read in the same reverse direction, but I have never explored the possibility. Was Shakespeare aware of this? Eng. Lit. friends tell me it is likely.

Call the Tune was heard periodically on radio for about four years, then it stopped. By 1966 Walter had moved to Television's Music Department, of which Huw Wheldon was then the head, and it was decided that the time had come to try out a music quiz on B.B.C. 2. A single programme called *Face the Music* was taped in December for transmission on Boxing Day. The founder members were Richard Baker, Paul Jennings and I. We recorded at Lime Grove Studios, and,

Face the Music: Joseph Cooper, Walter Todds, Robin Ray, myself and David Attenborough

as on my first radio appearance in *Call the Tune*, the professional musician was Denis Matthews. Ever since that day, off and on (I am happy to say it has often been on) I have had the fun of taking part.

I have not had a great deal of experience of other quizzes. I was twice on *Call My Bluff* and proved I could be a convincing liar, but the only other quiz programme I have been on was during the war when I took part in *Trans-Atlantic Quiz*, on radio, with Denis Brogan as my partner. Lionel Hale was in the English question-master's seat; Alistair Cooke in New York chaired his team of John Mason Brown, the theatre critic, and Christopher Morley, the novelist. Each team was tested on its knowledge of the other's country. I remember the Americans being challenged to list in order the counties through which the Thames flowed, from its source to the sea. I didn't know the answer, but John Mason Brown said it was the easiest question he had ever been asked; the answer was none – from start to finish the Thames is the boundary between counties. At that time I read the *New Yorker* magazine with extra care, and found I could cope with general topical questions, but I left the political and historical ones to Denis, who never failed to know the right answers. He knew all my answers as well.

A great deal of the popularity of *Face the Music* is due to Joseph Cooper. He sets the mood of the programme. When I am asked whether he is as 'nice' (of all the poverty-stricken words for a combination of 'friendly', 'agreeable', 'pleasant', 'warm' and 'kindly') as he appears to be, the answer is yes. (As with no less a person than the Queen the public image is the private truth. It makes a change.) I met him long before either of us ever thought we would be working together on television. It was in 1940, when he and Virginia's husband, Tony Thesiger, were attached to the same anti-aircraft unit, based in Bristol. It was there, a year earlier, that Ronnie Waldman gave me my first radio broadcast – a five-minute spot on a tea-time programme – in which, sandwiched between musical items played by a 'light-music' quintet, I performed one of the only two items then in my repertoire. After that I paid several visits to the West Country to broadcast. After one of my broadcasts the Thesigers invited Joe to dinner to meet me. I knew he was a classical pianist, but I didn't then know what a deft way he had with what is inaccurately called jazz, and in improvising in the manner of whatever composer we chose, as he does in the Hidden Melody spot in *Face the Music*. (We have, since then, from time to time improvised together, preferably not too much in public since the success of improvising comes from unselfconsciousness and, in my case anyway, it can't be done to order.) After dinner we sang some songs we both knew, and then Joe played us a tune he had written that hadn't yet got a lyric. Virginia was already writing for *Punch*, and we suggested she should try and write it. She called the song 'No News' – it was full of topical allusions to the absence of events at that time of the phoney war, and I sang it in one of my broadcasts. It deserved a wider hearing than it got.

Face the Music has always been produced by Walter Todds, who prepares the questions with Joe and, after taping, is responsible for editing the programme. Walter is one of the friends in my circle with whom I share a wavelength; what makes me laugh, makes him laugh too, and, as I did with Ronnie Waldman in the far-off days of variety radio, I save up items to tell him, assured that he will be as entertained as I am. One particular anecdote, source long forgotten, has been a kind of bond between us. Writing it down is risky (not *risqué*), for if it isn't lightly told it might offend those – usually non-churchgoers – who hold that all religious subjects are taboo. The scene is a Sunday School class of

Richard Baker

unresponsive urban ten-year-old boys. The teacher in desperation decides to try a new way of arousing their interest. In a falsely cheerful tone she tells of coming across the park that morning; glancing up at a tree, she beheld such a beautiful little creature with a bright red coat and a big bushy tail, his eyes very bright as he sat there nibbling at a nut. 'I wonder,' she says, 'if anyone can tell me who it was?' Long pause. Then in a voice of infinite boredom one of the boys says: 'I suppose it was Jesus.' (Come to think of it, it is really a sad tale of non-communication.)

Richard Baker and Robin Ray (in alphabetical order) have been the two most regular regulars on the panel, and very valuable to it they are. My heart rose when I found that either, or better still both, were on at the same time as I was. Not only were they informed about all kinds of music, but they added to their knowledge fresh, inventive and witty ways of answering questions. On and off the air they are good company.

Richard Baker, who is best known as a news-reader on B.B.C. television, is a man of many interests. He combines his wide experience and love of music with writing books. These include (so far) an introduction to music and two biographies, both of sailors. He served in the

Navy during the war. Richard also introduces, on television, Promenade concerts and Galas from Convent Garden, and chairs his own *Start the Week* programme on radio. He has a quiet understated wit.

Robin, whose store of opus-numbers reveals a phenomenal memory, once thought of becoming a professional pianist, but came to the conclusion that the world was over-supplied with performers. With modesty he questioned his own performance and decided to pursue another career. He has in turn been actor, stage director and taught at the Royal Academy of Dramatic Art. I think he would now describe himself as a T.V.-radio-journalist. His interviews with musicians on radio are first-class. I remember with special pleasure a long one with Alfred Brendel. His series of Saturday morning gramophone recitals is one of the most attractive I've listened to. My musical taste seems to match Robin's, and I never hear one of those programmes without discovering new work that I want to hear again. His manner on radio is informative and un-pompous, and his genuine enjoyment of what he chooses to play adds greatly to my pleasure.

Other regulars on the team were David Attenborough, Bernard Levin, Patrick Moore, John Julius Norwich, Valerie Pitts, Arianna Stassinopoulos and Dorothy Tutin. After taping the programme, some of us usually went out to supper together. These *après*-programme parties made a good finish to the evening. On one occasion David Attenborough, just returned from Australia and in splendid form, told us about a new reference book he had been shown in Melbourne on the use of the English language as now spoken in Australia. A word new to David, and to us, was defined as 'a heightened sense of indifference'. It was 'imbuggerance'.

Bernard Levin, for so long a strong member of the panel, found his writing commitments did not allow him time to travel to and from Manchester, where we recorded, and he had to withdraw. (I missed him as a travelling-companion. For choice we both sat silent in our corners of the carriage – he spent a good deal of the journey having a long late luncheon – but silent or otherwise, I find him an attractive, provocative and courageous character, even though I don't always agree with him.) Bernard's departure was a loss, because he not only knew a good deal and added a certain edge to the programme, but sartorially he provided pleasures for the eyes, such as when he wore a pink linen dinner-jacket. That same summer Robin Ray came back from a holiday under the southern sun with an impressive tan, and a long loose white garment of Arab origin that set off the tan and surprised us all at first; but it looked splendid on the screen. Sometimes Patrick Moore's neckties were of the roving kind, they wandered a little from under his collar, and gave him the air of an absent-minded professor. That is not at all the truth about Patrick. The little-boy look of that independent tie aroused my mothering instinct (as it had done when Richard Hoggart's tie rose up) and I felt an urge to put it straight, but I realised that the image of careless rapture was indeed part of his character, and I held my hand.

John Julius shared with me an undisguised pleasure at being part of the programme. I enjoyed the quiet enthusiasm he brought to it. He is well informed about music, and a lot more besides. Every year I look forward to the little anthology he compiles and sends to his friends as a Christmas card. It is always a personal collection of unusual and unexpected quotations.

The panel for *Face the Music* was always made up of one woman and two men, so the other female members and I were never in the same programme, although some of us met on other occasions when the quiz was staged live in aid of charity, and once as part of the King's Lynn Festival.

In the early days of television games the women players, led by Isobel Barnett and Barbara Kelly in *What's my Line*, only had to concentrate on their head-to-waist appearance, for that was all viewers saw of them, seated as they were behind a table. Week after week I noted the ever-increasing extravagance of their chandelier ear-rings and the elaboration of their necklaces. Their neck-lines, full of variation, ranged from the plunging and the 'sweetheart', to the ruffled, and the puritanical plainness of a simple white collar. I don't believe either of them ever repeated an ensemble. Below the waist for all I know those girls (it was a long time ago) had on gardening trousers, and old tennis shoes or wellies, hidden by the table and its ground-length cloth. For the women on *Face the Music* no such relaxation was possible. We were seen from head to toe, seated before a low coffee-table. If one appeared often this made demands on one's wardrobe. I tried to be clever in combining different tops with two or three skirts, but in the end I gave up the struggle always to wear something hitherto unseen, and happily settled for repeats. I have a certain well-loved blue-green jacket, made of Thai silk brought home to me by Virginia after a round-the-world trip at least twenty years ago, that is still likely to be seen again. I take comfort from the women who have said they were glad to see me in something they recognised from a previous programme.

In Pleasant Places

Being a member of the panel on *Face the Music* is one of the best 'fringe benefits' that has come my way. I think it is far the most enjoyable of all parlour games played on either radio or television. It is not only fun to be in it but, as I know from seeing it when I am not part of it, it is good fun to watch and try to play at home. I think the reason it succeeds – and for a minority-interest programme with a viewing figure rising to over six million it must be counted a success – is because it is an amicable occasion, chaired by an agreeable man with a gift for establishing an atmosphere that is both relaxed and lively. This, to start with, is reassuring. Secondly, although the game is played with alert interest and pursued with keenness, it is not fiercely competitive. It is not considered cheating to drop a whispered hint into the ear of a fellow panel-member; but what is *not done* is to accept the hint and then gaze into space, and pretend that you yourself knew the answer. I name no names, but there have been players who did just that. This was not popular, and the next time help was needed it wasn't always forthcoming. The fact that there are no marks, no prizes, no winners and no losers lessens the tension. In spite of this there have been rare members of the team who played the game with a grimness and perhaps a fear of failure that turned it into some kind of desperate contest. There was a novelist who didn't know the answers to his questions, and covered his discomfiture by making remarks like: 'I suppose you want me to name that crashing Gallic bore, Massenet.' 'No,' said Joe with commendable restraint. Such mistaken attitudes were rare. On the whole we played, as I think we were meant to play, as informed amateurs, in the best sense of that word.

Clearly I know rather less than some others who appear on the panel. (I am surprised when strangers ask me how it is that I know so much about music when I know that I don't.) I half-know a lot of general answers, but not many about opera. Joe once played a track from an opera that was familiar to everyone in the studio, and me. I could have hummed the whole aria, but what it was called entirely eluded me. I made several wild guesses, all of them wrong. The day after the programme was shown I joined a queue in our local delicatessen. The young man behind the counter who had never before struck me as being an obvious opera-lover, saw me come into the shop and couldn't wait for me to get to his counter. Over the heads of the other shoppers he called out with joyous relish: 'Fancy you not knowing "Vissi d'arte"!' Failing to answer a question can sometimes be successful. I have seldom given more satisfaction than by not knowing that answer. It isn't that I don't like opera, it is that I like chamber music more. (Murmur it low before Bernard; although I know it is my fault, Wagner does not speak to me.) The human voice, when it is as radiant and 'natural' as Janet Baker's, thanks to her superb technique and a beautiful instrument, is for me the best of all musical sounds. On the whole I prefer to hear singing in recital rather than on stage, but with artists of Janet's calibre I'm not choosy *where* they sing.

Our audiences in Manchester were of special quality. They came from all over the north-west of England in groups, from music clubs, choral and dramatic societies, Women's Institutes and Townswomen's Guilds, as well as individually and in family parties. They were ready to enjoy themselves, often musically knowledgeable, and – unlike London studio audiences, who do not always get tickets to the programme of their choice and have to accept whatever show is available at the time – they had specifically chosen to come to *Face the Music*, so knew what they were in for. (I recorded one of my solo programmes at the Television Theatre in Shepherd's Bush in London, watched by a coach-load of women up from the country who had expected to see *The Clitheroe Kid*. They arrived at the T.V. Centre after taping had begun, were not allowed into the studio and were hurriedly sent on to Shepherd's Bush to see me. Just before my recording began someone tactfully told me how disappointed they all were. After the programme was over the Commissionaire reported that one of the ladies had said she had quite liked my show; it was 'sort of different', whatever that meant.) In Manchester our audiences for *Face the Music* always seemed well-disposed towards us and contributed a sense of warmth to the broadcasts that was encouraging, they turned the sessions into 'occasions' and added an element of anticipation.

One of my cherished memories is of the night when Joe introduced a new question (it was complicated then and is far too complicated to go into now) which involved using the initials of composers' names. The team was Brian Redhead, Robin and myself. We were slow in getting on with the game, and to help us Joe said: 'I need a P.' This artless remark was soon picked up by the audience, although the three of us with supreme self-control showed no sign of having registered the suggestive hint until the audience giggled. To put things right Joe said something like 'P for Polka'; at which Robin sighed and said, *'That's* a relief!' Even then, although the strain was considerable, we did not entirely break down. Watching the programme later showed that this determination not to crack made it a good deal funnier than if we had. The more innocent of our viewers probably never knew what had transpired. I was not present on another night when a member of the team, asked to identify the link between a piece of music and a portrait shown on the screen, said he knew the music but had no idea who was the woman in the picture. He was urged to have another look. No, he said firmly, he had never seen her before in his life. With some embarrassment Joe said it was the Queen.

Until her tragic death in 1973 Joe's wife Jean was very much a part of *Face the Music*. They made a happy partnership. Jean's beguiling blonde country looks and remarkably youthful mien endeared her to all of us. She had a child-like quality of simple directness and an out-going friendly enthusiasm. Her support of all that Joe was doing gave her a justifiable feeling of true partnership. It was a big job they did together, touring up and down the country, with Joe giving lecture-recital programmes about various composers, and Jean in charge of the many mechanical details – microphone, tape-recorders and tapes – and much of the driving.

When Joe married again his friends were glad that Carol, who was already known to us as his charming and helpful agent, was able to take on the jobs that Jean had done. The new partnership is a good one.

CHURCHILL FELLOWSHIPS

For some years I have been a member of the Council of the Winston Churchill Memorial Fellowship Trust that was set up to provide travelling grants principally for those who might not otherwise have the opportunity of going overseas to find out more about their particular subjects. Sir Winston knew of the proposed memorial and approved it. What makes the Trust different from other sponsoring bodies is that applicants for its grants can be of either sex, of any age, and do not need degrees or any other educational or professional qualification, only their own know-how, experience and enthusiasm; and, in many cases, a desire to serve the community.

Every year between eighty and ninety fellowships are given, under approximately ten headings of agriculture, adventure, the arts, conservation and the environment, industry, the law and its maintenance, medicine, science, social and public services and sport. (Because there are fewer women than men on the Council too many grants go to the sports category; or so I think – and I'm not the only one.) The grants cover travel and living expenses for up to three months, depending on distances and, therefore, fares. Obviously it costs more to get to Tokyo than Florence. Churchill fellows come from every walk of life, from urban and rural backgrounds and to date their ages have ranged from sixteen to sixty-five. The Council gives priority to those who have never been abroad other than for short holidays.

It was Sir Trenchard Cox, a founder member of the Trust, and formerly head of the Victoria and Albert Museum, who suggested that I should join the Council. He is a modest and kind man who has an interest in many modern forms of expression that is unusual for one of his academic background and generation. I admire his open-minded attitude; he is ready to explore experimental plays and movies that I should be lily-livered about going to see. It was an education to sit with him on the panel, judging candidates for fellowships. Through his humanity and enormous knowledge he made the interviews interesting as well as unalarming, and this helped candidates, particularly the shy ones, to appear at their best.

Over the years, like most of the other Council members, I have taken the chair of a category. Mine is 'the Arts'. But to begin with I was a supporter on other panels, mostly concerned with social services, chaired by Margaret Alexander, widow of the Field-Marshal. Her death was a serious loss to the Council; she had been concerned with it since it began, and in interviews her quiet but penetrating questioning and her warm heart produced, as Trenchard does, the kind of climate in which candidates relaxed and did themselves justice. It was always Maggie's deep concern to remind us of the unique character of the Churchill Trust. 'Don't forget,' she said, 'the Trust was set up to provide opportunities for unusual and even eccentric individuals, as well as the professionals and the rest; and that it is primarily meant for those who would not otherwise have a chance of travelling abroad.'

In 1977 I took the chair of the Crafts and Teachers of Crafts category. It was a big job, and I found it fascinating. As I saw it I was not there to judge ability – I was not qualified to do that – but to try and assess the character and calibre of the candidates, and decide which of them had the capacity to gain most from a fellowship. That year there were six hundred and eighty-nine submissions for my category. I went through them all three times and gradually sorted them into groups under 'likely', 'possible', and 'not good enough'. The dining-room in Elm Park Gardens was piled high with papers. The third and final read-through was painstaking – I felt I was juggling with people's lives – and it was difficult not to be influenced by the look of a submission paper. Beautiful script writing (though I don't like script writing) seemed to show decorative skill and, although it didn't tell me much about the writer, it appealed to me more than slipshod writing with scored out mistakes and corrections. Obviously all this had to be weighed up against answers to the questions.

Trenchard was away during the crucial weeks of my paper-readings, but Sir Richard Powell, who was also on the Arts panel, kindly helped me reduce my final choice of sixty 'likely' candidates to a short list of twenty-five whom we would interview for fourteen fellowships. By that time I almost knew by heart the papers I had lived with for so long.

The interviews are always the real test and, as the candidates came before us, it was reassuring to find that my hunches about them so often, but not always, proved accurate. Sometimes appearances surprised me, even though, with such a category, I was ready for the men to have Tennysonian beards, and for both sexes to wear hand-woven garments and have an assortment of carefully organised 'careless' hairdos. It was impossible not to be more charmed by some than by others, but with my hand on my heart I can vow that my colleagues and I bent over backwards to be fair, particularly to the less appealing applicants, purging any personal prejudice and lack of enthusiasm for some of the projects on offer, by sharper looks at motives and reasons.

Art categories by the nature of their egocentric calling do not always demand the same selfless dedication and concern for humanity that impressed me so much when I helped to interview candidates in the social and public service categories; but I remember, one year, when we saw 'Workers in the Theatre', a number of them looked on their job, not as a way of expressing themselves but as a means of involving underprivileged groups in worlds wider than their own limited urban settings. The aim of all these would-be Fellows was to be of service. Several of them wished to learn more about ways of 'getting' to city children through improvised play-performances and story-telling in parks and youth clubs. An older actor, whose straggling hair, purple shirt (open a very long way down) and battered leather jerkin, had not signalled the kind of man he really was, had found that 'pretend' and acting games helped to break down violence in ten-to-twelve-year-olds. He won a fellowship that took him to America to gain further experience from the work going on in overcrowded urban areas in Detroit.

The variety of main categories is already enormous and continues to grow. There have been butchers and bakers, and if not candlestick-makers then makers of every kind of object from aids for the handicapped to pots, paintings and stained glass. Two dustmen from Battersea went to Germany to study new ways and means of waste-disposal. All kinds of decorators, restorers, musicians, communicators and maintainers of law and order and many others have sought to further their knowledge in foreign parts. I remember with pleasure an elderly ex-fireman from the north of England who applied under 'Preparations for Retirement'. He was eager to get to the Scandinavian countries where he had been told retirement was not dreaded but looked forward to as the time of one's life. This made sense to him (as it does to me). At his interview he confessed that he had been suspicious and sceptical about the fellowships and was sure that the likes of himself would never stand a chance of getting one. But he felt concerned because he had spent his life with firemen (whose working lives are shorter than in other industries), and he thought on their behalf he might as well have a go. To have been short-listed and invited to come south for an interview was, he told us, the best thing that had ever happened to him, and was, as he had said to his wife, as good as winning a grant. It had quite restored his faith in human nature. I should like to have seen his face when the letter arrived to tell him he had won a fellowship.

General Anthony Lascelles, who with Anne Seagrim and a small staff runs the Trust's organisation at Queen's Gate Terrace, does a huge job in dealing with the increasing number of submissions. Their help in the different stages that follow the awarding of grants is unending, and is well appreciated by the streams of new beneficiaries, as well as Fellows who drop in when passing to keep in touch and report developments in their careers that are directly the result of experience gained through their fellowships.

Serving on the Council of this very special Trust is one of the most heartening 'fringe benefits' that has come my way. Through meeting such a wide selection of candidates I am reassured that this country is well-endowed with numbers of admirably enterprising, responsible, knowledgeable and enthusiastic men and women. They operate in every kind of field and are, it seems to me, an insurance for the future.

THE SOCIETY OF WOMEN WRITERS AND JOURNALISTS

In the early 1960s Clemence Dane, who was President of the Society, suggested that I should join it, and after she retired I was elected to take her place. This Society, of which I am fond, is a small one – not just for reasons of exclusiveness but because of the feeling that a membership of not more than six hundred is about right for the kind of intimate and agreeable assembly it is; and also for the services it aims to provide. It is not a hard-bitten or thrusting group caught up in the rat-race of journalist-writers, but rather a collection of women who write professionally for many and various markets, including all the media.

The other day I was interviewed on radio by a show-off young man who tried through derision to prove his male superiority. Didn't I think the idea of a gathering together of women writers was a bit dated? Did we meet for tea and ask each other whether we had read any good books lately? The implication was that we must be a lot of ancient fuddy-duddy amateurs, sheltered, middle-class, and wearing picture hats (he mentioned these, and horse-drawn vehicles to take us to our meetings), who filled our spare time by doing a little scribbling. I didn't find this picturesque image tallied with the robust membership as I know it, and without rising to his bait I said so. Quietly. We are, I said, for the most part an energetic collection of professional writers of all ages, from every walk of life, who happen to be women. The object of the Society, which was founded over eighty-four years ago by an imaginative businessman, is to share working experiences, for the benefit of each other, to further our craft and to disseminate information useful to writers. There are writers' discussions – the 'in' word for this is 'workshops' – talks and summer-school week-ends; and a variety of other activities go on throughout the year.

The Society's lively quarterly magazine is edited by Pat Garrod, a short-story writer who with Joan Livermore, the organising secretary, and others on the council, do a good deal beyond the-call-of-duty for the rest of us. Literary competitions are held, and the work submitted for the Society's two main awards – for a poem and a short story – seems to me to be increasingly imaginative and original and of top quality.

As President, my job is to be a figurehead and an observer – benevolent and concerned, in a parental kind of way – but nevertheless a figurehead. So I feel a degree removed, and free to speak in the Society's praise. As I have never been much of a joiner, I can't compare the S.W.W.J. with other Societies and Associations, but I suspect that there is something unusually refreshing – in an age of fierce party-political allegiances, vested interests, prejudiced and elbowing competitiveness – about a non-political, open-minded group such as this small and friendly collection of writers, whose love for their chosen craft is their reason for coming together. I added to my enjoyable list of 'fringe benefits' the name of the S.W.W.J.

PULPITS

Allegiance to one's own faith, if it is a vital part of one's understanding, is total. It is also private. I have found that the wearing of a denominational hat is a divider. Announcing that one is an Anglican, Baptist, Buddhist, Christian Scientist, Jew, Methodist, Muslim, Presbyterian, Quaker, Roman Catholic, or of any other denomination is, at the present stage, a signal for blinds to come down, prejudices to rise up, and minds to close. If I am asked, I am glad to tell anyone which faith I follow, but I do not go about broadcasting my allegiance. I am not a flag-waver or a placard-wearer, because I have learned through experience that meeting-places of understanding and mutual trust are more readily found when flags are not waved. Preconceived and pre-received ideas of what we believe are so often distorted. It is the practical evidence we can share that is important. The way lives are led and solutions to problems are worked out should, I think, be enough to show the validity of a chosen faith that has proved trustworthy, supporting and, above all, practical. I am grateful for the opportunities that have come my way that have enabled me, without a particular hat, to speak in general terms about beliefs on which I base my life; to share ideas that have proved dependable and are changeless. Truth, as I see it, wherever we find it in or out of churches, is the reality of God's being.

There was a time when the Religious Department of the B.B.C. had the courage to call its daily early-morning programme *Lift up Your Hearts*, implying by this that there *are* reasons for joy and grounds for hope that can be trusted, and an understanding that right answers do exist and can be found. At least some nourishment was offered in the year's output. When Joanna Scott-Moncrieff edited the programme its name was changed to a non-commital *10 to 8*. She rose above that and, for the duration of her time in the department, found speakers convinced of some aspect of faith in life that they appeared glad to tell us about – not in a churchy way but with a religious feeling. Some of the talks reflected a valuable sense of wonder, a commodity that seems to be scarce just now. I remember with particular pleasure broadcasts by

C. A. Joyce, who had been on the programme from long before it was called *10 to 8*, and 'A Country Doctor' who, I believe, was a relative newcomer. Their formal beliefs differed from mine, but their shining awareness of the good that they found in their busy daily lives, and their natural humility, left an impression that continues to bless.

Today the early-morning programme, announced inaccurately as far as I am concerned as *Thought for Today*, seems to aim at being all things to all men, and is so general that it has no focus. The main ingredient missing is practical spiritual nourishment. If the idea behind this humanist approach is not to put off but to include the non-believer in a brief semi-reflective five minutes to cheer him on his way – or even make him think – I do not believe it succeeds. The *Daily Service* in the middle of the morning still lives up to its name; it serves by providing some sustenance, and its message of comfort speaks clearly to the con-verted. But the non-churchgoer, who might be open to finding out the possibility of Jesus's teaching that God is a reality and worth discover-ing, is not being catered for. I sometimes wonder if all those concerned with religious broadcasting actually believe that God is a fact.

I think the first time I spoke publicly, if somewhat obliquely, about my thoughts on things spiritual, was in a series Joanna produced, called *Private Collection*. Speakers were asked to quote from sources they had found reliable, that reflected their own philosophy or faith. I chose to speak about eternity – what Addison called 'Thou pleasing dreadful thought'. I quoted from Wordsworth, Traherne, Shelley and St Paul, all of whom said some of the things I believe about eternity; that it is a present timeless fact, and not miles and miles of nothing.

That original five-minute piece led to other early-morning broad-casts; and then, out of the blue, I was invited to give the Lanchester Lecture, an annual event at the College of Technology in Lanchester. It had never before been given by a woman. Flattered, but hesitant, I wrote to thank them for the invitation, and asked on what subject they wished me to speak and for how long. 'Talk about anything you like for an hour', they said generously 'as long as it is not engineering.' This left the field alarmingly wide. An hour was a long time. I talked it over with Reggie, and we decided that the business I was in and thought I knew something about, was communication. At that time non-communication was a fashionable subject. Bleak plays by Pinter and more affectionate plays by Wesker were being written about the failure of understanding between people. I was rather more inter-ested in exploring how and why communication worked, as I knew it did through my job: particularly as I had done it under tough conditions during the war, and more recently in my solo programmes on stage. To put it bluntly, I learned that communication is, in a non-church but religious sense, only possible where there is concern for each other. I have found this to be true in personal relationships as well as in a public hall.

It took me eight weeks of head-down application to write the lecture. I tried out parts of it on Virginia and other long-suffering friends whom I thought might be in sympathy with the idea. It is no good showing tentative material to an unsympathetic audience; only when it is set and grown independent of the writer is the time right to expose it to a harsher world. And I read it aloud, often to Reggie who kept an eye on the timing for me. Eventually called *View from a Small Corner*, I delivered it on a spring evening to a large audience in a modern auditorium in Coventry. It was the biggest challenge I had ever faced. The college had the text printed between bright blue covers and sent me a supply of copies. I was proud to see it in print.

As a result of Lanchester I had the courage to take on a few smaller talks in other places. Then about eight years later came another and even more particular challenge: to give one of five Lenten lectures in Truro Cathedral, in Cornwall. This time the subject was chosen for me – 'The Christian and Communication'. Not too difficult, I thought; I had been there before although not in a specifically Christian way. I told Truro about Lanchester and asked whether they would object if I were to quote substantially from my first paper. They were agreeable. So I took another look at my *View from a Small Corner*; as I read it, I realised that I no longer stood where I had when I wrote it; the view had opened up; I had had different experiences and made new discoveries. The lecture would be on the same subject, but the horizon had altered. It always does.

This time it took me six weeks, hard, to get it written. In the end I was able to include some of the illustrations from the original paper, but most of the material was different; better I hoped. By this time, very relevant to the new situation, I had read Bonhoeffer's definition: 'To be a Christian does not mean to be religious in a particular way but to be a man – not a type of man but the man Christ creates in us.' Every day, as I watched, listened and read, I was struck by the way man's dignity, his natural right, was increasingly lost sight of in the pursuit of a 'good' news story. On the spot, even in-depth interviews at moments of drama, tragedy or triumph did not often show much concern for the man or woman being interviewed. Concern – or to put it more precisely, love – was not always evident at such times. This I think accounts, among other things, for loss of trust between human beings, and for so much non-communication.

As I stood in the rose sandstone interior of Truro Cathedral, wearing a new off-white spring suit, I looked at the packed congregation. It was a mixture of all ages and evidently a mixture of faiths, too, judging by the clothes, habits, different kinds of dog-collars, Salvation Army bonnets, and uniforms. I had to admit to myself that it was probably the familiarity of my comedy movie actress's face (and the expectation of a laugh here and there) rather than the subject of my talk, that accounted for the enormous crowd. I hoped that what I was going to say would come out as I meant it to, clearly and perhaps usefully. As I had already learned, *not* wearing a denominational hat made for quicker understanding; so, I had begun to discover, did humility. The occasion was a happy one.

From time to time I have taken part in the lunch-time dialogues successfully established by Joseph McCulloch in the beautifully restored church of St Mary-le-Bow in Cheapside, of which for many years he was the Rector. The dialogues began as exchanges between himself and another cleric in the second of the twin pulpits. But Joseph found, as he wrote in his book, *My Affair With the Church*, that they were talking *about* the world and not *with* it, so he began to invite those to whom, for one reason or another, the world was listening. They came from the worlds of entertainment, business, politics, science, art and journalism, and did not have to be religious. Looking at the formidable list of famous names it is difficult not to wonder just why some of them were there; not always, I think, for their philosophic thought or proven ways of wisdom. Joseph's truthful answer to those who accused him of celebrity-hunting was direct. He said he found people interesting, especially intelligent and attractive people; and he acted on the assumption that others felt the same way as he did. The starry names certainly drew the crowds, and a regular audience, including many non-church-goers, filled St Mary-le-Bow during the lunch-time seasons. The dialogues were almost always stimulating and provoked thought; and often, Joseph told me, individuals reported that they had been helped by what they had heard. As his stated aim was to bring non-members into some relationship with the Church, he can surely be said to have achieved what he set out to do.

Fringe Benefits

Joseph led most of the dialogues himself, but from time to time he invited two big names to talk to each other. Yehudi Menuhin and Malcolm Muggeridge are a pair I remember. But I think the exchanges worked better when Joseph put the opening questions and kept the discussion moving, for he was adept at getting the best from his partners. He never dominated the talk, but skilfully helped it to flower. Left to themselves other pairs didn't always seem to get on to each other's wavelength.

The dark, rather austere outside of St Mary-le-Bow does not prepare you for the luminous interior of the building. It is light and airy; at once peaceful and heart-lifting. I was always glad to be in it. At the risk of sounding over-humble I must say that I felt a particular sense of privilege whenever I was one of the occupants of the second pupit. At first I wasn't sure how to approach the dialogue. Not as a preacher, that was certain. So why was I up there, with a microphone hung round my neck and a velvet cushion to lean on if I felt like it, and forty minutes of discussion time lying ahead. I decided I was there to share my findings of ways that work in my daily doings and relationships; and, out of a sense of gratitude and wonder, to bear witness to my increasing certainty – that is central to the way I try to live my life – of the power of God.

I agree with the statement of Ronald Knox that: 'We must accustom men's minds to the notion that it does not matter what the politicians do, does not matter if our bishops seem to let us down. We belong to a spiritual kingdom, complete in itself, owing nothing to worldly alliances.' I do not think it means we must ignore the world, let it go to pot. As we find out more about the spiritual kingdom, which is the infinite presence of God, who is all good, fills all space, is changeless, perfect and eternal – now – so we can see and experience this world in a new light. Even when my limited human mind does not perceive this I *know* it is so. We cannot ignore the world. It is too beautiful and too holy. How we view it, how we experience it, depends on from where we see it.

The most unlikely of all the pulpits I found myself standing in was the splendid and lofty one in Westminster Abbey. I was invited by the Dean, Edward Carpenter, to give the address, on 13 May 1977, at a non-denominational service of thanksgiving, for old-age pensioners of the diocese, to celebrate the Queen's Silver Jubilee. I was escorted from my seat beside Reggie in the choir stalls and led up the shallow steps, made so familiar by television films of great occasions, to the ladder-like stairs of the pulpit. From there, as I had done before in Truro, I looked down on a sea of upturned faces. It was of course an elderly gathering, and once again very mixed in its allegiances – there were Roman Catholics from up the road at the Cathedral, Methodists from across the way at Central Hall, and probably the same number of representatives of other faiths as I had spoken to in Cornwall. I wrote my talk on the recurring theme that continues to run through my own explorations – the discovery of that which is good, therefore true, therefore eternal, therefore changeless and present *now*. I called the address, 'You can only discover what is already in existence waiting to be discovered.'

Afterwards there was tea for everybody, in the cloisters, where a nippy wind tore at best hats and lifted the modern short veils of some nuns. Everyone was given a Jubilee souvenir tea-towel, very purple, with a black-and-white print of the Abbey in the middle. It is not easy after such an occasion to know how a talk has been received but, because there had been little coughing while I spoke, I hoped interest in what I had said had been held. I met friendly smiles in the cloisters, and was much moved to be told in a whisper by three separate people in turn, each of a different persuasion, that I had said exactly what they believed. Denominationally we were miles apart, but a meeting-place existed and had been found.

This experience echoed an incident I wrote about in my first book. In a radio discussion programme called *We Beg to Differ*, the team was asked how it would define to a child the word 'spirit'. When my turn came I said: 'You know the feeling I have for you, and you have for me – it is called love. And love is spirit – the greatest power there is.' Afterwards all of us had letters about the broadcast, and among those addressed to me were half-a-dozen or so from people holding very different religious ideas, and all of them thanking me for putting their point of view.

Believing that there is only one Divine Intelligence, these incidents did not surprise me, but I continue to find them moving; and encouraging. The story of the small boy who was asked: 'What do you think God is?' and who said 'God isn't a think – He's a feel' sums up my own view. It is this experience of feeling that proves for me the very presence of God.

A breakthrough in my own understanding of the spiritual kingdom as our own eternal being came about in the spring of 1955 when my mother was dying in North Carolina and I was finishing the provincial tour of *Joyce Grenfell Requests the Pleasure* in England. I was going to be with her as soon as the tour ended. One Sunday in April I drove the three dancers, who were in the show with me, from Liverpool across country to Oxford for our next week's engagement. The countryside was at its most exciting and beautiful, as only spring in England can be. A moment of promise rather than fulfilment, new green appearing in hedges, a confetti scattering of tiny leaves. Bluebells. Orchards frothing in blossom, and late primroses. Two of my companions sat in the back of the car reading the Sunday papers; the third, beside me, was a Welshman with an eye for such things as dandelions and lapwings. We informed each other all the way – 'Look – oh look!' I thought, how awful, my mother will never see another spring. And then with a stab of joy I suddenly saw that spring is a spiritual concept, a symbol of renewal. It is part of God's spiritual kingdom, part of our own spiritual consciousness. As the loved child of God she could not be deprived of anything that was eternal and therefore true. My mother – everyone – *included* spring.

Some years later I tried to put that discovery into verse.

> What eye beholds the Spring?
> No retina nor lens
> With signals to the brain
> Could compass such a thing.
>
> If on this earth we see
> The green immensity
> And hear the music's ring,
> Where can the real Spring be?
>
> From time to time the mind
> Sees more than mortal range,
> The universe made plain,
> A seeing for the blind.
>
> It is the eye of Mind
> That sees and hears and knows
> The law that holds intact
> The man, the star, the rose.

CHAPTER TEN

South Africa

I NEVER performed in South Africa, because the English Musicians' Union refused to let Bill Blezard play for me in that country; and as I considered him part of the act I was not willing to do the show without him. But I have often been there as a visitor – ever since 1950, when Reggie's cousin Harold, who is Chairman of the Messina (Transvaal) Development Company, invited him to join the Board.

Politically South Africa is a mess – an understatement if ever there was one; but physically the country is mysterious, exciting and vast; alarming and very beautiful. I am grateful for many sunny weeks of holiday, filled with bird-watching and swimming, and as few days as possible spent in Johannesburg, a city without a heart: ugly, ruthless, and elevated at six thousand feet, so that when you first get there you feel faintly fey. When you have got used to the altitude, it still has, for me, very little to offer in any way. In the old days, before the Company's head office moved to Johannesburg, we used to spend most of our time in the Northern Transvaal at the small copper-mining township of Messina, eight miles from Beit Bridge, which crosses the Limpopo to link South Africa with Rhodesia. It is an arid part of the country; the land is red-soiled and rolls on for limitless distances covered in low veld scrub where baobab trees, the only ones of any size, stand out like great clumsy dark-grey-trunked elephantine monsters covered with lumps. Their skinny branches are wholly inadequate for the rest of their bulk; the proportions are all wrong. Fist-sized nuts covered in grey velvet hang down from stringy stems and are the source of cream of tartar. When a baobab dies it doesn't fall in a noble manner; it collapses in a heap, and then it is seen to be made, not of useful wood but of fibre. South Africa protects these trees, and they are looked upon with respect. They also relieve the monotony of that endless sea of rolling veld with its skimpy bush and rocky outcrops. In spite of its beauty I prefer to keep the bush at a distance, but I can understand the charm this unlikely country holds over people. Seen from a rise its vastness has a compelling beauty as its colours change with the light. Clouds floating over it are reflected in truly blue shadows. I once looked closely at Constable landscapes in the Victoria and Albert Museum to see how blue was the paint he used for distant trees and hills, and it was as truly blue as the shadows on the veld in the Transvaal.

I loved being at Messina. We stayed at the Chairman's white house. It was spacious and airy, and the staff were friendly. Robinson (a name given to him long ago, when he was Harold's personal 'boy' and before he rose to rule over the kitchen) was a monosyllabic and loyal member of the household. When the time came to find a cook for the newly-built house, Harold asked him if he could fill the post. 'Anything Master say, she can do,' he said. And on that bold boast he was hired, and did well. William, the major-domo, was a good organiser, dependable, quick-witted and with a responsive sense of humour; and so has Ralph Smaile, Harold's driver. From the house, built on a rare high hill in that sea of low veld, and from its green grassed terraces you can see for endless miles in all directions. You also get a clear view of the smelter chimney; its smoke told Harold that the mine was working, and us which way the wind was blowing. Below the hill and over the roof-tops of two rows of upper-echelon houses were the shunting-yards of the South African Railway, and – though we always slept well – the noise of its operations, particularly at night, broke the silence you might expect to find in such a remote place. Virginia described staying there as a cross between being in Government House and Paddington Station.

The swimming-pool in the garden is a beauty. It is sunk below the level of the terrace and surrounded by whitewashed walls with a background of trees at one end and a creeper-covered loggia at the other. It was in this pool that Virginia and I, grey-headed by now, discovered that it was possible to feel like ballet dancers when we rose up, buoyed by the water, in a series of graceful under-water leaps.

It made us laugh at ourselves, as did another occasion, in London, when we found we were both swaying and vo-doh-di-oh-ing, in our old-world way, to the rhythmic cocktail-hour music relayed to entertain the queue waiting to see *Hello Dolly*. We were wearing hats at the time (my obsession had not yet run its course) and Virginia had on her over-long fur coat, so our conventionally respectable appearance, coupled with our jazzy movements, must have been a little startling. It gave me the idea for a new number; I began writing it later that

Swimming at Messina

evening, and it was called '*Unsuitable*'. Bill Blezard set it to a spirited 'bepop' accompaniment, and I enjoyed doing it wearing an urban shopper's hat and pretending to push a shopper's basket on wheels. The song tells the story of an elderly housewife who can't help responding to rhythm:

> I swing and I sway in a groovy way,
> As I push my little cart through the super-mart.

When I first went to Messina the women dressed formally. They came to what Miriam Grenfell described as 'tea-potties', not only hatted but gloved, stockinged and high-heeled as well. Miriam was Harold's first wife and mother of his two sons, an attractive, small, brown-haired woman of Welsh and Irish extraction with, unexpectedly, quite large, talented, long-fingered hands, who carried her head on one side in every photograph ever taken of her. She was funny, intuitive, quick-witted, warm, and I was very fond of her. She wrote entertaining letters, in a large, flourishing hand, which read as if she were speaking – the most successful way of letter-writing. She exaggerated with pleasing effect.

The temperature during what was reported to be locally known as

176

Harold and Miriam
Grenfell

'the Grenfell season' (January and February) ranged between eighty and a hundred degrees, so wearing formal clothes was not what we wanted to do. But perhaps the residents of an isolated mining community, meeting each other continually, welcomed a change of pace, and our visiting presence may have been useful in providing occasions for dressing-up. Miriam and I brought no hats to wear and took off our stockings the minute we arrived. I now wonder if our informality may not at first sight have appeared a little arrogant, as though we didn't think the company worth dressing up for – *not* our intention. The result was certainly a lowering of dress standards, and it was soon adopted by everyone. Hats, gloves, stockings and high-heeled shoes were abandoned, and I hope the change wasn't a disappointment. There were still dressy occasions; sundowners, for instance, when Mim and I both wore our best, but the 'tea-potties' at ten-thirty a.m. were a lot friendlier when we met less formally. I suppose providing an excuse for a little social life was how Mim, as the Chairman's wife, and I, as wife of a director, justified our presence in Messina. Our husbands, in shirt-sleeves, worked down at the head office until four in the afternoon, appearing briefly to lunch with us under the vine of the paved loggia. We gave dinner-parties, sundowners and went out to other people's parties. Occasionally I put on a short entertainment with the help of local talent at the piano. Our least favourite form of outing was a *brai-vleis*, an unsatisfactory form of South African barbecue, where tough meat (it has improved down the years) is burned to a crisp on an outdoor fire in pitch-dark gardens; and it is impossible not to get sleepier and sleepier as you sit around waiting for the feast to begin. As well as these duty diversions we had some quiet evenings, reading our books.

Miriam was one of the best gigglers I have ever known. In case this reads as a criticism I must make it plain that I know of no more companionable relationship than that of a really good giggler. The trouble was that we caught each other's eye, and it became difficult to control our *fou rire*. We did our best, and I hope no feelings were trampled on. Perhaps it is rude to be amused by other people's ways of speaking, but as it has been a weapon of my trade to use different accents, I have always been aware of them, and enjoyed discovering new ones. Until I went to South Africa I had never heard that way of using English, and coming to it freshly the impact was powerful. At an early 'tea-potty' a nice but nosy woman said to me: 'Mrs Grunfeel do ewe and meester Grunfeel hev twin beads?' When I understood what she had said (twin beds) I garnered the question and have treasured it ever since. Miriam enjoyed such things as much as I did, and in private we practised talking with a South African accent whenever we were at Messina.

The doctor's large wife was the subject of a pleasing Messina story. Coming back from a remote farm in the bush, she got out of the car to open a gate for her husband to drive through; and drive through he did, straight home some sixteen miles away. Later that evening he called his cook-boy to ask where supper was. 'Where is the Madam?' asked the cook-boy. The doctor was not too pleased at having to drive back all that way to fetch her, on a hot sticky and darkening night; neither was his wife very welcoming when he reached her.

At Messina we did most of our shopping at the Limpopo Stores. It used to be a series of rickety shed-like buildings, but is now a two-storey emporium where you can buy almost everything you need including bicycles, food, clothing, dress materials, electrical and pharmaceutical goods and stationery. Messina has become a town, and it boasts branches of the larger city stores: a motel, hotels, banks and petrol stations. The company provides hospitals, a golf course, a social club with cinema and swimming-pool, bowling greens, tennis courts and playing fields. There are also a variety of churches; most of them to my eye joylessly austere and uninviting.

Going to the movies, in the days when movies were a treat and not an ordeal, was the pleasantest of evening pastimes; the open air auditorium has the most comfortable cinema seats in the world. They are made of slung canvas, deep and spacious, widely set on terraces, and when the movie fails to hold attention you can lie back and look up at the astonishing African night, brilliant with stars that to European eyes sit in unusual places. The seats were designed, after much experiment, by Gus Emery, an American of enterprise and initiative, who was at that time General Manager of the Company. He also built an outdoor dance-floor next to his official house, and there, for his parties, the employees of the mine put on black ties and danced the dances of the day to gramophone records, even in the pulsating heat of an African night. Gus's guests did not dress up to dance only in Messina; at his ranch, twenty or more miles away in the wild bush, they also changed to dine and dance on another polished floor. There, at Skutwater, he had built a series of cages made of wire mesh, unprotected from the skies, and set on cement platforms. In these he and his wife, and their children, and his guests were quartered. I suppose the idea was to get as close to nature as possible. Sleeping out like this was quite an adventure; legend says that when elephant came in their silent way through the camp, they sometimes breathed through the netting on whomever was within. There was no shortage of lions either. When Reggie and I went to Skutwater for a week-end I was relieved to find we had been put in a more conventional mud hut; there was no glass in the windows, but at least we didn't feel totally exposed. I remember, after a dawn walk looking for animals and birds, taking an open-air bath behind walls made of thick branches. The aluminium bath was red-hot from the sun's rays, and all I had to do was pour in cold water. A bee, attracted by the delicious scent of my Floris soap and talcum powder, made my ablutions and drying-off awkward, for it would not go away until I managed to swipe it with my towel. Clearly I am not made of the stuff of a true nature-lover.

Reggie's knowledge of South African birds came from week-ends spent across the Limpopo at Harold's Rhodesian ranch. There, in a dark belt of tall thickly-growing trees along the bank of the Umzingwani River, space was cleared and the camp was built. There was a large two-storey rondarvel to house the farm manager's family, a cottage for Harold and Miriam, and three smaller rondarvels for visitors, with a bath-house and lavatory behind in the bushes. Each of these little round whitewashed mud-brick houses with thatched roofs had a wash-basin, two iron bedsteads, a chest of drawers and two chairs, and it was in one of these that we stayed for week-ends while we were up at Messina.

The ranch is twelve miles up a track from the main road, and it was the nearest to the wilds I have ever been – and quite near enough too. I am not much of a camper and was always glad to have Reggie beside me when we stayed there. At night there were animal noises, rather too close for my liking, and on the way to bed after eating by the camp fire, as we did before the place got sophisticated and electricity was introduced, we saw the eyes of unknown creatures watching us from the bush. Elephant have been known to go through the camp; leopard, wild dog, buck, eland, hyena, zebra, wildebeest and giraffe are free to roam in the land that Harold has decreed a game park. I can't pretend I didn't welcome the electricity when it came (so much easier than candles or hissing lamps), but those early days had about them an element of adventure that was lost when the improvements arrived. Less insecticide was then used in the garden and on the crops, and the place was a haven for birds. All you had to do was sit on the grassy space in the dappled shade of great trees, thickly leaved, that covered the clearing, and watch birds come in to bathe in the sprinklers. On my first visit a paradise flycatcher had built a nest on a branch just above where we sat, and the male, with a splendid fourteen-inch curving scimitar tail, darted in and out, executing an elaborate manoeuvre when changing places with his wife, who was sitting on the ridiculous nest the size of half a small orange. She moved off as he slid in, dragging his tail behind him. I loved the peace of the place and the feeling of cool dawns when the sky lightened behind black trees. Kingfishers started the early morning chorus as we went out, with our binoculars, to look for and find so many beautiful little birds, as well as the occasional secretary bird, the bateleur eagle and the enormous kori bustard which was usually to be seen on the airstrip.

It rains very little up there, and I forgot we had come to Africa hoping to see the sun, and joined in the wish that desperately needed rains might come. We were at the ranch one year when they came in a dramatic way; the sky went black, a wild wind lashed the trees, and we smelt the approaching rain coming across the bush – a delicious flowery scent that brings with it relief and rejoicing. The farmer's children ran out to meet it – hands outstretched – and danced in the

*Rondarvel at
Harold's ranch*

spashing downfall, their hair flattened to their heads. It rained all
night, and early next day an African came running in to tell the glad
news that the river was coming down. Most of the year the Umzingwani River is a very wide sandy strip; but there is always water under
the sand, and this is pumped up to irrigate the orchards, the cotton
and wheat lands as well as to supply domestic needs. Now the rain
came, and with it the sudden spectacular flow that spread across the
dry sand and flooded the banks to a height of twelve feet. We all went
to see it; already there were fish in the water and birds yelling in
celebration. We joined in the general delight.

One evening on our way back to Messina we picked up two African
boys walking towards the main road to catch a bus to Bulawayo. One
carried a carnival paper straw-boater hat. They each had a tiny cardboard attaché case, no shoes, unbuttoned shirts over shorts. They were
in their early twenties and neither had a word of English. They sat
behind us in the car, bolt upright, on the edge of the seat. They
seemed scared and wary. I wondered how to begin to communicate.
When we came to a deeper gully than usual I looked back as we
lurched through it and smiled. No reaction. We passed a white stork
on top of a dead tree and I pointed it out. No reaction. I had hoped

that some sort of vibration of friendliness might have reached them, but there was no sign of any contact. We continued on the rough track, the car rolling and dipping, and as we got to the top of a small rise, one of those vast African landscapes came into view before us, about sixty miles of it: flat land with a low range of hills in the far distance. Rains were badly needed at that time too. It was a day with sun and clouds. Suddenly from the left I saw, as I had seen it once before in North Africa during the war, a grey curtain of rain stalking across the landscape towards us. 'Look!' I said excitedly. *'Look* – Rain!' The boys forgot their shyness; great grins spread across their faces. They burbled a low, wind-instrument noise to each other and smiled at me. At last we had made *some* contact. A simple basic need for rain, and joy at its arrival, had been the meeting-place. They appeared to trust us a little more after that, and when we dropped them at the main road they made more woodwind sounds.

When I went to South Africa with Reggie in the last years of his time with the Messina Company, we always stayed out in the country, forty-five miles north of Johannesburg, with Bill and Mary Wilson. Bill joined Messina about the same time as Reggie and is now Managing Director. He and Mary live in a long, low white farmhouse with a green roof, at the end of a mile and a half of lane off the main road. It is perched on the edge of a ridge overlooking arable lands that grow down to the reeds on the bank of the river below. Beyond the river the shallow valley suddenly rises up steeply to a crowning outcrop of rock, like a fortress wall, that continues the length of the escarpment. In the distance to the right shine the broad waters of Hartebeestepoort Dam.

Both the Wilsons are of Scottish origin; Bill was born in South Africa, Mary comes from Glasgow. When I first knew her she was still involved in athletics – before her marriage she had worked as a physical-training teacher. At Messina she encouraged the young people of the mining community in their swimming and tennis. In those days the Wilson children, four boys and a girl, were noticeable for their fair hair, like their mother's, straight backs and prowess in sports. I treasure a picture of the youngest, aged about five, walking slowly home from the pool, naked as the day he arrived, with his dripping trunks on his blond head. Now Mary's naturally curly hair is white, and the only swimming she does, and in which every afternoon when I was staying with her I joined, takes place in her own blue pool, where we swam side by side talking of everything under the sun. It was a stately progress, none of your head-down splashing crawl kind of swimming, but civilised exercise taken when the sun was far enough down the sky not to burn our bare heads. There is something liberating about conversation in warm water. Mary is reserved, a woman of few words; she is balanced and wise. In the blue pool, under those high clear skies, we spoke of things dear to our hearts, and without reservation. Another test of real companionship is the ability to enjoy comfortably quite long silences together. I can do this with Mary in or out of the water.

The Wilsons have built, behind the main house and across the drive the other side of a paved back-yard, a thatch-roofed guest cottage, far enough away for privacy, near enough to feel part of the family. It is there that Reggie and I have stayed, and where I wrote some of my first book and began work on this one. The days there fell into a pattern. Bill, who has has kept his youthful figure, went for an early morning jog at daybreak. Then he and Reggie drove into Johannesburg for their day's work. I wrote all the morning in the cottage. Mary and I met for luncheon and then, one of my most favourite indulgences, we went to our rooms for an afternoon siesta and read. Our swimming engagement was for 4.30. Bill and Reggie came back from the city bringing the newspapers, we dined early and watched television, then a novelty. South African T.V. has a small viewing public and a correspondingly small pool of talent to draw on. Five hours' viewing every evening was ample (there or anywhere else, come to that), and it was divided between Afrikaans- and English-speaking programmes, each in turn having the prime viewing hours. The set provided by far the best quality reproduction I've ever seen anywhere. The definition, colour and sound were all exact. Because of British Actors Equity's ruling that no production employing its members may be shown in South Africa, no plays or variety shows made in Britain are available. Only a few documentaries get through. These are eagerly watched. Local productions, although increasingly technically improved were generally poor, and the fill-in material we saw, made up of old American situation comedies and a few tatty German and Scandinavian 'light' entertainments, so dated that the women's clothes looked like period costumes, made pretty dull fare. I believe in free trade in entertainment and in sport as a possible way of finding meeting-places. Laughing together is a useful start to understanding; I'm not quite so sure about games playing, now that sportsmanship and losing gracefully seem to have gone out of fashion.

In Pleasant Places

I once wrote a verse called 'Egotism' that began:

> I find it an amazing thought to think
> That all the places I have ever seen
> Go on existing when I am not there.

In my memory the places hang in the air like stills, and I look at them with lasting enjoyment. As well as the Wilsons' farm at Skeerpoort there is another 'pleasant place' in South Africa where both Reggie and I love to be – Rawdon's Hotel, Lanzerac. It was once an old wine farm and sits against a background of mountains that change colour from pink to apricot to pale lilac, on the edge of the small university town of Stellenbosch, thirty miles from Cape Town.

For my taste no domestic architecture has surpassed that of the eighteenth and early nineteenth centuries. In that period the Dutch were particularly good at designing houses that continue to be practical and pleasing both to look at and to live in, and the tree-shaded streets of tranquil town-houses they built in Stellenbosch bear witness to this fact. So does Lanzerac, now skilfully converted by David Rawdon into a most comfortable and attractive modern hotel. The central whitewashed two-storey gabled house, typical of Dutch Colonial architecture, faces you as you approach it up a straight dirt road through the vineyards. Inside low white walls, that divide the grounds from the fields, the drive is brick-paved and makes a wide sweep around an oval lawn. Great oak trees give shade to the bedrooms, built from old stables, outhouses and slave quarters on either side of the main house. These trees seem to bear more acorns than our English oaks, and given a breeze in February, the time we have usually been there, and the antics of lively squirrels, they come down fast and hit with force whatever happens to be in their way – the roofs of parked cars, the brick paving or one's head. I have very few other complaints to make about Lanzerac. Every bedroom is decorated differently, with pretty chintzes, bed-covers and antiques. I like it best when we are put in a room with a back-yard where we can sit in privacy to read and write, and where I can hang out to dry the the clothes I wash daily. There is a special satisfaction in knowing that in that warm air what is laundered before breakfast will be ready to wear in time for luncheon.

Reggie and I, twice with Virginia, have often stayed there. For us one of the pleasures was that there was 'nothing to do' except *be* at Lanzerac. True, we often drove to the immense beach at Strand, half

Lanzerac

an hour away, where I swam in the sparkling Indian Ocean. Virginia won't bathe unless the temperature is in the nineties; even then Reggie stays on dry land. They sat on hired deck-chairs and gazed out to sea, Reggie with binoculars, while I went through the punishing ordeal of changing in the Municipal Bath House, a low, hideous, shiny, red-orange brick bungalow built on the beach. Here (Men to the Left and Women to the Right) for a small sum you buy a ticket and give it to the *tricoteuse* within, who downs her needles to pass you a wire basket and a thick red rubber bracelet stamped with your allotted number. In a dark, sandy-floored cubicle, usually damp underfoot as well as gritty, you strip and change. You fold your clothes, put your shoes on top of them in the wire basket, and the *tricoteuse* stacks it under your number and hopes 'yew weel enjoyee yaw swum'. I did. When, after an hour of sun and sea air Reggie and Virginia began to get restless, I took the hint and retired to the Municipal Bath House where I showered and rinsed out my bathing-suit before the damp struggle into my clothes. Was it worth it? Every time. Not only was the sea refreshing, but the sand was firm and clean and the view beautiful. Far away to the right a bloom-on-the-grape blue skyline shows Table Mountain and the rest of the range that separates the Indian from the Atlantic Ocean. Nearer, on the left, a darker blue skyline of rocky hills rises above Gordon's Bay.

In Pleasant Places

Sometimes at Strand, before I went in for my dip, I made quick watercolour note-sketches to remind me of sights seen on the beach. The pale colours of the sand, sea and sky accentuated the brightness of children's sun-hats and everyone's sun-tanned body. Afrikaaners of both sexes can be very generously proportioned and seem unconscious of their size and shape. They also wear the minimum of bathing costumes. I think of myself as a large woman but in South Africa I seem almost delightfully petite. There was always plenty to record in my sketch-book, as well as land- and sea-scapes.

An added pleasure to the looks and comfort of Lanzerac and the goodness of the food, particularly the Saturday night cold buffet for which the place is famous, is the fact that so many of the staff have been there for a long time and give us a friendly welcome when we go back. So did Michael Olivier, the congenial and entertaining manager who was in charge for most of the years we stayed there; and helped to make us feel we belonged. The regulars whom we always saw in their usual places on the terrace are, because they fly south from the European winter, known to the management as the English swallows.

A few miles from Lanzerac the hospitable Barlows, Peter and Pam, allowed us to walk and watch birds on the lands that surround Rustenberg, one of the loveliest of the early Cape houses. There they made gardens with deep borders filled with English summer flowers; hundreds of roses, and thick hedges of blue and white agapanthus lilies. On his farm lands, before his untimely death, Peter had planted a garden of protea on a hill above a pond, and there the sugar birds took honey from those strange dry flowers that look to me as if they had been made of coloured grease-proof paper and make the same noise as paper does when they are handled. In their own light, and growing in bushes all over the hill, they make a splendid show and are handsome, but close to, or indoors in a vase, they look like artificial flowers and make me uneasy. South Africans will not like this foreign view of a flower they regard with special favour. But I prefer flowers with green stalks and soft petals.

The last time Reggie and I went to the Cape we travelled on the Blue Train in pre-World War I luxury I did not believe possible in these days. The train takes twenty-four hours from Johannesburg to Cape Town, and moves in comparative silence (which is part of the soothing treatment) and at a delightfully civilised speed, so steady that in the dining-car there is no tintinnabulation of glasses and china. Bowls of soup do not spill over. It is a tourist attraction, and places on it are so heavily in demand that accommodation must be booked well in advance. All the 'rooms' are comfortable, a few are *de luxe*, and one compartment, reserved for Presidents and Princes and other visiting V.I.P.s, is super *de luxe* with its own completely equipped bathroom with full-length bath, living room with sofa, armchairs and dining-table, and a bedroom where the twin beds are arranged lengthwise and not across the train as they are in our sleepers at home. Reggie and I had long wanted to make a journey in the Blue Train, and on his birthday, in November 1976, we boarded it in Pretoria at the start of its journey south.

The long, stately sixteen-coach train came into the station, and, as it stopped near where we were standing, we saw in one of the big plate-glass picture-windows a pyramid arrangement of mixed pink and white carnations, obviously the V.I.P. suite. We wondered who would be travelling in it and went closer to have a good look through the glass at all the creature comforts. The captain, or whatever the genial official in charge was called, asked to see our tickets. He bade us get in, and we climbed up into the coach and followed him – into the suite with the carnations. No two people ever enjoyed its comforts more than we did.

We left Pretoria at noon and made a leisurely progress around the outskirts of Johannesburg – where most of the passengers joined the train – through mile on mile of manufacturing estates and monotonous suburbs, as ugly in South Africa as they are everywhere else in the world. As soon as we had silently rolled away into open country, flat but impressive because it was so vast, we left our suite and walked through the lounge-car to the dining-room for the first sitting of luncheon. We studied the long menu (the food is one of the tourist baits) and made a modest choice. Back in our suite, we looked out on a sea of bending grasses blown by breezes under an empty blue sky, and enjoyed the sense of space and light. A lone rhinoceros, presumably in a game park, trotted by on the open veld, and groups of buck, nibbling the verge at the edge of the railway-line, took no notice of the train. The sun went down in a flaming sky; and at the mining town of Kimberley we had a fifteen-minute wait and time to get out and look at the main street as the lights came on. Not a sign of a diamond anywhere.

The most interesting scenery began, while we were asleep, in the high Karoo. I knew, from an earlier visit, the fascination of its bare hills, and understand the charm it has for those who like deserts. Heath and a few hardy shrubs grow in the shallow soil, but for miles it seems there is only endless rolling emptiness that changes colour with the light. The train passed through Matjiesfontein, where, with Virginia, we once stayed at another Rawdon Hotel. David acquired the entire small deserted railway village, built in Victorian times as a health resort, where Cape Towners, who came to exchange the damp days in the city for the bracing, clear, dry air of the Karoo, stayed at the turreted Lord Milner Hotel, conveniently facing the railway station. The place had been empty for years when David took it on, modernised the plumbing and restored its Victorian look with Turkey carpets, period furniture and large portraits downstairs; and upstairs he made the bedrooms light and comfortable with chintzes and good beds. The terraced cottages where the railway employees lived were turned into family motel rooms; the village shop is again a village shop, and the pub caters for those who don't go to the hotel. A museum is established in a cottage. Around the Lord Milner gardens grow, and pepper-trees in the courtyard give a pretty, lacy shade. Tennis-courts and a putting-course have been added since our visit; the pool, filled with fresh underground water, is a boon in hot dry seasons. The only mild drawback is the hardness of the water, and to combat this David supplies luxurious Badedas to soften the bath-water's impact. On the train Reggie and I asked to be called with a cup of tea at five-thirty a.m. so that we could see the village, once more, as we passed through it. For our pleasure, the captain arranged for the train to slow down almost to a walking pace.

During the years of Reggie's regular trips to South Africa he took me on two enjoyable bird-watching holidays to Kenya; one year we also went to Uganda. He had been there before with Herbert Axell, ex-warden of Minsmere Bird Reserve in Suffolk, on a tour conducted by the great naturalist John Williams. John Williams not only knows all about birds, but also about wild flowers, bats, butterflies, snakes, spiders and, I dare say, all the rest of the animal kingdom. On a ten-day trip they saw and identified over six hundred different species of birds. Reggie was determined to show me some of the wonders he had enjoyed, and in 1971, with Daphne Ball as our guide, we drove in a small rented car from Entebbe to Ruwenzori Lodge, near the Mountains of the Moon, and on to Queen Elizabeth National Park. Our bird tally was not as great as Reggie's had been on his first visit, but we saw hundreds of birds, most of them new to me, and including my most exciting bird-sight – a black bee-eater. So knowledgeable is

John Williams (and so local are the birds) that he was able to tell Daphne at exactly which point on the road between a certain tree and a stone bridge we would find this specific creature; and we did. At Ruwenzori we took a meandering walk through the chest-high, down-sloping tea-gardens below the Lodge, and came to a deep gully with steeply rising forest on its other bank. As always we had our binoculars hung round our necks, and I caught sight of something the colour of badly-dyed auburn hair up a tree at eye-level across the gully. It was a red-headed colobus monkey, with two companions. They are not common or easy to find, so our pleasure was enormous. We stood still, and either we didn't bother them, or they hadn't seen us, for they swung themselves slowly from branch to branch on a half-dead tree, with almost no leaves to hide them. We watched for about half-an-hour as they lowered themselves in such a leisurely way that they appeared to be moving in slow motion, hanging on with one elongated arm until the very last second before rhythmically dropping some distance to grab with the other hand – almost in passing – a lower branch. Then, as slowly, they climbed back without effort, only to start the whole process again. It was an enchanting sight of natural grace at its most casual and looked as if it were being carried out for the fun of it. As they moved about we saw they not only had red heads but long tasselled tails.

I made rough drawings of the beautiful Ugandan women and girls we passed on the road, tall, long-necked and elegant with pretty arms, wrists and hands. They wore a sort of uniform made of different flowered stuffs; a picturesque dress cut in an un-modern fashion with a low square neck, short sleeves set with gathers at the shoulder (a corruption of a puffed sleeve?) and the voluminous skirt tucked up over an under-petticoat in the shepherdess style you sometimes see in old prints. We learned later that the design for the dresses dates back to Victorian times when the first missionaries came out from England and decreed what the women should wear.

We met a great many army trucks on the road as we drove back to Entebbe the day before we were to fly to Nairobi *en route* to South Africa. Daphne was surprised to see them. She hadn't heard of any army manoeuvres. We did not suspect that Amin's take-over was about to happen. We flew off from Entebbe at ten-thirty the next morning. At two-thirty the airport was bombed, and all roads out of Uganda were closed. Amin had moved in.

CHAPTER ELEVEN

Family and Other Gatherings

On the whole I enjoy preparing for events more than the event itself. The idea of Christmas always fired me, and even as a child it was the getting-ready period I liked most – making presents and cards, gumming coloured paper rings together for chains, and posting my personal list of requests up the chimney to Father Christmas.

The feast itself was always, from as far back as my memory goes, spent staying at Cliveden with Aunt Nancy and Uncle Waldorf Astor and their five children. My ambivalent feelings about the place exercised me a good deal. I was torn between wishing we could have our own family Christmas at home – decorating our own tree, putting up our own holly and mistletoe – and the greedy certainty that at the big house there would be lots more people, presents, festivity and foods. As the day drew nearer I settled for greed and hoped there wouldn't be a family row and that pleasures would be plentiful.

We usually arrived on Christmas Eve in the dark at tea-time, the car sent to fetch us from Taplow Station loaded with our baggage and the parcels Tommy and I were not supposed to notice. 'Mummy, what's in that?' 'Wait and see – it's Christmas.' As we turned the corner by the giant marble shell fountain, at the end of the straight quarter-mile approach to the house, the glassed-in porch as if by magic suddenly blazed with light. How did anyone know we were coming? I only discovered years later than when a car passed through the main iron gates of the park the lodge-keeper telephoned, on a hand-wound private line, to warn the house that it was coming. The butler was at the open door to greet us. 'Shake hands with Mr Lee.' We did and said we were quite well, thank you, to him and to the footmen waiting to carry in the bags. We shooks hands, too, with the parlourmaid, hovering behind them, in her dark brown alpaca uniform with a gossamer-fine organdie apron, high collar, and head bandeau cap tied with brown velvet ribbon.

We sniffed the special Cliveden smell as we stepped into the porch, where, as well as tennis racquets, hockey-sticks and golf-bags, there was a giant Chinese jar, full of golf-umbrellas, walking-sticks and a special 'pusher' – a polished wooden device, like a wide, shallow, spread-out crutch – which legend said had been designed to fit the waist of some elderly, stout party, to push her up the long and steep yew-tree walk that rises up to the house from the riverside below. It had been sold with the house when old Mr Astor bought it from the Duke of Westminster. We took it in turns to push each other up and down the front hall with it, until some grown-up stopped us. The delicious smell came from pots of humea; a delicate plant with a feathery cascade of reddish-brown flowers that give off an incense-like scent; not much to look at, but lovely to sniff. (It is increasingly hard to buy humea. A year or two ago Reggie discovered that one of the few places where it is grown is in the commercial nursery garden at Windsor Castle. He managed to get hold of a pot, and for about ten days the flat was heady with its scent.)

In the front hall we saw the giant Christmas tree was where we expected it to be, at the foot of the oak staircase. The banisters were festooned with garlands of box, yew, bay, ivy, holly and other ever-greens that, as well as the humea, gave off a subtle aromatic scent. Only once were we allowed to help decorate the tree. The job was usually done by a gardener on a step-ladder, with the housekeeper handing him the tinsel and coloured balls. I always made sure that certain favourite decorations were still there; the glass birds in little tin cages were regulars I looked for.

Aunt Nancy, wearing a sweater over a silk shirt, neat tweed skirt, golf socks and ghillie shoes, came out of her boudoir to greet us.

'You children go on upstairs – and take your coats with you. I will not have them left all over the place.' She was rather fierce, and, after kissing her proffered cheek and feeling, as always, as if I had done something wrong, I scrambled up the polished stairs.

'Come on down right away as soon as you have washed. You needn't change today. Tea's ready.'

Ordinarily we always 'changed' for tea. As little girls my cousin Wissie and I (the only girls of the party until our Brand cousins, Virginia and Dinah, were old enough to come for Christmas) put on frilly muslins and our bronze dancing-slippers with elastic that crossed our ankles. As we grew older we graduated to velvet and fine wool. The boys began in their sailor suits, but once they were old enough to go to school they wore the small boys' uniform of grey flannel jacket and shorts with black elastic-sided 'house-shoes'.

We came down and sat at the children's table near the fire, where Uncle Waldorf chose to join us. He poured out our milk and sliced the wholesome loaf and plain cake baked for us to eat. At the grown-up table, where Aunt Nancy presided, there were delectable little scones in a lidded silver dish, kept hot over a spirit lamp. There was also a special, almost black, rich fruit-cake topped with marzipan, chocolate éclairs and very short crisp shortbreads, all made in the still-room by two full-time cake-and-pastry-cooks. Sometimes we were allowed special treats from the grown-ups' table, but Aunt Nancy kept an eye on the goodies, and we were strictly rationed.

After tea Aunt Nancy went to her present-room, a small dark panelled study next to her boudoir used for storage. No child was allowed to go there, particularly at Christmas-time, but, once when I was about sixteen and was sent in there to fetch something for her, I saw it was like a little shop. Piles of sweaters of all colours and sizes, men's, boys', women's and girls'; silk stockings, silk scarves, chiffon squares and boxes of linen handkerchiefs, from the Irish Linen Stores, initialled for everyone in the party. There were evening bags, men's ties, golf-balls in boxes, little packs of tees, diaries, toys, games, books and candy. *Lots* of candy. There was never a more generous present-giver than Aunt Nancy, but she was always careful about her candy store; most of it came from American friends, and she didn't let it out of her keeping except in very occasional bestowals of a caramel here and a sour-ball there. She also had a great many boxes of chewing-gum and was never without a supply in her pocket. Presents from the store were given to everyone in the house, family, friends, staff and visiting staff – in those days ladies' maids and valets always accompanied their employers. Aunt Nancy's private secretary helped by doing much of the present buying, and all the wrapping up in layers of best quality tissue-paper tied with inch-wide red satin ribbon. Aunt Nancy wrote the tags.

At about half-past six the bell-ringers and carol-singers, steaming a little from the outside damp and exercise, arrived in the hall. I thought of the bell-ringers as old men, but I don't suppose they can have been, as they had walked all the way from Burnham to play for us. We were all summoned to hear them. Each man had two bells, and they stood in pairs facing each other. At a nod from their leader they began to ring. First they rang *The Blue Bells of Scotland*, a tradition of their

Aunt Nancy on the ice

visit and not the most Christmassy of choices. They didn't just play it once – they played it again, and again, and again. The bells were very loud. And then it was time for the carol-singers. All I remember is a small group of men and boys in dark clothes; one a hooty tenor who, before the group joined in, swooped through an opening solo verse of *See Amid the Winter Snows* with all the notes run together. This, for some reason, gave me bad church-giggles. Wissie caught it. The boys became infected, too. Aunt Nancy gave us fierce frowns. It happened every year. I half-hoped, half-dreaded the swooper would swoop again; and every year he did.

After the carols we were sent upstairs to bed, and on our way we stopped at Uncle Waldorf's dressing-room, where his valet had put out a selection of stockings for us to choose from, in anticipation of Father Christmas's visit later that night. My father was a non-sporting Londoner who neither played golf nor shot. His short City socks were no good for hanging up; Uncle Waldorf's beautifully hand-knitted knee-length stockings were ideal. As very small children we didn't open our stockings until we took them to our parents' room, and there in their bed we discovered what it was that crackled and tinkled and bulged so enchantingly. As we grew older we opened them in our own beds at whatever hour we woke up and felt the precious weight, and heard the sounds a really good stocking can make. Nursery breakfast was upstairs. After giving us all time to go to the bathroom and 'be good', and after waiting for our parents to finish their breakfast in the dining-room, we were allowed to go downstairs.

A transformation had taken place in the front hall. On every chair, all over the sofa and on the big high-backed oak bench by the fireside, were piles of presents. Everyone, grown-ups and children, had a pile marked with his or her name. (There is a story that when A. A. Milne was a young man he went to spend Christmas at a large house-party like that at Cliveden. He was the first down that morning and to his dismay found that everyone in the house-party had been given presents. He had not brought anything for anyone. Thinking quickly he went round the room and added his name to that of the real giver: 'With love from Granny – and A. A. Milne.' 'Happy Christmas Uncle Pat, with love from Joan – and A. A. Milne.')

When I was little I went straight for the biggest parcel; later I discovered it is true that good things come in small parcels, and one year, when I was nine, the littlest parcel held a brooch, a proper, *real* brooch: a duck made of a blister pearl with a green enamel head and neck. 'From Aunt Nancy.'

At one stage in my childhood a new school-story by Angela Brazil appeared every Christmas, and I hoped for and was always given it. From experience I knew that Boxing Day would, except for the Beagle Meet, be an anticlimax, and I saved up my Angela Brazil for a treat to be begun on 26 December. But I had to have a quick look before I put it aside, and was comforted to see things had not changed . . .

'By Jehoshaphat!' ejaculated a tall slim girl, with a mane of unruly red-gold locks, wielding a cricket bat. 'This *is* going to be a spiffing term!'

The noise in the front hall was deafening. New bicycles had bells to ring, toy motors had hooters. We all screamed a good deal.

'Look – oh, look what I've got!'

Of course we were spoiled and given too much of everything. I cannot defend it. Once, when I was first married, I was given the twin copy of my cousin Wissie's raccoon fur coat, from America. I felt I was in a collegiate movie of the twenties when I wore it. In that house it was the custom to give on a scale unknown to most people, even from the same background. If the giving had been limited only to those who already had, it would have been indefensible, but my aunt and uncle were sharers on the grand scale with all and sundry, and their imaginative generosity, undiscovered for the most part, was their special gift. And not only at Christmas.

Christmas at Cliveden in the early twenties (the fat little girl is me)

A little before eleven we got ready for church. I was probably wearing something new for Christmas-tide – gloves or a scarf or my new duck brooch. We piled into several cars and were driven to the little hillside church at Hedsor for the morning service. Here another giggle-hazard sound, like the hooty tenor, lay in wait for us. The hazard lurked in the strange way the vicar spoke. He had a deep rumbling voice and was popularly supposed to have *two* stomachs – an ordinary one, as it were, and an echo-chamber. Thus, when he said 'Let us pray', it came out –

'Let us pray . . .

    . . . us pray.'

Can it really have sounded like that? He came to luncheon sometimes but never echoed outside church.

The great thing about Christmas at Cliveden was the way the pattern was adhered to. We could count on the day's shape remaining the same. After presents, church and luncheon, we were made to go out, whatever the weather, for air and exercise. In my memory it was usually mild green weather with blackbirds in bare tree-tops anticipating spring in bursts of early song. Only once do I remember a white Christmas, and then it was the slushy kind: no good for snowmen or sledging. About two-thirty in the afternoon of Christmas Day everyone, grown-ups and children (that made it more fun for the children) went down to the immense lawn below the terrace, to the south of the house. Sides were picked up, and we played 'French and

English', or if you prefer it, 'Flags'. I was always the last to be chosen, partly because I was lazy and un-athletic, and partly because I was a tiresome, bossy, plump child. I stood about a good deal, watching. It was pleasing to see Reggie Winn, newly married to Cousin Alice Perkins, dodging the enemy and triumphantly snatching a 'flag' for his side. He played all games to win and has kept his zest longer than most of us. My pa, a slow mover like me, was always caught and made a prisoner. Aunt Nancy never stuck to the rules. My ma wasn't good at rules either, but ran like a deer and was cheered on. Darkness fell early. We went back to the house, and Aunt Nancy said:

'You-all get your books and sit quietly for an hour.'

After tea there was a half-hearted attempt to get a carol sing-song going. At school carols were lovely, particularly when we learned descants and I was one of the piping trebles allowed to sing them. But only Aunt Phyllis and my mother were really musical. And none of the other children except Bill Astor, who knew the words, was at all enthusiastic, and it faded away. As we grew older we were allowed to stay up for dinner – a treat for those whose bed-time, until they were twelve years old, was seven-thirty. And dinner on Christmas night was a fancy-dress occasion.

Dressing-up was my favourite sport. At home I was allowed to put on my mother's dresses and shoes and, while she lay on her bed resting before going out to dinner, I teetered about her bedroom playing at being a grown-up. It was the fashion, in the years directly after the First World War, for women to have 'false curls', often, like my mother's, made from their own long hair. The curls were fastened to silk-covered wire hairpins that tethered them over the ears, under a cloche hat, to give the illusion of the newly fashionable bobbed hair. Wearing these curls, and one of my ma's hats, gave me the feeling of being a real grown-up.

The other day an acquaintance who had once had long hair and wore it in a bun, as I now wear mine, found in her cupboard a for-gotten boxful of such hairpins, made in Paris probably in the early twenties. She passed them on to me, and has revolutionised my life. The fine silk round the metal prevents the pins from slipping, and at last I know that my hair, even when I've come straight from the hairdresser and it is clean and silky, is going to stay up. I've rarely had a more welcome present.

At Cliveden dressing up for Christmas-night dinner was a big excitement. On the first floor, called the French Landing, there was a large black-and-gold Chinese chest, and in it was kept a tumbled collection of dressing-up clothes. Some were genuine fancy dresses. There was an exquisite white taffeta Pierrette costume, decorated with fluffy black pompons, made for Aunt Nancy to wear, when she was a bride, to the famous ball at Devonshire House, some years before the 1914 War. It had matching shoes, black satin with white pompons, and squat low Louis heels. Neither Wissie Astor nor I, even when we were young and slimmish, could get into the dress, with its eighteen-inch waist, or the small, elegant shoes. There were also mandarin coats, parts of an eighteenth-century-style shepherdess's dress made of glazed chintz, kimonos, scarves, an odd skirt, blouses, hats and masks – funny-face masks for pompous colonels, wicked eye-patched pirates and yellow-faced Chinese villains; and two Hogarth-like Ugly Sister masks, one with a long nose that turned down and one with a ski-slope of a nose that turned up. I didn't like any of them; they were macabre and frightening. There was also a foolish pink-cheeked female mask, with blonde crêpe hair in pigtails and a small rosebud mouth. I particularly disliked that one. But Aunt Nancy liked nothing better than putting on one of these faces and pretending to be the character that matched it. She acted the fool with the rosebud mouth, and we half believed she really had become that rather alarming blonde ninny.

The children made a general scramble through the chest and mask-box hoping for inspiration, and if, as usually happened, there was nothing I could use, I got help from my mother. I never put on a mask. There was something disagreeable about wearing a face that didn't belong to me, and I hated the stifling smell given off by the waxy canvas.

My mother and Aunt Phyllis, in borrowed straw boaters, their husbands' hard collars and ties and the longest skirts they could find, dressed as they had when they were 'belles' in Virginia at the beginning of the century. The carried tennis racquets. Even as a child I knew they looked romantic and charming. My cousins and I turned ourselves into cliché Arabs, cowboys, apaches, pirates, gipsies and 'grown-ups'. One of the boys always pounced on a mandarin coat and stuck with determination to his chosen disguise. He spoke only in Pidgin English and walked in a funny oriental way.

After dinner there were charades, and people did turns. Aunt Nancy's annual and favourite turn was always a success. She borrowed Uncle Waldorf's pink hunting-coat, white breeches and shiny black boots, jammed his black velvet huntsman's cap (too big) well down over her small face and became a little *nouveau riche* hunting-man, rising – with his imaginary wife, 'my Rosie' – up the social scale. Snobbish? Yes. Funny? *Very*. In this disguise she was entirely possessed, improvised after-dinner speeches, danced in character, walked in character and conducted dialogues with my mother, who 'fed' her, that held us all entranced. We came to believe in the reality of the little man. Until Aunt Phyllis, her favourite sister, died in the early 1930s, she never needed persuading to put on the pink coat; but after that time it was never seen again.

Years later Aunt Nancy invented other characters. She got hold of a set of 'prop' plastic teeth (the kind Dick Emery wears as the vicar in his T.V. sketches), was unrecognisable, and became an upper-crust British woman with prejudices against Abroad and 'Emmericans'; and until within a few years of her death at eighty-two, she could turn herself into one of those gallant women (her exact contemporary) who served in the W.A.A.C. in World War I, and show how some twenty-eight years later this heroine marched in the peace parade after World War II. This old girl, with knees bent, stoop exaggerated and head thrust forward, lurched by, giving the salute to an invisible Personage on a dais. It was funny, tragic and admirable, at all levels.

The children, who never quite understood what was being laughed at, got sleepier and sleepier, and quieter too. The quietness was deliberate, so that it might not be noticed that the clock said ten-thirty – eleven – and, oh joy, *midnight*. And so to bed.

'Goodnight, and thank you, Aunt Nancy.'

'Have you had a happy Christmas?'

'Rath-*er* – and thanks *awfully* for my presents.'

Then slowly upstairs, where the rouge I had applied over-generously didn't shift with soap and water, so I left it on and fell into bed. Awful to think Christmas was over. But – oh *good* – Boxing Day tomorrow, the Beagles; and my new Angela Brazil.

When we married, Reggie and I still spent most of our Christmases at Cliveden. It was a long time before we celebrated our own at home. There were occasional Christmases with his side of the family, happy but different; some of them seemed a bit thin after the lavish feasts at Aunt Nancy's. None of them smelt quite right either.

After the War, when we were living in London in the King's Road, I decided to decorate the flat even though we would be going away for the actual holiday. Christmas was a time when friends came to see us, and I needed no excuse to indulge my pleasure in what my ma called 'fixin' up'. I bought gold metallic paper, folded it and cut out stars to hang from cotton threads, and spin in the warmth of the kitchen-dining-room. It took me a long time to discover how to cut out a convincing five-point star, and, when I had learned how, I made dozens. We still use some of the original supply made over thirty years ago; and the same lengths of broad red velvet ribbon are now hung on the carved frame of a gilded baroque looking-glass and over the pictures in the living-room at Elm Park Gardens.

I think Americans make Christmas look prettier and gayer than we do, and I borrowed ideas from U.S. magazines and invented my own – flat, tailored bows with swallow-tail ends made from velvet ribbon and wired to the base of a pair of two-branched glass candlesticks; and an army of little standing gold-paper angels. I gave them long folded wings, and discovered it was possible with a Biro to draw details of feathers, haloes and faces on the metallic surface. The ink doesn't take, but the design is etched in. We have never had a live Christmas tree, because I didn't want to have to sweep up fallen needles. (I believe there is now a spray that holds them indefinitely.) Instead we have made do with a small token tree built of wire and shredded silver paper, and to hide its inadequacy I cover it with gold tinsel roses, more stars, shiny gold balls and strands of a zigzagging kind of golden tinsel, all from America. Last year, for the first time, we lit our tree with a string of tiny coloured lights. It was a big improvement.

Our Christmas and Boxing Day luncheon parties began in a modest way with Miss H. M. C. Johnson, an old friend of my father's, in her dark-blue hat and her mother's diamond ear-rings, and at most two other friends. As we became more confident about the limited space in the dining-room, and in my cooking, we expanded, and now we expect to seat up to twelve people on a variety of chairs at two tables made up as one. We have collected visiting young Australians and Americans, sometimes homesick for their families, and added them to a group of regulars who came, or come, annually to one or other of the big days. Among these have been Athene and Beau (Nicholas Hannen) – it was he who advised me to go to the Royal Academy of Dramatic Art, where I lasted exactly one term, before Reggie took my mind off the stage and I left; Ingaret and Laurens Van der Post, bringing Ingaret's mother, rising ninety; Hazel Armour Kennedy, the sculptress, introduced to us by the Hannens; Margery and Geoffrey Castle; Joyce Carey, Murray Macdonald, and Tim and Rosalie Nugent.

They have all been part of our Christmases. Some of them are no longer here, but recent additions are Trenchard Cox, Betty Hardy, a friend ever since the 'How' radio programme days, Patrick Woodcock, Laurier Lister and Julia Burney. Virginia comes to both Christmas and Boxing Day occasions.

Athene's husband, known as Beau because of his good looks, was an old friend of my pa's from the days when they were both articled to Sir Edwin Lutyens. My pa became an architect, but Beau decided he preferred the stage, where he was a handsome and charming addition to any play in which he appeared. Some time in the early 1950s he and Athene established an annual Spring Luncheon that became a tradition for the rest of Beau's life. The regular members of the party were Virginia and Tony, Reggie and I. Sometimes A. A. Milne and his wife, and occasionally Victor Stiebel, joined us, but the old dependables were the Thesigers and Grenfells, and they put the date in their diaries with pleasure as soon as the Hannens announced it. The luncheon took place in a private room at the Garrick Club, and Beau went to a great deal of trouble to make it the special occasion it always was. The ladies wore their new spring hats and Athene her parure of Victorian moonstones. Beau presented each of us with a little spray of pink rosebuds and gave the gentlemen carnations for their buttonholes. He worked out menus (one year all the foods were chosen to match his green-and-pink striped Garrick Club tie) and he invented names for the dishes – 'Coupe d'Athene' – 'Saumon Virginie' – and wrote it all out in French. After the luncheons we signed our names on a menu card. Athene has kept a complete collection that, to this day, comes out on the occasions of the Spring Luncheons that the four remaining originals – herself, Virginia, Reggie and I – now enjoy in her riverside flat in the Mall at Hammersmith. Athene usually makes for us her own special cream 'dessert', flavoured with sweet-scented geranium. One year she hadn't been able to get hold of any geranium-leaves and had decided to give us peaches instead, but passing a butcher's shop she noticed a flourishing plant in the window among the chops and other meats. She went in and asked if she might be allowed a few of the scented leaves. The butcher asked her what she needed them for. 'To eat,' said Athene, and went home to concoct the most delicate of creamy delights for the next day's party.

We don't give many parties because we prefer to see our friends in small groups. I don't enjoy any kind of occasion unless there are

Beau and Athene Hannen

enough seats for everybody. Because I feel like this we have never given any gathering that didn't provide some sort of sitting-place. But I do like getting ready – fixin' – for any kind of home occasion. I cannot pretend it is all done entirely for the love of others; I have decided that even if preparing feasts is a kind of self-indulgence, it is a sin I am prepared to risk. So once or twice we have entertained on a scale we hadn't expected we could manage until we tried.

In 1962 we celebrated the eightieth birthday of my father's younger brother Bill Phipps. He and Aunt Pamela had always been an important part of my life, although, because he was a sailor and away a great deal of the time and when he retired they went to live in the country, our meetings were spaced out. But, during a period when they took a flat in Chelsea, Reggie and I saw a lot of them, and it was good; no generation gap. There is in my family a definite Phippsy look, and Uncle Bill had it. He was bonier and slighter than my pa, but they had the same long jaw-line as does Tommy, many of our cousins and I. My first memory of Aunt Pamela is still clear, because of the pale mauve linen dress she was wearing when Uncle Bill brought her to meet my parents, the day after they had become engaged. I had never before seen a dress of such a romantic colour, and, with her thick ash-fair hair and petal complexion, the whole picture pleased my eight-year-old eye, and I have never forgotten it.

I have come to the conclusion that I do not have very powerful clan feelings. This does not mean that I am not fond of my kith and kin,

W. D. Phipps by J. S. Sargent

but that those I love among them would be my friends if we were not related. Nevertheless there is a tug towards the tribe, so when Uncle Bill's eightieth birthday fell due, it was fun to assemble a family occasion to do him honour. Twenty-three of us met at our flat. They included two of his best friends, Marjorie and Geoffrey Oaksey. There were short toasts before he cut the savoury birthday cake I had had made for him – cheesy and tasty and decorated with nuts and olives. Uncle Bill, who, as Reggie is, was a great weeper at moments of happiness, cried a little, and together we all laughed a good deal. I am glad to record that Phippses usually do.

In 1954, while Reggie was in South Africa, my father died, and Uncle Bill, then living in the border country near Edinburgh, came south to go with me to Golders Green for the little thanksgiving service in my father's memory. We came back to 149 King's Road where Mrs Gabe had luncheon ready for us. As we went in the front door Uncle Bill noticed that the film *Genevieve* was playing at the Gaumont opposite – where Habitat now stands. He said he'd heard it was a good picture and that my cameo part in it was funny. I said 'Let's go and see it this afternoon.' He was a more conventional man than my pa, and for a moment he wondered whether that was quite the thing to do on that day. But we agreed that my pa would have thoroughly approved of the idea. So we went, and laughed, and cried at the touching part where John Gregson denied himself the Old Crocks' Race in order not to hurt a garrulous old man. We thoroughly enjoyed ourselves.

Because of Uncle Bill's health the W. D. Phippses – he always signed his letters W. D. Phipps even to his children – spent their winters abroad, and eventually they settled in Spain. But sadly soon after they had found the very flat they wanted, Uncle Bill was taken ill and died. Aunt Pamela came back to London. We were very pleased when she came to live, just across the grassed square, on the other side of Elm Park Gardens, where for half the year, while the leaves are off the plane trees, I can see the lights of her fourth-floor rooms and maintain a niecely watch on the hours she keeps. There is no doubt about it, goodness and selflessness (far stronger than unselfishness) added to a sensitive awareness of other people and their feelings is attractive. Not only does Aunt Pamela possess all these qualities, but she is also independent-minded, interested in what goes on in the world, reads her *Times* from cover to cover, and gets through her library books far more quickly than I do. At eighty-seven she is still pretty as a flower; white hair becomes her; she continues to take an interest in clothes and always presents an enchanting, fresh appearance. The smaller and frailer she appears to be, the brighter shines her gentle spirit.

Our most ambitious effort was the wedding reception we gave for Jean Stewart when she married Jack Gunn. For that we hired extra glasses, china, cutlery and a dozen little gold chairs; and somehow, by using the passage and the space at the foot of the stairs, all twenty-eight of us sat down to the cold collation, eaten on our knees, prepared by me and Mrs Gabe, who had not yet left to live in far away Burnt Oak. Mrs Gabe, too, enjoyed preparing for parties. I left the main dishes for her to make at home, and on the morning of the great day Reggie drove round to Flood Street to collect her and tray-loads of food. She has her own special way with egg mousses and chicken salads. She enjoyed cooking on Mrs Beeton's scale, and for this party my diary says she used three dozen eggs and eight chickens. I made ready the green salads and sliced tomatoes, each slice done with a dash of sugar, a drop of French dressing, made with plenty of sugar, garlic, vinegar and a little oil, and topped with freshly cut up mint. I also hulled eight pounds of fine firm strawberries, and arranged them,

Jean Gunn

dusted with icing sugar, in snow-topped mounds in big white china cabbage-leaf bowls. The appearance of the table laden with good foods was photogenic enough for an American glossy magazine. It seemed a pity to destroy it, but after some appreciative remarks from the bridegroom and the rest of the party we soon forgot the look of the spread and ate it up.

Jean and I share a feeling for colour, and I decorated the flat entirely with the kind of roses we both like – fat garden roses in every pale colour available, bush roses, roses of the old fashioned cabbage variety, moss roses some with stripes, and tea roses. They filled the flat with their fragrance, and when Jean, looking serene in her pearly grey-cream dress and amber petal hat, walked through the front door with Jack, she stood still and breathed in the summery scents. 'Oh – those roses.' She and I have known each other since we were girls and she is one of the friends on whom I know I could call for any favour, and, if it were at all possible, she would grant it. She is another of the special friends who share my faith in God, and her friendship, like Virginia's, is woven into my life.

To list everyone I love would be meaningless, but I must add to the names already mentioned in my first book of memories that of Christine Harrison who taught me to think more clearly about metaphysics and helped me to understand the indissoluble relationship of God and man. Before she married she had taught at a day school in Queen's Gate, where I went for a fill-in term before going away to boarding school. She is only a few years older than I am, and we made friends.

There is also Verily (Anderson) Paget who came into my life through the unexpected agency of the Girls' Friendly Society. In

1951, when I was at the St Martin's Theatre playing in a revue called *Penny Plain,* I had a letter asking me to grant an interview for the G.F.S. magazine, a publication of which I had never heard. It offered a refreshing change, and after a matinée performance Joe Dockery ushered into my dressing-room a very pregnant Verily Anderson. As it turned out, I think it was I who did most of the interviewing during the hour we spent together. I learned she had an invalid husband and four children; was a freelance journalist; ran a hotel for children in Sussex; and was a cousin of Peter Scott, whom I had known since he was a chubby lad, famous in Chelsea where we both lived, for his unusual clothes. In summer and winter he wore a short-sleeved linen tunic, with bare legs and sandals. He scorned a coat in the coldest of weathers. Since that first meeting Verily and I have been friends, and Reggie and I follow with affectionate interest and admiration her career, and that of her remarkable family. Marian is a painter. Rachel writes and broadcasts; her book, *The Purple Heart Throbs,* about the writers of romantic novels, was enthusiastically reviewed. Eddie, a born naturalist, has graduated from gamekeeper to maker of documentary films with a television company. Janie designs, makes and markets clothes under the trade name 'Janaë'. Alex is training to be a masseuse. All are happily married with children. All are gifted, inventive, intrepid; most are musical; and all five are a credit to their mother who was widowed when Alex, the child she was expecting when we first met, was very small. Verily brought them up to be independent, original and loving.

In 1962 she was in hospital, and the five young Andersons came to us at Christmas, bringing with them presents of their own making. I only remember Janie's models of two Victorian figures constructed out of pipe-cleaners and coloured crêpe papers. 'They're meant to be you and Reggie.' The couple stood on the desk, he in top-hat and tails, she in scuttle-bonnet and crinoline, looking as if they were about to swing away into a waltz. If the likenesses were not exact, the skilful making and the vigour of the figures were successful. For a twelve-year-old child it was a remarkable achievement. We kept them until they fell apart. The Andersons are fond of animals, and Verily was used to giving house-room to many kinds. To this day Eddie's special taste is for predatory birds, and if he and his wife Tina have to go away, Verily takes over the supervision of his barn owl and whatever other creatures he currently happens to have. She is given typed instructions, detailing precise menus to be followed, and times for feeding. I was glad he had not brought with him any of his feathered friends that Christmas. But Janie could not be parted from her white mouse. Mercifully it spent most of its time sleeping in her pocket within a little grey woollen tunnel she had knitted for its comfort. I am not drawn to mice, but I did my best to appear brave about this one, and tried not to show that I wished it hadn't come to the party. During the times when it was awake and Janie let it out to explore the room, I I was able to keep my legs up on the sofa.

Also with us that Christmas Day was Clive James, a young man I had met in Australia in 1959, when he and his fellow-members of the University Journalists' Club in Sydney gave a luncheon in my honour. My diary says: 'Highly intelligent group of girls and young men.' They were well versed in Anglo-American humour, knew all Stephen Potter's works, collected recordings by Flanders and Swann and Nichols and May, were amused by Peter Ustinov, Mort Sahl and, it seems, me. 'They were nice to me. Friendly, relaxed and not at all frightening as the young can be.' After luncheon when the President, John Howard, and Clive saw me to my taxi I asked them if they were journalists. 'Not *yet*.' They wondered whether if they were to write to me when I got back home to England I would write back. Yes, I said, not thinking either of them would remember our conversation. But for the next few years Clive – and for a good deal longer, John – wrote; and I wrote back. They were the kind of letters that articulate, imaginative and lively young creatures have always written. What they needed was an open ear, conveniently removed a good distance from themselves and their cronies; and I provided it. They showed off, like gambolling lambs, and were often amusing, outrageous and sometimes thoughtful. But mostly they were getting rid of excess energy. They were, of course, anti-establishment, anti-authority and (and this appealed to me) anti-received ideas. They flirted with the concept of anarchy. In other words they were feeling their oats and growing up. Clive sent wild scraps of writing and occasionally poems that I thought showed evidence of more than exuberance. John reported on the Sydney scene, and was soberer. Clive's ambition was to get to England, and with his energy and thrust I was sure he would. In time he arrived with a postgraduate grant in his pocket, and went to Cambridge.

When he first came to see us in London, one Sunday for luncheon, every inch of him from his casual polo-necked sweater, decidedly unusual in our adult world in those far off days of 1962, to his unpolished shoes expressed protest. He was ready to throw out most of the ways of life he found in Great Britain, told us tales of the jazz underworld that widened our eyes, but was hungry enough to tuck well into a good meal. We watched him settle down, enjoy Cambridge, acquire a dinner-jacket, practically take over the Footlights (the University theatre club) and now, at the time of writing, he is a member of the new establishment: the journalist he, and I, always knew he would become. He works, as once I did, for the *Observer* and is the most readable (if sometimes prejudiced) television critic currently writing. He is married to Prue, a fellow Australian. They have two beautiful daughters.

I treasure a picture of Clive with an empty match-box lid on his nose, on that Christmas day in 1962, trying to pass it from his fully-grown one to Janie's tiny tip-tilted nose. We played Poisoned Handkerchief, and – in another nosey game – we lay flat on the floor and tried to wiggle a sixpence off the end of our noses without moving our heads. Clive was enchanted by the little Andersons, helped them into their coats and was driven back to his digs in their family car by Marian. Two days later he wrote me a Collins. It was the 'time spent' that he loved and thanked for. Reggie had taken photographs of us all, and Clive said please he must have one of Janie to wear next to his heart; he was sure it was bullet-proof.

A very few years later Janie was making her own clothes, and, out of an old voile dress patterned in a design of green and white marbling like end-papers in an antique leather-bound book, she made for herself, and wore, a pair of green marbled stockings.

In 1971 Reggie and I went to her wedding, in the little Victorian village in Norfolk where the Andersons had gone to live. It was a truly hot summer's day, and we drove through farmlands, pale with wheat and barley, with verges spilling over with wild flowers. The bridegroom, Charlie Hampton, wore an Edwardian morning-coat and wing-collar, and Janie, on Eddie's arm, came down the aisle in the dress she had been embroidering for months – an exact copy of the Primavera's in Botticelli's picture – a wreath of fresh ivy in her fair curly hair, and carrying a sheaf of corn and wild flowers from the ditches. She was barefoot. The small bridesmaids and pages that followed her came linked together by ropes of more wild flowers that her sisters had been making all the morning. The little girls had daisy-chains on their heads and bigger field daisies tucked into their shoes; the boys, with round-necked tunics, looked like Augustus

*Charlie and
Janie Hampton*

John's pictures of children. The whole scene spanned the works of
Botticelli, Kate Greenaway and John. Suitably we sang 'All things
bright and beautiful'. Janie and Charlie drove away from the church
in an open 1920 vintage Roll-Royce, sitting on top of the back seat
as if they had won an election.

Verily had just become engaged to Paul Paget, a distinguished
architect who, until his retirement, was the Surveyor of St Paul's
Cathedral. It was in the garden of his house, Templewood, that the
Hampton reception was held. The guests were a mixture of Norfolk
county in top-hats and conventional printed silks, and way-out King's
Road. There were several fancy-dress 'gypsies' mixing ancient velvet

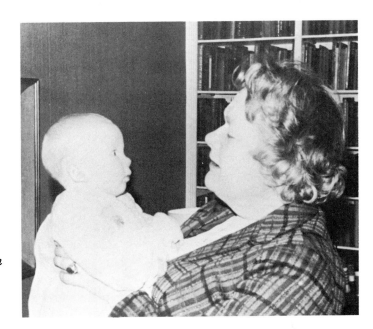

Daisy Hampton and her grandmother Verily Paget

bridge-coats with raggle-taggle finery, more bare feet and flowing hair everywhere. Reggie and I meandered away from the crowd and were surprised, because of his unexpected appearance in a wood, to meet a young man in a collarless low-cut blue singlet, a tail-coat, grey flannels and tennis shoes, being dragged along by a panting bull-terrier on a lead. I seem to remember he was one of the few with hair cut *en brosse*.

Two and a half weeks later, Verily and Paul were married in the Lady Chapel of St Bartholomew the Great in the City of London. The young Hamptons got back from France that morning, and Janie, with half-an-hour to do it in, washed her hair and came to church with it tied up under a pirate-style handkerchief. Charlie had a large daisy stuck through the wool of his fisherman's jersey. It was the dearest occasion; small, quiet, devout and affectionate: Marian, Rachel and Janie with their husbands, and Alex, in scarlet, wearing the picture-hat Verily had worn at Janie's wedding. Eddie gave the bride away, his flame hair more ordered than it had been in Norfolk. John Betjeman was Paul's best man. I was Verily's somewhat mature bridesmaid. There was a small party afterwards in Paul's pre-Fire-of-London house in Cloth Fair, next to the church. I believe it is the earliest surviving house in the City that is still occupied. John said this was the first country wedding he had been to in London. That exactly summed up the village-and-friends feeling of the occasion.

Charlie and Janie went to live in Staffordshire where together they rebuilt by hand an almost derelict cottage. After the birth of their first child, Daisy, I had a letter from Janie telling us they were growing all their own fruit and vegetables, keeping chickens and ducks, and had acquired a goat. She was also baking all their bread. They were now pretty well self-supporting, and hoped to be more so, since she had just found a recipe for making lavatory paper out of nettles.

One more wedding note. That same summer Reggie and I went to see Celia Johnson and Peter Fleming's second daughter Lucy, who is my god-daughter, married to Joe Laycock. It was another pretty village wedding. The bride, in dotted white Swiss voile, and her young husband wandered among their guests out in the garden at Merrimoles, where the lawn goes to the edge of arable acres, that day yellow with ripe wheat, a particularly decorative back-drop for a party. The house was designed by my father for Celia and Peter soon after they were married, and stands in a field of that ancient name. This, so far, is the only wedding we have been to where the happy couple took off for their honeymoon in a helicopter. The wind from its blades tore at the ladies' hats and lifted their skirts, and made the wheat wave about like the sea.

Nowadays Reggie and I don't often go out at night because we have become idle about making the effort, and, selfishly, we prefer to entertain at home rather than be entertained out of it, particularly in the winter. I agree with Mr John Knightley in *Emma*. His views on the folly of going out on a winter's night, unless obliged to do so, parallel my own. At home I sit with a rug over my knees, even though the flat is centrally heated. But you can't always expect rugs in other people's houses. Some Britons seem to take a pride in being stoic about discomfort, as if there were something noble about it. There are those who, though they could quite well achieve comfort, don't provide it even for their guests – perhaps as a kind of protest against self-indulgence. Such puritanical practices are not for me. If I have to, of course I can stand ruggedness without wilting, but not just for the sake of proving something. Being my American mother's daughter leads me to think it is pretty silly not to be comfortable when possible. Another country week-end hazard is being taken *out* to dinner. Those of us who lead busy lives during the week in London or wherever it is we work, look forward to quietly restoring relaxation at week-ends, whereas, understandably perhaps, some country hosts count Saturdays and Sundays as times for social whirling. Speaking for our elderly selves we have become lazy about packing and dressing-up. It is our hosts we have come to be with – if possible on their own. Of course there are exceptions to these generalisations and, in spite of our burrowing instincts and idleness, we genuinely rejoice when certain friends ask us to dine or stay with them – even in the winter.

I hope Reggie and I are both sociable; I know that, unlike my ma, we are not very social. She was both social and sociable; every lighted candle beckoned to her; it did not have to be flaming in a candelabra – any light drew her.

In general I have always preferred occasional small gatherings of friends, with a little new blood introduced for variety and flavour. What I am not fond of – is anyone? – are large cocktail-parties, where there is nowhere to sit, noise of a parrot-like horror, and not enough air. Nothing is worth shouting at the top of your voice, and at such parties unless you shout it is impossible to communicate. I do realise that cocktail-parties serve a purpose; in one ghastly evening it is possible to pay back social obligations and tick off a great number of names on a long list. There are even laudable reasons for giving them – to celebrate engagements, birthdays, anniversaries and to honour visiting friends. But unless such private parties are given in gardens or a building the size of Blenheim the decibel-count, the sardine-packed standing about and the heat do not offer joy. Some public relation parties, on the other hand, provide enough fascination to compensate for the physical discomforts. In the last few years we have been to one or two high-powered literary gatherings where the novelty of spotting the author kept us absorbed for far longer than we had planned to stay.

'Don't look now, but I think that must be Antonia Fraser/Simon Raven/Lawrence Durrell/Kingsley Amis/Dick Francis/What's-his-name Waugh. . . . And, look, isn't that James Herriot?'

In my experience full-dress occasions are exciting because they are rare, and the unaccustomed impact of a grand spectacle remains vivid. In 1963 Reggie and I were invited to what was probably one of the last of the really splendid balls of an historic kind given at Windsor Castle, in April, to celebrate the wedding, a few days later in London, of Princess Alexandra and Angus Ogilvy. Gala is what it was – crowned heads, lesser royalty, jewels in profusion, orders, ball-gowns and hair styles all in the grand manner.

Women's fashions that summer were romantic and becoming – small tight waists and full bouffant skirts. Rose Baring, in her primrose yellow wild silk, and I in my latest and 'best' stage dress from Victor Stiebel, of lime-green paper taffeta, had difficulty in fitting our voluminous skirts into the car. Later that year when I was planning what luggage I would take by air to Australia for a theatre tour, I found the weight of four stiffened net underskirts so heavy that I asked Victor if he thought some of the petticoats could be dispensed with. Then and there he had them all cut out. We both liked the straighter, newer, more casual Edwardian line, and on the strength of this he had all the stiffening removed from the rest of my stage dresses. The ball at Windsor was the last time I ever wore such extravagant skirts on or off the stage.

We dined with a party of friends, nearby at the Hind's Head Hotel in Bray, and afterwards joined a long line of cars, whose rear lights, ahead of us, made a ruby ribbon strip all the way up the Long Walk through Windsor Great Park to the Castle at the top. The floodlit grey Round Tower, like a child's cut-out toy, stood against a sky still streaked pink from the West. Crowds of watchers lined the way into the Castle precincts, waving and calling out, 'Turn on the inside lights so we can see what you look like'.

I imagined that the Queen and Prince Philip would open the ball. I was determined to see them do so, and of course, as usual, wherever we go, we were among the first to arrive. Even so we had to get in line and make a slow progress, with the rest of the eager early-arrivers, up shallow stairs flanked by pink and white potted cherry and almond trees in full flower. There was a good deal to look at – the place, the pictures and the people. I was amused to think that, in that enlightened year of 1963 when we all considered that our lives had become simplified and streamlined (or so I believed, *vide* my diary), hardly a woman present had been able to manage her own hair arrangement, and the placing of her tiara, without professional help. The word 'arrangement' is accurate. There were Nefertiti-like 'beehives' with the hair back-combed over elongated, domed shapes, Victorian ringlets lacquered rigid, and many over-life-sized mops – one mistaken lady had allowed her hairdresser to tease her hair into an explosion of frizz, like Struwwelpeter (this was before we had grown used to Afro hair-dos). In her blonde loofah-hair lurked a very tiny sparkling diadem. I was one of the few women present who did not wear a tiara, and in an unworthy way I felt rather distinguished.

We reached an ante-room and waited for the doors to open into the Waterloo Chamber, where we were to dance. As they opened an unseen band began to play a Viennese waltz; other doors, across the vast space of the empty ball-room, were flung wide, and through them, waltzing, came Princess Alex and Angus, followed a few turns later by the Queen and Prince Philip. Both couples made a complete circle of the room before the rest of us took to the floor – just time enough for me to see that the Queen's white dress was made of fine lace in tiered flounces and the Princess's of heavy white ribbed silk. Their big skirts swung as they revolved. There was about the young bride-to-be a radiance that was beguiling. Like her mother, Princess Marina, she had an air of romance and glamour. She was the prettiest girl in the room. I had been in Australia four years earlier, at the time of her first public tour, when her intuitive and natural warmth towards people had made her an instant hit wherever she travelled. Instinctively she had broken away from the formal arrangements and done her own walkabout, talking to the crowds long before such informality had become a part of royal public-relations. The press, radio and television knew a 'natural' when they saw one, and were as enthusiastic about her as were the rest of the Australians.

Reggie and I danced a little and stared a lot. We had never been inside the castle, and we were taken behind the scenes to see some of the pictures hanging in the curved corridor leading to the private apartments. I noticed an order form, on a table near the bedrooms, on which visiting royalty had written what they wanted for break-fast, and the hour it was to be brought to them. Most had speci-fied nine o'clock and modestly asked for toast and coffee, but one healthy young European princess ordered cold meats – ham *and* beef – to come to her room at some unearthly hour the next morning. Back in the Waterloo Chamber the floor was too crowded for me to see all I wanted to see of the dresses, so we wandered through the drawing-rooms where other like-minded guests were also taking a good look, and what with the flowers, the splendour of the rooms and the people, we decided, as we drove back to London in the breaking light of an early spring dawn, that the evening had been a fair treat.

CHAPTER TWELVE

Three Originals

WHEN I first met Mr Clews he was on all-fours on the pavement, wearing a long overcoat, a large black Anthony Eden hat and a pair of lady's fur-lined boots. He was a tiny jockey-sized old man, and with another passer-by I helped to get him on his feet and sat him on a low stone wall in front of a house, round the corner from South Kensington Station. He wasn't looking for something lost, he wasn't drunk, he had 'come over queer' and fallen down. The other passer-by excused himself – he had to get back to his office. I offered to drive the old man home, wherever that was, but he said, 'No. I'm all right. It's just weakness.' He told me it was no wonder he'd fallen down because it was silly to expect anyone to live on the Old Age Pension (this was in the mid-1950s); it ran out by Thursday. He was half-Irish and had been raised in Birmingham, but his accent was faintly American. I asked about this. It was the first time he smiled: 'Lived there twenty years – Coloraydo – oh, and all over. I should never of left it.' He had been a master tailor, and to prove it he took out of his pocket a battered tailor's thimble with an open end. 'I don't see so well now.' He was, also, 'deef, and didn't hear too good either', but I sat there with him for twenty minutes or more to make sure he was well enough to manage on his own. I asked him his name and where he lived, but he would not tell me. Before I left him I wrote my name, Mrs Grenfell (not Joyce Grenfell) and my address on a piece of paper and gave him two pounds. 'If you need help let me know.' 'I don't want help,' he said.

I didn't expect I should ever hear of him again, but three days later a letter arrived, written on blue paper in a clear and pretty hand, signed George Clews. He thanked me for my friendship and said the money had gone on 'several good meals', and had bought him a new raincoat, a pair of grey flannel trousers, a shirt and some boots. It seemed a well-spent two pounds.

The letter was written from a Beds for Men hostel in Camden

Town, and I wrote back to him to say I was glad he felt better and that I was amazed at the way he had stretched my small present. 'I'm a good shopper,' he wrote back, 'because I know where to go – Maggie's stall in the street market.' He had bargained with her; Maggie and he had words for at least half an hour:

'Well, Maggie, you don't want to sell, so good-bye.'

'Come back here, you old skinflint.'

'Maggie, really. You treat me like a stranger. Honestly Maggie, it's a lot of money, but being that you are a few days older you are much better-looking than I am.'

'Don't give me that sort of talk – give me the money and clear out, you make the place look untidy, you old goat.'

He got the goods at his price.

We corresponded regularly, but meeting him was complicated by his deafness. It wasn't just a question of speaking up, I had to yell at him; unless I yelled, full-pitch, he couldn't hear me at all. He shied away from coming to our flat; he'd rather meet me out because, he said, he didn't want to take his cough indoors. So we evolved a plan. I drove my car to the bus terminus in Camden Town where the number 74 bus turned round, and he was on the look-out for me. I was forbidden to go anywhere near Rowton House where he lodged, in case 'they' saw him get into my posh car. It was a modest Ford that lived in the street, but he was impressed by the way it moved so 'easily', and I realised it was his deafness that made him suppose it ran as silently as a Rolls-Royce. We went for drives and ended up in the car-park at the Zoo. This was usually pretty empty in the morning, and I drove to a far corner, where I wound down the window and we yelled at each other, unheard by eavesdroppers.

He never questioned me, and for a long time he didn't know I was an entertainer, but he noticed my wedding-ring, asked about 'hubby' and always sent him greetings.

During our drives and picnics in the car-park, where he devoured easy-to-eat crustless sandwiches, soft cakes and hot soup that were all he could manage because of his other handicap – no teeth – I learned about his life as a hobo; he had jumped trains all over America and had been a slinger of hash as well as a master tailor. He was woolly about facts and dates, and versions of his stories varied, but he always stuck to his master tailor claim, and was never parted from the thimble that he kept in a little concertina purse. Sometimes I was allowed to hold it. No, he had never married: 'too quick for that'. His chin

Mr Clews presenting me with flowers at Colindale Hospital Fête

curled up when he laughed and the corners of his mouth went down. It was a young laugh to look at, but it sounded like old twigs crackling in a fire. He always wore his hat at an angle and had a jaunty walk.

He told me about his step-sister who was 'pretty like a little doll'. He 'more or less worshipped her as a kiddie'. He never knew his own mother, but his stepmother was all the world to him, and when he heard she was dying he left America and came home to England to see her. But she died before he got here, and his little step-sister, grown-up and married, didn't want him hanging about. He got drunk and was put in the cooler until he sobered up; and when he got back to the house she threw his suitcase through the door at him and told him to get out and stay out. And that was that.

On one of our pre-picnic drives we stopped at the top of Primrose Hill to look at the view. He had written to ask me if I liked poetry. He was making me a poetry book of all the poems he could remember, and that morning he searched through his many pockets under the layers of wool he always wore and produced a shiny little red notebook about four inches long by two-and-a-half wide. Before he let me see it he told me there was a poem he hadn't written down but he'd say it for me – *now*. He fixed me with an accusing look and spoke firmly:

> I've heard it said and I've proved it true
> That the ones you trust the most
> Are the ones who let you down.

Pause. Silence. Point taken.

On this particular day he was in a reciting mood and told me that the next poem he was going to say for me was too long to write down, but he knew I would like it. He blew his nose and hawked to clear his throat and then he gave me a full-blooded performance of 'The Face on the Bar-Room Floor' with all the stops out. He sat beside me on the very edge of his seat in the front of the car and used his poetry voice. I was spell-bound on several levels at once: it is a period piece and it holds. The sound of Mr Clews belting it out on fire with the drama it told, combined with the noise of wild winds hurtling leaves at the windscreen of the car, and the sight of his small feet in their lady's boots, ankles crossed, straight out of a Belcher drawing, made a rich and lasting memory. When he finished I patted his hand to show how much I'd liked it. It didn't seem the moment to yell my appreciation. 'Yes, it is lovely,' he said.

The poems he sent me in his letters were less dramatic. He had found them in papers and magazines; he told me the *Christian Science Monitor* was a good place to find the kind of poems he liked, and when he liked one well enough he learnt it by heart. This is the one he liked the best because it described things he knew and was fond of, and reminded him of America. He didn't know who had written it. Nor do I, and I apologise if I am infringing copyright. This is most of it, exactly as he sent it to me.

> I have a map
> of Old New England

roads drawn with
a blunt blue pencil
on my heart. The
roads where lilac
bushes can be found
by white doors in
Vermont, by a haying
cart, rain faded,
near a red
New Hampshire barn.
The lilac roads
twist sea-ward down
to Maine.
However deep the
night I could
follow lilac
backroads home.
I could find
New England
even in my sleep.

He was a great believer in cleanliness and told me he washed all over most every day, and did all his own laundering. There were facilities at The House and, besides, he knew his things were properly clean if he did them himself. He was a bit of a dandy even at seventy-nine and wished there was an iron to press his shirts.

I had an idea: a drip-dry shirt that needed no ironing. It was not easy to give him presents. He was too independent, proud and inclined to be tetchy. I bought a plain white shirt, took it out of its cellophane wrapper and deliberately put it in battered brown paper. My plan was to make it all as casual as possible, as if I hadn't actually bought it but had accidentally come upon it. I hoped I had arranged the affair with delicacy.

'What's this supposed to be?' he said when I handed him the parcel.

'Just something I found.'

Slowly and unenthusiastically he took the string off it, rolled it up and pocketed it; then he unfolded the paper and stared at the shirt. Eloquently I explained how easy it all was – 'You just wash it and hang it up.' I had left the instruction-tag hanging from a button. He grumbled about newfangled gadgets; but I was used to his disgruntling, and I left him that day believing I had had a modest success and fulfilled a long-felt want.

The next day came his letter. '*Please*,' it said, underlined, '*Please* take back that shirt. I don't understand it. I've read the instructions and it's *impossible*. I'm worried to death with it and I haven't slept since you gave it to me. *Please take it back.*' He won the round and the match, for though I tried again later he refused to accept the shirt.

It isn't always easy to be a good neighbour. I once made a bid to please an elderly friend, Mrs Thomson, who lived near us at World's End in Chelsea. She had a passion for listening to boxing on her little wireless set, but was so afraid the battery might fade out before the end of a bout that she hardly dared switch on at other times. When I arranged for her to have a supply of batteries she became a keen listener to the rest of the programmes. 'But boxin',' she told me, 'is best. Oh, I do *love* it. *I really do love it.*' I had a good idea, the perfect treat for Mrs Thomson: a visit to a live boxing match. I knew I wasn't brave enough to go myself; I have always thought boxing one of the sillier masculine exercises, notwithstanding the skill, grace and all the usual reasons given for its worth. But Reggie said he would take her, and I hurried to tell her the good news. Her voice rose to a high squeak. 'Oh, *no*,' she said 'I couldn't *look* at it. I wouldn't like to *be* there. I only like the sound it makes on the wireless.'

On another occasion an energetic American friend of my mother, Hoyte Wiborg, went at her own expense to help evacuate refugees from the Spanish Civil War across the border to France. She spoke no Spanish but was undaunted by that handicap and full of resolve to do good. An elderly man and woman arrived at the inn where Hoyte was organising shelter; they were tired out, angry and very voluble. She took no notice of their noise and soon had them safely tucked up in bed together. Next day they were less angry but still voluble; it was discovered they had never seen each before their arrival over the border.

Mr Clews had another queer 'come over' about eighteen months after we first met. He fell down in a tea-shop, on a depressing and snowy day in January. The police telephoned me. Did I know an old man called G. H. Clews; they had just taken him to St Mary's Hospital, Hammersmith. I asked how they had found me, and the policeman said: 'We asked him if he had any family and he said, No, and we asked him if he had any friends and he said, Yes – One. You. And he had a letter on him with your telephone number and address on it.'

I hurried to the hospital in a taxi. He looked smaller than ever lying under a grey blanket on a stretcher in Casualty. He grinned at me. He had a very purple black eye, but it wasn't a new one; a bicycle had knocked him down the week before. 'Big man on it', he told me, and he just lifted Mr Clews out of the road, dumped him on the pavement and rode off. Mr Clews was furious about it; but it had nothing to do with him being in hospital now. He had just come over queer. He was all right again and going back to the House where he wanted to make sure of his own cubicle. He had a corner bed, and that was the best place in the building; he wasn't going to risk losing it and his 'things', thank you very much. The almoner at St Mary's said he wasn't ill enough to be admitted, but she could get him into the Infirmary. He wouldn't hear of it. The hospital offered to send him back by ambulance. 'No fear,' he said, getting down off the stretcher 'and have them all enjoy a good stare? No, I'll pop on a bus.'

'No, you won't,' I said. 'You'll pop into a taxi with me.' I leaned over and said into his better ear: 'Shut up and do as you are told.' This delighted him and he cackled his twig laugh. When we got near he made me stop the taxi round the corner from the House in case any of his mates were watching. Neither the driver nor I was allowed to help him get out.

We wrote to each other once a week for the next few years and had our occasional drives and picnics whenever I was in London. One day a mobile x-ray unit visited the House, and to his delight (and my surprise at his reaction) he was found to have a spot on his lung and was admitted to Colindale Hospital where he became king of his ward and ruled everyone with his own particular magic. His only complaint was about draughts. He wrote to tell me I had better do something about it; but he would not wear a smoking-cap, 'thank you very much' – a phrase he used a great deal. I searched the shops for something suitable, and in the end found a pale blue knitted ski-ing cap ringed in yellow with a pom-pom on top. He was not enthusiastic. 'Take off that thing,' he said, ungraciously hitting the pom-pom, 'and I'll try it on.'

When we met he was always fierce with me, but he wrote to say 'You may be assured I was pleased to see you – so pleased that after you left I sang two songs and the pations liked my singing very much. After you left the Lady Doctor gave me a through examination.'

When the weather got warmer he discharged himself from hospital and went back to the House. Summer time was not much good for the zoo car-park; too many coaches, but I found an even better place for our picnics – one of the private drives in the Nash terraces facing Regent's Park. At that time the great houses were standing empty while the Crown Lands Commission made up its mind what to do with them. As commanded I made his sandwiches out of two-day-old bread. He couldn't be 'doing with' new bread. It 'gummed him up'. One beautiful sunny day, he told me he had heard of a good place for old men where they could do their own cooking and come and go at will. But he said he would probably stay on at the House; he liked it there, was used to it, and he would rather have it than the unknown. He was anxious for me to meet the 'Super' in charge of the House and his wife. 'Nice people', he told me. They had been good to him. That was the last time I saw him.

We had made a date, and I was about to leave my flat to keep it when the Super rang to say Mr Clews had died in his sleep. They found him with his hands folded (as Ruth Draper's were when she died) and a smile on his face. I went up to see the Super that morning and he asked me how I had met Mr Clews. When I told him, he asked me whether I would like to hear Mr Clews's version. This is it:

Mr Clews had a very beautiful voice and was singing in South Africa. It seemed I was there too on a concert tour. He got malaria and lost his beautiful singing voice, but so strong are the bonds between fellow-artists that we had remained close friends ever since.

I had two other elderly 'special' friends, Joe Dockery and Miss H. M. C. Johnson. Joe was for many years the stage-door keeper of the St Martin's Theatre in Tower Court in London. He didn't retire until he was over ninety, and then only because he was mugged on his way home. It took him a while to get over it, and by the time he was fit again he reluctantly agreed that the moment had come for him to hand over to a younger man. 'But I could *easily* have gone on,' he told me. He was a small terrier of an Irishman, very straight-backed and nimble. He was no respecter of rank; according to him he kept the various managements running the St Martin's in their place: under his thumb. Every encounter was a small foray and he preferred to be the top man. He had a way of raising his eyebrows to show he was the winner in any conversation or discussion; indeed all his tales ended in score-off tag-lines to prove it.

Like Mr Clews he was inadequately equipped with teeth by the time I knew him, and he raged when the last of them went and he could no longer grip his pipe. He used to sit in his little cubby-hole at the stage-door in a thick haze of smoke – coughing away – and could be quite intimidating if you weren't used to him. Visitors seeing him within, waited for some sort of acknowledgement of their presence, but he didn't stir until they had knocked, and then, still sitting firmly, he looked up, opened the top half of his door and said accusingly: 'Yes?' I think he felt it was up to him to hold the pass. He was certainly a good watch-dog in my interest. I had to remember to tell him if I was expecting any visitors, and then he was very gracious and welcoming. If an unexpected caller asked to see me he pattered up the stone stairs to my dressing-room and said with scorn: 'There's a person below wants to see you. *Says* his name is Smith. . .'

Reggie and I went regularly to visit him after he left the St Martin's and to show us how fit he was he used to go into a 'buck and wing' around the table in the living-room, where his devoted son, Tony, kept him well supplied with coal that burned fiercely to keep the old man warm. When he was about ninety-four these little dance interludes left him panting, but he told us the doc said he had the heart of a man of forty and – puff puff – he wasn't in the least – puff puff puff – out of wind. Until his very last years he came down from his top flat to let us in and *ran* up on the return trip just to show us he could do it. I loved his guts and his memories.

He was a born 'character'. We sat in his hot little room asking him questions to get him going. Tales of his childhood – 'I was a bright lad' – and of his flurries with the Church all made intriguing hearing; so did his endless scores against authority and anyone who tried to put him down. He told us how he got on the stage. Passing the old music-hall where the Palladium now stands, he saw a man posting a notice advertising for four small boys to play in the forthcoming pantomime. He got one of the jobs and was cast as a Saucepan. The saucepan, made of papier-mâché, went over his head and came down to his hips, with a gauze cut-out for him to see through. Piecing together the stories – 'You wouldn't believe some of the things that happened to me' – we learned he had been to Russia and worked as a clown in a circus, and had assisted Houdini – 'Remarkable man, Houdini!' – in an engagement in London. He produced old programmes, letters and cuttings from *The Stage* and *Variety*; and sang us splendid songs of the music-hall, followed by twinkling dance-steps to illustrate what followed. He remembered and quoted pages of dialogue from melodramas, in which he had either understudied or stage-managed. He took all the parts, male and female, and made the pieces vivid and deliberately ridiculous. 'Plays were like that then.' He always swore

Joe Dockery by John Ward

the first-night telegram he sent to Agatha Christie for *The Mousetrap*'s opening at the Ambassadors Theatre next door to the St Martin's, read: 'Have a happy week!' signed the Mayor of Tower Court.

He became gentler with time; in the end he was too deaf to hear the television, but he could get something from his little radio and liked to be told if any of his stage friends, particularly Siobhan Mc-Kenna, were to be on the air. He hoped to reach his century and nearly made it, but one winter when we were abroad he slipped away, remarkably cheerful to the last. I wish he had carried out his threat to write a book.

Miss H. M. C. Johnson was a friend of my father's. When the bombing drove him from his house in Royal Avenue he moved to a flat in Chelsea Cloisters (a Sing-Sing-like block in Sloane Avenue), where she was another tenant. She became our friend, too. As an architect my father marked on plans the position of the housemaid's cupboard as

223

'H.M.C.', and my father used to address her as Miss Housemaid's Cupboard. She bristled slightly but enjoyed it; and I never think of Miss Johnson without remembering this. She was an elderly spinster of rigid habits, prejudice and northern humour. She came from Manchester, the only sister of several brothers, to whom she was devoted.

Miss Johnson lived her life for her brothers, subscribed to papers and magazines they might enjoy, and sent her copies on to them in distant lands. It was she, together with another stalwart Miss of whom I wrote in *Joyce Grenfell Requests the Pleasure*, who gave me the idea for my song 'Three Brothers'. This is the second verse:

> All of my brothers,
> Harry and Jim and Bob,
> Grew to be good and clever,
> Each of them at his job.
> And I was allowed to wait on them,
> To be their slave complete,
> I was allowed to slave for them
> And life for me was sweet,
> For I was allowed to fetch and carry for my Three Brothers,
> Jim and Bob and Harry.

She and my pa enjoyed what he called a good 'crack' over their luncheon, at adjoining tables for one, in the Cloisters' then frugal restaurant. Miss Johnson had strong views about Roman Catholics and in the old Victorian way referred to Protestants, who had 'turned', as 'perverts'. This sung out at full voice in the dining-room caused heads to lift up. She also felt strongly about the National Health. She did not like it. She told me she always wore pinned to her corset, in case she was run over by a bus, a label that gave her name, address, age and blood group, the name of her private doctor, his address and, written large, in block capitals at the bottom: 'I DO *NOT* WISH TO GO ON THE NATIONAL HEALTH.'

Miss Johnson's other running complaint was that *Punch* was not what it used to be, or *ought* to be. She wrote to the editor about this, and regretfully felt compelled to cancel her subscription. She didn't much like the *Spectator* or the *New Statesman* either, but thought it was safe to continue with the *Listener* – although she wondered whether her brothers would get from it what they had enjoyed in the old *Punch*. Such things exercised her greatly.

She was minutely honest about everything. Returning from visiting

Miss H. M. C. Johnson for Christmas

an office in the City she took a ticket on the Inner Circle Underground for the train to South Kensington, but found she was caught up in the rush-hour. She decided to come home the long way round – on a much less crowded Circle train. For the next few journeys, to repay the extra charge she felt she owed the London Passenger Transport Board for the longer trip, she bought a fourpenny ticket for a threepenny ride.

When she came to us for Christmas luncheons she always wore the same stylish navy-blue velvet hat, and pearl and diamond drop ear-rings; the fur stole that had been her mother's exuded a faint scent of camphor. I knew she was very appreciative of the decorations, the food and the occasion, but little was said at the time. Later on she refused all further invitations. 'I'm too old to go out,' she said, although she remained mobile and still visited the Victoria and Albert Museum.

She ended her days in a holy home run by Anglican nuns. After she died we had a letter addressed to 'My dears, Both,' telling us that when we received it we would know she was dead. She also wanted us to know that my father's friendship, all those years ago, and our continuing affection had made a great difference to her life.

CHAPTER THIRTEEN

My Kind of Magic

WHEN I first took part in the 'Woman's Hour' programme on B.B.C. radio, the editor was Joanna Scott-Moncrieff, and very good she was too. In my view it was her particular genius that made the five-days-a-week magazine the excellent one it still is. Her vision of listeners' potential interests was reflected in the wide range of subjects she introduced, and the quality of the books she chose to have read each day. She raised sights, never played down to her listeners, stimulated new interests and, in effect, was an encourager. She expected intelligent responses and was rewarded by getting them. What had been originally designed to appeal to a minority females-only audience, listening in the early afternoon, began to attract other listeners, some of them in motor-cars. In those days there were, I think, more occasional pieces – reflective spoken essays, well written and read by thoughtful, literate broadcasters – and it was not unusual to find, as an integral part of the contributor's thinking, a personal ethic; a sense of spiritual values. Joanna's gift (through her choice of speakers and the pieces they produced) was to convey an unspoken philosophic content acceptable to both churchgoing and non-churchgoing listeners.

Joanna eventually moved from 'Woman's Hour' to the department of Religious Broadcasting. She successfully brought new points of view and new voices to its early-morning programmes on both B.B.C. 1 and B.B.C. 2. I was an occasional contributor, and was glad of the opportunity to try and sort out (and share) findings of the practical and sustaining truths that are central to my own thinking. Putting these into plain terms within the five-minute 'slot' was good exercise. Joanna was always fierce with me, both in the 'Woman's Hour' pieces and the 'holy' talks – steering me away from too many ideas. She taught me the valuable lesson of sticking to one main point; and helped me to make it clearer.

She had great skill as an editor and got the most out of a script. Every time I submitted a talk to her I knew it would be improved before I came to record it. One of her general rules was – 'cut the opening paragraph'. I tried to anticipate this, by doing my own cutting before she saw the piece, but in the end I found it wiser to leave the job to Joanna, who continued to lop off my first sentences to good effect; it strengthened the whole. While she was in the Religious Department she compiled and edited anthologies selected from the early-morning talks. They include some of my pieces, one of which was 'Wishes for a Godchild'.

It was for 'Woman's Hour' that I wrote my contribution to a series called 'My Kind of Magic'. I knew just how I wanted to deal with the subject, and, thanks to Joanna's guiding hand, my script unexpectedly turned out to be one of those little essays that not only worked on radio, but later became a magazine article that was published in most English-speaking countries, including America. I mentioned my radio talk in a letter to two writer friends in New York, Marchette and Joy Chute, and they asked me to send them a copy. Joy wrote back saying they believed that, if I could clear it with B.B.C. for publication, they could place it with a national magazine, and in June 1965 it appeared in *Woman's Day*, and was sold in a chain of supermarkets all over America. Here is an edited version of it.

MY KIND OF MAGIC

By 'magic' I don't mean abracadabra and fairy godmothers with wishes, nor do I mean witches and spells and funny goings on at seances.

I mean the heightened quality of certain, often quite small, experiences lit by unexplained excitement, powerful with innocence. It can come from looking hard at a shell, arriving at an unexpected view of the sea, hearing a bar of music.

> 'To see a World in a Grain of Sand,
> And a Heaven in a Wild Flower,
> Hold Infinity in the palm of your hand,
> And Eternity in an hour.'

Some of my contemporaries don't agree with me that this kind of magic is far more potent in middle age than when one was new. It is so for me because now I bring more to each experience, and 'magic' is very nourishing.

Places induce it. East Anglia. The bush in Australia. I get it particularly in a certain small valley in Cumberland. The first time I went there, having chosen a place to stay from an unillustrated guide-book with just an inch of unexaggerated prose, we drove across a high bare pass and as we came near it I knew – this is it! I said it out loud, too. It was recognition, and I get it unfailingly every time I go back there. (I get it whenever I make a new discovery of *anything*.) I don't think I knew what people meant when they said a place was their spiritual home. But I do now.

Of course magic can happen anywhere. Even in Birmingham, the wrong end of the Edgware Road or bleak bits of Scotland – that's place magic.

There are other kinds. Seasons each have separate magics, small signals sometimes, usually ahead of time. Blackbirds in January, for instance. But I'm usually in the middle of summer when I feel it. I had it once at dusk in East Anglia, driving up a track between two huge fields of cereals (I never know for sure the difference between barley and wheat) both as pale as a child's hat and wreathed with scabiosa, poppies, camomile daisies and pink-ish mallow, as well as lemon-yellow snapdragon and little blue speedwell. Dusk is a good time, when all the colours become luminous. And autumn is good, when there is a very clear light and suddenly, without leaves, every-where looks spacious; it anticipates next spring; the birds think so too and sing again. And I like winter moonlight with sharp pencil shadows, of trees and wire fences, on a pale star-sapphire landscape. They give me the feeling.

It is possible, I think, to have a nostalgia for a past one could not have known. The mid- and latish-Victorian era is my time. I like to view it from the convenience and comfort of today. I like to savour selected bits of what can now be seen as a serene and orderly past. It wasn't, of course, but magic selects what it wants to see, and from our present chaos it can be made to seem a world of positive, rounded-off conclusions. Very restful. I also like its slow tempo. An escape? Yes. Why not? An escape to sure, eternal qualities.

Visually that age appeals to me. The clothes they wore, the furniture they lived with; I refuse to be psychological about the significance of flounces and frills covering chair-legs. I share the Pre-Raphaelites' passion for detail, and nature in detail; the dedicated reproductions of a bird's wing, a wild rose, ivy, and the weight and quality of thick Victorian dress silks. Oh, and the sheerness of muslin and mull and dimity and print.

I treasure those books made of thick creamy-coloured pages with little drawings at the start and end of chapters – exquisite little drawings of bryony and traveller's joy, of a robin's nest with eggs in it, and everything penned with very loving care. There's a good smell to those books too; musty and safe. They usually have heavy bindings and embossed titles in gold and, though often deadly dull to read, are lovely to handle and look at.

Then there's colour magic. That's nourishing if you like, so long as it is one's own palette. I can't abide relentless orange, the kind without mercy of a touch of white. I don't feel easy with Kelly green, purple, or fierce pillar-box red in any large amount.

People's houses reflect their awareness of colour-sense, and I have a painter friend who has a really magic touch with muted colours. I've never seen it bettered. Her rooms are for thinking in. She has, too, an artless way with flowers that makes most arranged arrangements look like an abuse of privilege. Some field-daisies and cow-parsley in a pale yellow jug against a putty pink wall, with an added white hydrangea head – or two clashing geraniums in a glass. Her taste rings my bell and has magic. [She is Mary Potter about whom I wrote in my first book of memories.]

I think flowers and music give me the most pleasure – flowers, white ones in particular. I like them so white that they appear to have built-in light and green shadows. Very white roses. White lilac, not the forced feeble kind that flops almost at once, but the tough open-air variety with clusters big as bunches of grapes, and the last buds at the top still tight bright green. And the smell! It's the most romantic of all scents. Roses are for any time, lilac is for fleeting fancies! White Christmas roses, well, they're cream really, little button ranunculuses with green middles, and best of all, wild white violets.

One of the best magic moments is finding the first white violet of the year. No year is complete until I find one. And a cowslip – the downy pink stem is very satisfactory, and the flower smells the way honey tastes.

The third important annual find is a wild strawberry. It is best when you find a tiny scarlet fruit hanging from the same plant as a white strawberry flower.

Listening to music has been the most constant, ever-increasing and developing pleasure I know. When I was young I listened because I saw pictures or liked the rhythms. Certain music stirred me, made me cry, yearn, sigh, gloat and wallow. I stood night after night at the Proms, from the age of fourteen, emoting and getting nourished. Later I began to hear what I was listening to. The wallowing decreased, but the nourishment increased.

I once heard a musician say he felt it was impossible to communicate completely with anyone who wasn't in some degree musical. He felt that non-musical people were in some way handicapped, as if they lacked a dimension. Music is a bond, a language even if you don't know all the grammar.

The thing about my kind of magic is that it is ever-present, and past experiences of it can be taken out and looked at again; 'recollected in tranquillity', like poetry, any time, anywhere.

Like all moments of revelation magic is un*self*conscious, as is happiness. Perhaps it is another word for happiness? When one is entirely happy one is un*self*conscious. A divine experience – bliss!

You don't have to translate these small experiences into, 'This is me finding a first violet or recognising a felicitous phrase of music.' Perfection is recognised. Another proof of eternity?

'My Kind of Magic' re-appeared in *Woman's Day* five years after its original printing, when the magazine celebrated thirty-five years of

Cumbrian Landscape by John Ward

publication. Readers were invited to choose five pieces from previous issues that they would like to read again, and mine, I was surprised to learn, was one of those included in the birthday edition.

In the early days of television I took part in a magazine programme from Alexandra Palace, and one of the other contributors was Edith Sitwell. She was anxious about going before the cameras – was her hair all right, had she got on enough lipstick? I tried to reassure her: there were experts to advise us about such things and anyway she looked splendid. Her gothic appearance, her long and beautiful hands covered with many giant aquamarine rings made a fascinating picture on the small black-and-white screen. It had recently been announced in the press that she had become a Christian. The interviewer asked her what had made her change her mind. She said she had looked at the pattern of a frost flower on a windowpane; she had studied shells, feathers, petals and grasses; and she knew, without a doubt, that there must be a cause – a 'divine principle' – behind designs of such infinite variety and beauty. 'I have come to believe,' she said 'that the cause is God.'

The 'certain small valley in Cumberland' mentioned in 'My Kind of Magic' has been important to Reggie and me for over twenty years. I won't give its name, because already that part of north-west England is overrun with caravans, cars, campers and coaches. In summer the hills are not only bright with heath and small flowers, but they also dazzle the eye with hot orange and aggressive royal blue canvas tents and lean-tos. Selfishly I am glad the secret valley road is so narrow that coaches are banned from using it. They can get everywhere else in the district, but, so far, it has not proved practical to widen this road. Once a day a local bus takes valley schoolchildren and shoppers to and from the nearest town, but monster coaches on 'Mystery Tours' are forbidden entry.

The first time I saw the valley I had an unexpected homecoming feeling about it. Viola Tunnard and I were booked to do two weeks of concerts in music clubs in Lancashire and West Cumberland. We planned the route together, and decided to look for an hotel that would be a base for the second week of the tour, when all the engagements were within twenty miles of each other. We were sure there must be a central point, in that beautiful hill country, from which we could work; but neither of us had been to Cumberland, and nobody could advise us. I got out a three-inch relief map that showed very few villages and plenty of brown shading; that meant hills. My hotel guide had pages of coloured pictures advertising hotels in the specified area. None of them looked inviting, but at the back of the book were unillustrated entries, and among them we found a short paragraph describing a three-hundred-year-old coaching inn – with a reputation for hospitality, comfort, and excellent home cooking – set in a peaceful stretch of valley, with mountain views. There was fishing available, and the nearest rail-head (long since disappeared) and market town were eight miles away. We looked at the map. Between two small hamlets, just above a winding river, was the word 'INN'. It was situated at exactly the right place for our needs – none of the concert halls was more than twenty miles away.

I telephoned from London to ask for two single rooms, confirmed the booking by letter, and on a cloudless, cold April day in 1958 Viola and I left the town where we had played the night before and drove up a steep pass that came down the other side of a wooded mountain, to grassy slopes and the open view of the shallow valley ahead of us. We stopped the car. Creamy bird-cherry foamed in the hedges, and a few early bluebells were coming up through new bracken on the hillside. I turned off the engine. We could hear cuckoos calling, lambs bleating and waters, in the little beck some way below us, running over rocks. Splendour!

It was then that I said 'This is *it*!' not entirely knowing what I meant, but feeling confident in my words, as I said them. Viola agreed it was a good place, and later she told me she had had the same intuitive tingle of a right arrival as we first looked down on the valley that was to mean so much to me, and later to Reggie. Viola didn't return there as regularly as we did, but she shared our feeling for the place, and whenever she and I did concerts together in that part of the country we always stayed there.

We drove on through small fields between stone walls. I was glad to be away from towns and out of the touristy part of the Lake District. Even inside the car the air smelt fresh and sweet. Around a corner, up a rise, we came upon the long, low, whitewashed two-storey hotel, sitting in a garden filled with azaleas, tulips, forget-me-nots, wall-flowers and polyanthus. It accommodated about twenty-four guests. The visitors' book was full of bishops; their names and the names of many of the other guests, recurred year after year.

The Milburns, who owned the hotel, greeted us. Keith, the extrovert, a great fisherman and born host, came out from behind the tiny bar, too small for more than three visitors at a time. Drinks were handed through a hatch and consumed around a fire in the cosy entrance hall. Ella, reserved and shyer, emerged from the kitchen where she supervised all the meals and cooked a good many special dishes herself. Keith was tall and good-looking; she was small and trim in a dark red twin-set and neat tweed skirt. Her hair was braided around her head. Both were then in their fifties. Robert Branthwaite, then the general helper and waiter, fetched the bags. Our small bedrooms faced the view of High Fell, across an open valley – it gives a feeling of shelter and space – and to our left widening meadows spread to further hills and woods. I opened my window and heard a curlew crying. For luncheon there was perfectly cooked cold roast duckling, followed by apple crumble with a generous sugary crust and thick cream. Ella and Mrs Robinson, who helped her, produced the kind of menus you don't often meet in small country hotels, all of them delicious.

We had a good week. Viola and I spent our mornings exploring the woods; we found the lakes and walked for miles. One day she went fishing and I did some sketching. Every evening Ella gave us an early high tea in the empty dining-room before we went off to work. All the small tables in there had been found by the Milburns at local auctions and no two were alike. As she got less shy of us Ella opened up, and when she had given us our meal she came and sat at our table. At first, I think, she was a little suspicious of us. We were an unknown quantity – Viola a musician and I a 'theatrical' – but she was curious to know about our lives and the jobs we did, and we made friends. We left the hotel each evening at about six o'clock to drive across country to the various halls along the coast.

Joe Coulthard

In spring and summer, in this part of England, the daylight lasts until eleven at night. Driving back to the hotel, all that week of clear cool weather, I stopped the car each night at the same red telephone-box and reversed the charge for a call to Reggie, in London, to report on the day's doings. The telephone box, one of Sir Edwin Lutyens's beautifully proportioned designs, was the only man-made object, in a single-street village of mean little terraced houses on the edge of the moors, that stood up to the scenery. I enthused about the concerts – given to friendly audiences – and said: 'We *must* come here together.' It was *all* enjoyable – the countryside, the hotel, the food, the Milburns and the valley.

Ever since that first visit to a place, chosen more or less with a pin twenty-one years ago, Reggie and I have been back at least once a year, usually in May. Once we went in June in a year of spectacular wild roses that festooned the hedges like curtains, and sometimes we have made two visits, the second in October – burnished bracken, blackberries and mushrooms. There is a pleasing little excitement about mushrooming, perhaps because mushrooms are hard to find. (I once heard a sad tale of childish disappointment. When she was a small girl, a Balkan princess was offered a treat by a Grand Duchess aunt, and chose to go mushrooming. Full of anticipation she was taken in a carriage to a meadow and, with her little basket in her hand, she ran off excitedly to begin the search. But it had already been made on her behalf; beside every mushroom in the long grass a liveried footman had placed a marking flag.)

When Viola and I first went to the valley Joe Coulthard, the elderly gardener at the hotel, asked me where I lived. 'In London.' 'Must be very monotonous,' he said. Carlisle was the only town of any size he had ever seen. He once complimented me by saying: 'You'd think you were a Cumbrian.'

Every spring we visited Joe and his wife at Beck Cottage, less than half a mile from the hotel if you climb fences and cross fields. The back vegetable garden ran uphill and was well kept. He grew flowers in the front, and it was there he sat for me while I tried to do a sketch of him with his scarf neatly folded across his chest. We were there the year he died, and I wrote some verses after I had been to see him for the last time, up in his small bedroom.

IN CUMBERLAND
The cuckoo shouts the old man on his way.
Bluebells and kingcups celebrate this tardy spring
Like any other in these hills.
The old man, in his tiny upstairs room,
Has never seen a city
Or slept more than forty miles
From where the cottage stands
Beside the beck.
The green familiar hill
Fills every inch of window opposite his bed.
(The cuckoo shouts the old man on his way.)
His children honour him with love;
So do his neighbours.
His wife is silent and her heart is full
At this first parting.
He never uses words like 'joy'
But he is powerful with innocence, and joy.
His world is small
But it contains all that a whole man needs.
He brings to it expectancy of good
And finds good everywhere.
(The cuckoo shouts the old man on his way.)

I was afraid I might have over-sold the delights of the valley to Sylvia and Bob Ritchie when they came over from Australia and we brought them up with us one May, and I was relieved to find they were as enchanted as we are with this corner of the country. Chris Todd, a local farmer, put on a display of his sheepdogs. This was the highlight of the visit. Craftsmanship is always impressive, and when it includes qualities of trust and confidence as well as skill, as it must in the handling of sheepdogs, it is exciting to watch. We stood in a drizzle against

Bob Ritchie, Chris Todd, Sylvia Ritchie and Reggie

the fence of a small rising meadow while Chris put two of his pretty black-and-white collies through their paces for us. They could hardly wait to begin showing their prowess, and lay quivering with excitement waiting for his command. He showed them to us working singly and as a pair, rounding up a group of sheep and then, after isolating three of them, heading the rest into an enclosure – all with the minimum of whistled commands. The collies raced off with evident delight at the word 'Go!' and squirmed with satisfaction when the job was done and Chris called them to heel.

I once tried to do a quick water-colour of the valley while the nearby sky was duck-egg blue, the distant sky indigo, and in between there were white clouds, grey clouds and clouds almost purple with impending rain. The grasses in the meadows were vivid lime-green. The light changes quickly there, and by the time I had splashed on the bright colours the whole scene had turned to dull greys. But the brilliance had lasted for at least five minutes, and I was glad to have got some of it on to the paper. It wasn't a work of art, but it made a shorthand note to remind me of what I had seen. I never managed a complete painting of that view, it didn't stay long enough in one mood. But John Ward did.

When we introduced him and his wife Alison to the valley, he made a water-colour for us of Reggie's favourite view of a hill, with a single wind-bent thorn tree growing out of its prow end. We have added this picture, and a bigger, panoramic sketch he also made of a whole range of mountains above one of the lakes, to our gallery of his paintings.

I once talked to John about the reason why painters paint and poets write. Why do we (in my amateur for-pleasure way I include myself) feel we must reproduce and comment on things that already exist in their own form – an object, light on a view, an emotion or an idea. John said he didn't believe he painted to express himself; no artist did. Sometimes it was done in acknowledgement of delight; more often it was simply a job, and that in itself was fulfilling. There was enormous satisfaction in using hand, eyes and mind to put on paper something of acknowledgement. In the same way I think I write a poem or do a drawing to crystallise what I have seen or experienced; to record it. John is scornful of highfalutin' talk about art. He regards himself as a craftsman, that he is also an artist goes without saying. I have watched his work progress, simplify and soar from the days when he did attractive fashion drawings for *Vogue* till he reached his present stature. In all he does (including his illustrations to two small books of my monologues and song-lyrics) there is a measure of true enjoyment; and living with many of his pictures, as we do, we know this feeling persists.

Cumberland brings out in me a response to nature that causes Virginia to tease me – in an old-friend way. She had a botanically-minded mama who went wild-flowering, armed with her Bentham and Hooker, to remote places, but Virginia's tastes are more for man-made than for natural wonders. She responds to the general look of spring – chestnut 'candles' and bluebells – but her spirits rise more at the sight of an Adam fireplace. I appreciate architecture, objects and gardens bright with herbaceous borders, roses and drifts of daffodils, but my heart leaps up higher when I find a wood carpeted in wind-flowers, or a first spring daisy.

Twice on our valley visits Reggie and I have gone out at sunset in early June to see badgers, and seen them where they were supposed to be. On both occasions we settled ourselves under a bank, crouching as low as we could to be hidden from the badgers' view. The first time it was a very cold evening, and we were glad that they came out as soon as we arrived; two adults and three well-striped cubs. They took

A year of wild roses

no notice of us, and the young rolled in the sand by their sett, until it was too dark to see them any more. The second time the air was warmer, the wait longer, and we were attacked by swarms of midges that went up our noses and into our ears and mouths – until the temperature dropped and they suddenly vanished.

You may well think it foolish that, compelled only by reasons of delight and wonder, we should subject ourselves to the hard, hard ground, rising cold damp and this torture from midges in order to see a nocturnal creature come out of its hole, meander briefly on a nearby grassy mound and then race off as if on little invisible wheels into the encroaching dusk. But we found the moment good; it entirely made up for the discomfort, and we went back to the car well satisfied. We were further rewarded by a full moon. It was heralded by a pale glow, in the cloudless sky behind a nearby mountain, before the big white ball of light rose up as if drawn on a string. It rises that way, at speed, in South Africa and sometimes there the moon is red.

When we are in Cumberland Reggie and I spend much of our time looking at birds. I am not an expert birder; Reggie knows about them, whereas I am simply a spotter, good at spotting, but not always knowing what bird I have spotted. We much enjoy being up in that hilly country looking for, and, finding, peregrine, ring ouzels and my favourite British bird, the dipper, a beguiling little rotund butler with a white bib, brown apron and neat black tail coat. He pauses on rocks in rushing rivers bowing (dipping) as he looks around to make sure the way is clear for him to fly into his low nest under the bank or a bridge just above the water. We have never missed seeing dippers in our part of Cumberland, but every year the rivers seem to get lower as the cities take more and more water from the lakes, and each spring we fear the birds are fewer.

We are fond of many people in the valley and, now that Ella has gone, Geoffrey White the retired vicar, who still lives there, and Joan Robinson are our oldest local friends. When the post-office-cum-store closed down, Joan opened a little shop that provides a welcome service not only for those living nearby but also for visitors. She sells basic groceries, home-made jams, honey, postcards, films, candies, survey maps of the district and a selection of particularly pretty linen kitchen towels. I stock up with Christmas presents from Joan's shop. She combines this enterprise with being a J.P. Geoffrey's early retirement for reasons of health, the result of almost five years spent in a German prisoner-of-war camp, was a sadness for the two parishes he cared for; one in the valley, the other three or four miles away. Reggie and I used to go with Ella to the well-attended village church, and enjoyed Geoff's beautiful speaking voice reading from the Bible and leading the prayers. He sang a useful baritone in the hymns and turned the services into celebrations. He gave a great deal to a widespread community, including work with the young, and enthusiastic support to the amateur dramatic society. Geoffrey is a keen fisherman, and, on Reggie's first visit, he and Tim Armstrong, who works for the National Trust, took us in a boat on one of the lakes, in the light of a May evening, hoping to catch trout. There was no cloud, no wind; the nearest mountain was exactly reflected in the glassy lake. We floated in a silence broken only by an occasional dip of the oars. Geoff said to me: 'Sing us something.' I don't know what I sang, but it certainly wasn't 'Speed, Bonnie Boat'; none of us wished to be speeded anywhere on such an evening. When I finished, a bird up in the wood behind us broke into song. I didn't recognise the tune. '*Do* you have nightingales up here?' I asked Tim. He rested on his oars and with no change of expression on his agreeable face said: 'Not with feathers on.'

Another valley-dweller, Nora Tallentire, made available a barn in

238

Funny-looking in an oilskin fishing hat

Pied Flycatcher by M. E. Eldridge

the yard of her small stone farmhouse built against a hill, for Geoff to turn into a tiny house exactly suited to his needs on his retirement. There from his bed he looks down at a lake with a Druid's oak wood on its far shore, where we find pied flycatchers, and above it steep rising moorland.

Every year we make sure that the pied flycatcher is back in the oak trees where he should be. He is a dapper, small, black and white visitor with a clear sweet call, a little like a robin's, only more sophisticated. Until two years ago there had always been a pair nesting in the same oak trees in another wood, but now most holes are occupied by clever, pushy, noisy starlings. There are pied flycatchers in other places, but we miss them in this steep wood; we are sad not to find them in their accustomed place, where for twenty years in all weathers we had always found them on the first day of our holiday.

We are gluttons for punishment in a cause dear to our hearts. Here are some lines I wrote after a particularly disagreeable cold, wet spring visit:

BLISS

Funny-looking in an oilskin fishing hat
I know a simple bliss on this wet day.
I am watching a pied flycatcher feed

239

In Pleasant Places

Its invisible young above my head
In a small, dark hole high in an oak tree.
I am in a steep grove of mountain oaks
Where the sloping ground is carpeted close
In deeply springing cross-stitch patterned moss.
I am alight with the discovery
Of a small pied bird going in and out
Of a small, dark hole high in an oak tree.
Rain filters through the jigsaw-puzzle leaves
As limp as silk. The air is fresh and sharp
With scents of mould and mosses. I can see
New ferns unfurling. Bliss is a strong word
Wiping out all else. I know a simple bliss
Watching all this, and a bird in a tree.

Perhaps if we lived in the country I might be less acutely aware of birds and flowers; maybe short sharp visits to wild places concentrate my enthusiasm and my interest in looking and finding, listening and learning.

CHAPTER FOURTEEN

Friends, Letters and Diaries

IN STORIES fairy godmothers wave their wands and decree blessings of health and happiness for their elect. But when I consider the variety and quality of those near and dear to me I am conscious that friendship is the most precious privilege that this earthly experience can offer. I put friendship at the top of the list of blessings in my life. *Chambers Dictionary* defines it as 'attachment from mutual esteem: friendly assistance'. I would add 'affectionate respect'; but none of these definitions really describes the effortless glow that deep friendship generates. Nor the delight.

When I look closely at the faces of those I have loved for a long time I realise that I no longer observe their general appearance. It isn't that I take my friends and their looks for granted, but rather that what I know of them goes beyond the outward and visible. When she was young Virginia, with her height and a slightly withdrawn manner, gave an impression of hauteur that I knew had little to do with her real self – amused, amusing and warm. A recent objective scrutiny of her appearance confirmed that her always attractive rounded face, with a finely wrought nose that tilts at the tip, blue eyes that go up at the corners and eyebrows that put in the expression, as she thinks and speaks, is still evident. The mouth is well-drawn, slightly, charmingly crooked and has the lower lip that I was once told signified a performer – which Virginia isn't. She is the least dramatic person I know. Now that I have looked more clearly at my oldest and dearest friend I see that her appearance, far from suggesting aloofness, presents a restoring kind of comfort, a sense of confidence without hauteur; and with her head held as high as it always was, and her great height, she has become a most handsome woman. Feature by feature she is not conventionally beautiful, but the whole, the invisible and the visible, has something more than physical beauty in it.

I have been blessed with friends 'for all seasons'; friends who laugh in the same place; appreciate the same authors, poets, composers and painters; like the same foods, the same ways to spend an evening, a day, a weekend or longer, and have the same interest in spiritual matters. They are not always the same friends. Virginia would not enjoy bird-watching in a marsh or flower-finding in a field. Very few of my close friends would. Nor do I share her fancy for hacking at impenetrable tangles of brambles in other people's woods. But we do agree on more important things like faith, the temperature of rooms, *most* T.V. programmes, books, music straight and music rhythmic, and meals – except that Virginia doesn't like garlic. I prefer it to have passed by rather than loitered too long.

Playing the friendship-testing game with myself I put the question: could you share the same living quarters? When it is with Virginia the answer is yes, because I think our concern for each other would over- come minor differences in our views. One thing is certain, we would not have to share the kitchen, for she hates cooking. I would willingly be the cook, if she would take on the housework and that most boring of all domestic chores, the cleaning of the bath. I would hope to have a bed-sitter of my own into which I could retire to use my own radio and television.

Staying with Virginia in her country flat, which we do a great deal, with continuing appreciation and enjoyment, is not like visiting. When we first went there she allowed us to choose the wall-papers for our rooms. The flat is long, light and airy, on the second floor of the Victorian addition to a pink brick Queen Anne house, about thirty miles from London, belonging to a childhood friend of hers and mine. Opening off a broad corridor are four small bedrooms, originally for the staff, the dining-room and two bathrooms. I am usually a quick- wash-rinse-and-out type in the bath, except when we are there. This is because of the wall-paper in the bathroom. On a white background, sparingly distributed, hang red cherries among green leaves, and the effect is delicate and light. Here I like to lie in the full-length tub; gazing at the cherry-bower adds contentment to a long and lingering soak. I bath before supper, and in summer the westering sun pours in and floods me, the cherries and also a tapestry rug, worked by Virginia in a fantasy design of more cherries twined about a ribbon stripe. It is a warm, comfortable and somehow encouraging bathroom. The big living-room at the end of the corridor, at one time the housekeeper's room, is painted pale turquoise blue and hung with white curtains. Now it is the comfortable and pretty centre of our spring and summer week- end lives, where we read, write, listen to music and watch television;

Virginia Thesiger

or delightfully nod off in deep armchairs. Virginia writes on her knee in the living-room, and I write next door on the dining-room table. She is still a practising journalist. For many years she was the very readable film critic on the *Spectator*, and her articles, like C. A. Lejeune's, were read for their wit as well as for their views on the movies.

At Virginia's Attic (an affectionate misnomer), which we look upon as a second home, she provides rugs for those who want them. When we are there the arrangement is that she does the dusting and sweeps up the crumbs, Reggie gives a hand in whatever direction it is needed – tray-carrying, letting off the dishwasher, fetching the papers – and I prepare and cook the meals. All of us help with clearing up. We follow a simple programme. Meals are light; a 'proper' luncheon with vegetables and some kind of 'after'; and a supper of soup, cheese and fruit.

This is the pattern that Reggie and I follow at home. As cook I brew up batches of soup in London and bring them in large glass jars to the Attic for our supper. I have become quite deft at making and sometimes inventing soups. (Non-cooks can skip the rest of this paragraph.) My colour sense won't let me make two pale soups at one time, so when I blend a pale parsnip concoction, I provide a companion-batch made of dark spinach, compounded, as most soups are, of potato, onion with a touch – not a thump – of garlic and either chicken or beef stock. When I make a moon-coloured soup of leeks or artichokes I cook for contrast a jar or two of fresh watercress. This is the greenest of all the green soups. Here endeth the cookery note.

We spend our days at the Attic in individual pursuits. Reggie reads, walks and watches birds. So do I; I also very occasionally do a little sketching. Virginia's pleasure is to work in the woods, in all weathers, dead-heading rhododendrons and azaleas, weeding beds of primula and lilies, and in particular getting at and cutting down brambles. Every autumn we all go blackberrying, and in my zeal to garner the best, invariably growing among the fiercest nettles and in the most inaccessible places, I am always well scratched and stung. But the satisfactory weight of a full pail of shiny blackberries compensates for passing scars. *Il faut souffrir pour être* a successful brambler.

Every year, when I get back to London, I forget that it is not a good idea to use the pounding gadget on my electric blending machine to press the blackberries through a sieve. I did it again this year. Fired by the sight of so many superb and glossy fruits, I first lightly stewed them with dark brown sugar and very little water, and then poured a supply into the sieve and switched on. At the time Reggie was at the sink, kindly helping me by washing up some purpled pans. As you will know a blackberry is composed of a cluster of tiny, round, shiny globes, each one of them full to bursting with red juice. The minute the pounder touched the fruit all hell broke loose. The juices took off in every direction. Reggie, the walls, window, ceiling, cupboard doors and my nose, stone-coloured blouse and the knees of my pale beige trousers were all simultaneously splattered. It was so sudden and so unexpected (it always is) that all we could do was stand there and laugh. A supply of free fruit hardly balanced what looked like being the cost of repainting the kitchen, replacing two new shirts, Reggie's and mine, and my pants; and the possible resignation of our long-suffering housekeeper Mrs Agos, who has been our much appreciated helper even since Mrs Gabe retired. 'Are you going to *cook*?' she asks me apprehensively, and

Mrs Agos by
John Ward

withdraws to make a bed or scour a bath. Reminder: blackberries and an electric pounder DO NOT GO TOGETHER.

But all was well. I rushed our clothes into soapy water and miraculously there wasn't a trace of that most tenacious of fruit stains anywhere; and Mrs Agos did not see the kitchen until I had washed down all the affected surfaces; and the resulting blend of blackberry juices and puréed windfallen apples was delicious.

But to get back to the subject of friendship. There are friends who are less easy and have to be 'studied', as my nanny used to say to describe that particular awareness needed to get on with those who appear to have too few skins, and who take offence and get hurt by imagined slights. It is easy to dismiss difficult characters as not worth bothering about, but a great deal of quality would be missed if they were cut out of one's life just because they are unsure and over-sensitive. I know that with certain friends I have to think carefully before I speak, and even then I make mistakes. Trying to put oneself in other people's shoes is a useful if difficult exercise; the trouble is that it takes up so much time testing the temperature. And making quite sure that the lines are open isn't easy. Even 'old shoe' relationships between people who share a lifetime of experiences and the same wavelength have to be nourished and, for the joy of it, worked at.

I believe it was Stendhal who said in effect that it is only when two people are revolving independently – each on his own axis – that they are capable of revolving into one blended harmonious unity – one complete movement. If *one* is wobbling while the other spins steadily there can be no such unity. Uneven friendships are not likely to bring much satisfaction to either party, for if one is all take and the other all give practically nothing is achieved.

Friends one is lumbered with from outgrown past associations, and sense-of-duty friends that make unwelcome demands for attention, and the friend one loves but does not much like, are the difficult ones to include. Loving and liking are not at all the same thing, just as pity is not the same as compassion. Not long ago I was asked, in a radio interview, how I accounted for the fact that my 'show-business marriage' had lasted. 'It isn't, in fact, a show-business marriage,' I said; but the reason it has lasted is because we *like* each other. The liking is the vital part. Loving is something else and important; but liking includes amusement, respect, the enjoyment of sharing and the nourishment of understanding silences.

I wonder what is my contribution to those I look upon as close friends. They certainly have my interest and affection, and I treasure experiences shared. Their contributions to me include elements of surprise, humour, spontaneity, zest and enthusiasm, intuition, spiritual awareness and affection. And what certainly seems to be their genuine interest in what I think and do. I expect some criticism, as in turn I criticise; not, I hope, on a destructive level and not too often out loud. Criticism is perhaps too fierce a word; it is awareness of each other's little ways and practices that sometimes causes irritation. I don't find it easy to love the small faults I see in my friends, nor do I think it is natural to do so. It would not be truthful to say I do not notice that A bangs doors and B is messy in the bathroom. I do not fancy damp bathmats and toothpaste splodges on the mirror, but wisdom tells me to keep these dislikes to myself for as long as possible, because they are trivial and not important when measured against kindness and a loving heart. I now know that it is a waste of energy to lose patience over such things, and it can be hurtful. If, as I suspect, it is through one's own frailties that one can recognise frailties in other people, then the way of not letting these become too important is to look to one's own motes and beams.

Unpunctuality is another thing. I find it selfish, bad-mannered and inconsiderate, but one of my dearest friends tells me IT DOES NOT MATTER, and that it is egoistic to object to being kept waiting. 'There is no such thing as time,' I wrote in a song, and metaphysically this is true, but when one is leading a busy life of dovetailed engagements involving other people I think it makes sense to try and be on time. I *know* it makes sense. I inherited my dislike of unpunctuality from my father and take it to ridiculous extremes, setting off an hour early to go to a theatre out of a faithless suspicion that unless we get there before the crowd we won't find a place to park. (All too often I am proved right, and that is why I continue to start early.) I almost always arrive at the station or airport in time to get the plane or train that leaves before the one I came to catch. Reggie, left to himself, might be a last-minute man, but long years of living with me have trained him the other way. And we had an experience in New York when my insistence on getting to the dock two hours before the ship sailed back to England proved to be a good idea; for he had left the passports and tickets for the trip in the drawer of the bedside table back at an hotel half-way up town.

My Scottish-American great-grandfather held, as does the Brigade of Guards, that it is inexcusable to be late; you must allow time for unexpected events to occur. It may be true that *somebody* has to be last, but nobody need be; if you are late it means you didn't start soon enough.

Unless Reggie is with me I am content to be on my own for much of the time, but I do like to be in touch with friends and the need to communicate is strong in me. It is my instinct to communicate with those I love, and letters have always been an important part of my relationship with close friends. There was a time when nothing I did was complete until I had written it down either in a letter or my diary. It wasn't enough to experience an event or a non-event; it had to be considered, re-thought and shared – a self-indulgence only excusable if kept under control. Out of affection rather than a sense of unselfishness I do not pass on worries and sadness. My faith helps me about this, as it does in every department of my life; and the old adage is true: least said soonest mended. Large and infinitesimal occasions and encounters that have amused or interested me go into letters to Virginia and other friends who might be expected to respond. But it is important to choose whom to tell what, and I hope my antennae always work. Happy relationships obtain at different levels; all demand sensitivity and none can ever be taken for granted.

When the heart dictates, working at friendship comes naturally. Even then it takes some effort; it is not always a balanced exchange. Though I believe affection is strong, some of my friends don't always have the same drive to communicate as I do, and one or two of them are almost entirely unable to make the effort to find paper and pen and the time to write letters. I complain and nag to little effect. But I have decided that if I am fond enough I will continue to write, and hope. Occasionally there is a rewarding response, usually brief, and always lacking the detailed information I hunger for: namely the well-being of the writer and a résumé of the life he or she is leading.

I best enjoy hearing from friends who write as they speak – with their tone of voice strong on the page. Virginia's is. We have kept each other's letters, dating from about 1926. She has mine typed and filed. I have never got around to having hers so tidily preserved; they are stowed in dated manilla envelopes in three large drawers in my work-room, and now and then I open a batch and have a good time reading her succinct comments and accounts of her doings. Our combined correspondence has no literary and little historic value, but the letters reflect the times we have lived in. Some trivia can be fascinating. Shortly after the war Virginia learned that in Holland the Arnhem Band had lost all its musical instruments. Moved by this sad story she wrote a letter to *The Times* offering to pass on any replacements that readers might be able to supply; she added a list of requirements furnished by the Band. It included two items hitherto unknown to her – 'a completetion of harmony corps' and 'a Piston in E♭'. The response was generous. It was unfortunate that in her letter Virginia had referred to Arnhem as a picturesque village; this threw the local mayor into a rage, because it isn't a village, it's a town, and a proud one. It took all of a Dutch friend's tact and ingenuity to convince the affronted man that in England the word village is used as a flattering term of endearment.

I get pleasure from unimportant detail. Here are quotations from two of Virginia's wartime letters. 'I never know why it is supposed to be good for one to do unpleasant things; I'm always so much nicer when I'm doing things I like.' She went on to tell me about a visit from friends who 'ate like horses', had 'large cooked breakfasts, port and claret every night, the heater on all the morning, lights blazing. I feel we shall have to sit in darkness warming our toes on Price's night-lights and go to bed bathless to recapture some of our fuel target level. I *asked* them so I must not grumble. (I really have a very bad character and a heart full of dried milk.) I wish I could go to sleep in a warm white cotton-wool nest, circular in shape, and warmed by a constant pink fire. Can this be what I am fighting for?' She went to St Paul's Cathedral for a huge W.V.S. service. 'I don't know what we were giving thanks for, dedicating or remembering, but I know I sang quite beautifully. I was against the brick wall covering Cromwell's tomb,' to protect it from bombs, 'and it echoed so pleasingly that I appeared to be the only person singing, and that effortlessly.'

My mother's letters, while not literature, were graphic. She des-cribed a girl in the last days of her pregnancy as looking just about ready to make a touch-down. She also had a gift for inventing capsule descriptions of people. A Scottish politician, once red-haired but turned pastel and sandy, reminded her of an ear. Antony Bernard, a small dark aquiline musician, she likened to F♯, not the key, of which she would not have been aware, but the key signature on the page. (Noël Coward, too, was good at capsule portraits. He said of an orchestral conductor that he was like a Jewish Squirrel Nutkin.) I doubt whether my ma had ever heard of an aphorism, but occasionally she said something that fitted Webster's definition: 'a short pithy sen-tence stating the truth'. Here is one of hers: 'When royalty leaves the room it is like getting a seed out of your tooth.'

One way of making letter-writing less of a problem is to have the necessary equipment always to hand. I keep supplies of stationery by my bed; on the table beside the sofa in the living-room where I sit; and in a plastic bag ready to take with me on a journey or to the hair-dresser. Under the dryer is an ideal place to write air-letters. I find I can write two in the twenty-five minutes it takes my hair to dry. But I write too much, too fast, and my hand that was once legible and had some character, has deteriorated into a smaller, scrawly scurry across the page, hard to read and ugly to look at. I blame those damn-able, convenient ball-point pens that do not respond to the touch, and produce only uniform strokes of pin-thinness. Oh, for an equally con-venient ball-point pen with the flexibility of the Relief nib of my youth. Why don't I type? Because you have to sit at a table to type well (I like to write on my knee, often in bed); I have never learned how, and

Garnee Miall

my typing is too eccentric to inflict on anyone. If speed were all, I might qualify, but the unknown words I produce with two hurrying fingers – such as hwo, teh and dna – occur too often, and my corrected typescript ends up even less legible than does my spider-scrawl.

It interests me that writing has recognisable national characteristics. Broadly, the Latin countries write spikily, Americans make more rounds and loops than any of us, and, for my money, the most beautiful hands come from educated Britons of both sexes. (I don't seem to know any Scandinavian, German or Russian writing.) The kind of hand I best like moves rhythmically across the page, in straight lines, with both confidence and authority – never too large, sometimes almost too small – always clear, easy and a pleasure to read.

Good writing is still rare. But I have at least a dozen friends, who have the kind of calligraphy I enjoy; fewer men than women – but Rupert Hart-Davis and Johnnie Bevan are winners. Visually I admire Reggie's bold sprawl, but it loses marks by being hard to decipher. His brother Harry and their cousin Harold Grenfell both have good writing – Harold's is beautiful. The women whose hands I admire usually turn out to be people with inner resources and a sense of proportion.

Many of my other friends have these qualities, but their writing doesn't give sign of it.

All of us in the entertainment world get many letters inviting us to make appeals, to judge, debate and speak; to open fêtes, bazaars and garden parties. Most of the bids come typed, so it isn't often that one is beguiled into saying yes entirely because of the hand-written look of the invitation. But that is what happened in the early sixties when one came from an unknown woman in Derbyshire. Nan Scott's writing sat prettily on the page, her economic style had a light touch; the note was simple and informative and her invitation, tentatively offered, made me want to accept it. I had a hunch that anyone who wrote as she did, fist and facts, would be pleasant to know. With Bill I went north to do a charity concert for her in a village hall and thereby made two new friends – Nan and her mother Garnee Miall.

Nan's mother was called by her grandchildren (and afterwards by everyone else) Garnee, a corruption of Granny. She was rising eighty when I first knew her. I loved her looks – broad brow, wide-apart blue eyes and a glorious un-grown-up smile that reminded me of another child-like innocent, my nanny Lucy Sampson – innocent, not in the innocuous, blameless sense, but as Webster defines innocence, 'purity of heart'. Garnee was a free spirit; a Quaker who kept her simplicity. She responded to delight and joy. She also had a sense of the ridiculous. She was someone to tell good news to – a sharer. What we shared was a pleasure in wild flowers, birds, books and the idiosyncrasies of the human race; and affection. Garnee and I wrote to each other; our relationship was a continuing, growing one; we met when we could, and, on or off paper, we talked heart to heart. No age gap.

She kept me in touch with her family – unknown to me – living all over the world. Her interest in them was lively, and she made them real, reporting news from Peru, Australia and Japan. (Mialls get about a good deal.) When we met she used to say: 'Talk to me about God.' We explored and shared discoveries. She said she liked having her own discoveries confirmed. As I had done with Walter de la Mare we talked about death and agreed that our identity – the spiritual being – is the truth about us, and is that which is eternal.

Joseph McCulloch gave me this quotation from the seventeenth-century writer, Sir Thomas Browne:

> Thus we are men, and we know not how: there is something in us that can be without us, and will be after us; though it is strange that it hath no history what it was before us, nor cannot tell how it entered in us.

I believe this refers to our spiritual identity. I wish I had known it to tell to Garnee; it would have been very much to her taste.

I once suggested to her something that is becoming clearer to me. I begin to see that although we may think that what we love about those dear to us is their appearance, sound of voice, way of walking, laughing, tilt of nose, movement, touch, human presence, it is really their qualities we love. These are wholly spiritual, and endure. Garnee's identity was compounded of humanity, gentleness, courage, endless discovery of that which is good and therefore true; endless wonder in life and, in particular, continuing astonishment at the beauty to be discovered around us wherever we find ourselves. In a cell? I asked. 'Yes,' she said, 'perhaps the graining in a bench or the light on stone walls.'

Unlike another friend of mine, Garnee, very much living in the present, was fully aware of the loving presence of the good in her earlier life. This other friend, a widow of my own age, told me with bitterness that she never thought of the past. It had been happy; it was over. She had pulled down a blind (her own words) and couldn't bear to look back because those good days would never happen again. Because I believe that whatsoever things are good, past or present, are true, it is not only wise to 'think on these things' but, like Garnee, to go on enjoying them.

Garnee was alive with appreciation and wonder to the end of her days, and lived to celebrate her ninetieth birthday, when her friends, descendants, kith and kin flocked to honour her. To say everybody loved her is a sweeping statement, but I suspect it is nothing less than the truth. She put into practice a line I saw outside a Friends' Meeting House in Bath. 'Friends believe that when you speak to the good in a man you find right answers.'

After that first visit to Glossop (the name sounds to me like slurping soup) Garnee sent me *The Oxford Book of Wild Flowers*. It is a most useful, easy-steps-for-little-feet guide to flower-finding rather than a scientific botanical aid, and exactly suits my needs. The flowers are arranged in colours, and, should you need them, the Latin names are given; and now that I've added Keble Martin's more complete flower book and the newer Collins's paperback to our car-library – it includes a bird book, several maps and a National Trust catalogue of its possessions – I can identify the genus in Garnee's book and find the particular variety in Keble Martin. He gives very few common English names, and, if like me, you can only just tell Rosaceae from Ranunculaceae you need help. Reggie marks up the birds in the bird book; the date and where we saw them; and I do the same with flowers. You may well ask why. Answer: it satisfies something in us that likes discovery; and when we return to a part of the country where first findings were made it amuses us to see if the butterwort is still growing in the same marsh and the greenshank calling from the same pool.

When I took part in one of the B.B.C.'s nature unit films I was seen flower-finding up a mountain in Switzerland and on the edge of a wood in Hertfordshire. Flower-finding, I said in the film, is a rewarding thing to do. I held up my copy of Keble Martin's *Concise British Flora in Colour* towards the camera, and suggested that it was a great help and made the pursuit more interesting. I advised viewers to get hold of a copy. Some few weeks after the documentary was shown I had a heartening encounter with a youngish London taxi-driver. When I hailed him he gave no sign of ever having seen me before, but as we were creeping along in thick traffic he pushed back the sliding window that divided us and yelled at me:

'I did what you said. I got the book.'

I had no idea what he was talking about.

'Oh . . . good.' I wondered with whom he had confused me. 'Did you enjoy it?'

'Marvellous,' he said. 'I used it in Epping Forest.'

Light dawned, and we talked at the top of our voices, against the traffic's roar, about flowers, nature, life and the wonder of it all. He thanked me for putting him on to a good thing. 'I'll be using it often.'

Occasionally I paint flowers I've found – not to make a picture for framing or showing to other people – but for the pure pleasure of recording them. Sketching a tree or a house is like keeping a diary; it records the pleasure. The doing is the fun.

I have a pen-friend whom I have never seen, although she knows what I look like because she has seen me on television and in old movies. She came into my life when she wrote me a letter about a radio programme I had written in which I quoted a poem. She liked it and sent me something else by the same poet. And so began an enjoyable correspondence that has gone on for many years. We don't write regularly; at most three or four four times a year. She is one of the unexpected riches in my experience.

Her name is Katharine Moore. Her handwriting, like Nan Scott's, is the kind I respond to, because it is legible, attractive without being fussy, and has character as well as charm. I know she is older than I am, is a Quaker, and after a long and happy marriage is now a widow. I know she writes books that I enjoy reading; has children and grand-children she likes; and includes some 'adopteds' in her family circle. What I do not know about her is whether she is tall or short; fat or thin, pretty or plain. Years ago we decided to leave this mystery unsolved. I once spoke to her on the telephone and decided she sounded tall and slim, distinguished in a scholarly English way. Her voice seemed to go well with her handwriting.

A clear picture of what she is mentally like has been evoked through her letters, which are vivid, economical and warm. We share a taste for reading, the eternal pleasure of seasons, music, sounds and sights, and for people who pleasantly surprise us by their diversity. We seem to agree on some fundamental ideas and are interested in each other's lives. In 1964, K. M., as I address her in my letters – she calls me J. G. in hers – compiled a diverse and fascinating anthology called *The Spirit of Tolerance*, published by Gollancz.

Tolerance is a word I was brought up to respect. The dictionary defines it as 'the disposition to tolerate beliefs, practices or habits dif-ferent from one's own'. Different, but not necessarily worse. I was taught to think of it as an awareness of the many different ways that may lead to the same valid answer. It was supposed to show an open-minded regard for new ideas; it also warned against being emotionally certain one was right before taking time to stand back and look coolly at whatever was in question. But nowadays the word has come to be used as a synonym for permissiveness – an acceptance of everything, without criticism or a sense of true values. Anything goes. This new tolerance is permissiveness gone mad. It rejects discrimination; it does not allow anyone to say 'I believe this to be good, and that to be bad.' I dare to submit that, through experience, I have an inkling of which is which, but to say so is to proclaim one is intolerant.

For a very long time I know I was both critical and intolerant – and emotional – about anything I didn't understand or wasn't immediately drawn to. With the arrogance of youth I dismissed Stravinsky's music, Picasso's painting, great wealth, and the world of the horse – to name but a short list. I didn't like the idea of any of them. Eventually, time, the great healer, let me outgrow my intolerance; and my pa's open-minded attitude to new ideas influenced my thinking. I am still blind to the later Picasso and though I now recognise that the horse is a beauti-ful creature to look at, I am still glad I need not get on its back or have it as a friend (nor do I have to attend its race meetings – one of my

Carley Dawson

ideas of hell). But today Stravinsky is firmly established in my heart. Now it is Stockhausen whom I can do without. I couple him with another modern mockery, the high-decibel count of pop, rock or whatever the current blood-thump travesty of music is called – usually so loud that it is impossible to hear the words or discover the tune.

Here is part of the introduction K. M. wrote for her anthology:

Freedom of thought is necessary for any step forward. So the man of tolerance has often proved a true prophet. He has, in his day, patiently defended the despised, the outrageous, the persecuted; many times with little or no success. Yet, in time, what was held to be intolerable has become not only widely accepted but essential.' [She goes on to speak of women's place in society, child-labour, race relations and the recognition of genius.] Which has been proved right – Erasmus or Luther, Shaftesbury or his opponents, John Woolman or Carlyle, the tiny number who applauded Keats or *The Quarterly*? In a word, the tolerant or the intolerant?

Question: Must I think again about Stockhausen?
Answer: No.

I wrote the foreword to K. M.'s latest book, *She for God*. I found it 'a fascinating and intelligent review of the splendid regiment of women who, from Jesus's time to the twentieth century, have proved . . . that God is no respecter of gender'.

To some of the friends who write regularly to me I have periodically sent back large batches of their letters for them to give to their grandchildren. Smaller parcels have gone to K. M. I have returned at least fifty years' worth to Carley Dawson, and only a little less to Elly, both in America. They and their descendants will have to rally a good deal of stamina if they are going to read through the collections. Carley and Elly have written to me at least every three weeks since we first began to correspond. Carley is one of my dearest friends. These letters, like Virginia's and mine, may not be of literary value, but are full of contemporary details and because of their continuity may well have some sociological worth. They have given me a great deal of pleasure. None was written with an eye to posterity. It is their spontaneous unselfconsciousness that makes them worth preserving.

During the overseas hospital tours that I made during the war I kept a journal in a series of exercise books, and from 1946 I have continued to write a page-a-day diary. Why does one keep a diary? In my case for practical reasons as well as for pleasure. While I was leading a busy professional life, writing nightly – or first thing the next morning – was a useful way of recording occasions, engagements, places and the names of people I worked with. I put down details of my programmes and always noted the quality of the audience's reception. I also recorded the weather (hardly a June went by without my complaint that the days were as dark, cold and wet as November), meals and the clothes I wore. Such things bring back to me the flavour of the times of which I was writing, and I still list them. The entries are hurriedly written, like shorthand reporting, and often verbless. They are private in the sense that I never expect them to be read by other eyes than mine. *Very* occasionally I add a few 'great thoughts', hopes and resolutions. The diaries are neither libellous nor, except by comparison with those kept by an eccentric step-great-uncle of Reggie's, are they sensational. Great-Uncle Albert Lyttelton is said to have kept a diary entirely devoted to his ablutions. These were of an unadventurous nature.

Jan. 1: Bath
Jan. 2: Dry rub
Jan. 3: Bath
Jan. 4: Dry rub

Every one of the 365 days of the year had one or other of these reports, evidently of vital interest to Great-Uncle Albert.

I wish I had always kept a diary. As a child I often tried, but it came to nothing. After a few weeks the entries dwindled to 'forget what I did', and by the end of January they stopped altogether. In those highly-lit days my earlier self in adolescence went through some chosen hoops of a rum kind such as (willingly) attending point-to-point race-meetings, sailing on uneasy seas off the rocky coast of Maine, and running after a pack of beagles over heavily-clodded fields. These things were all done for love. I was seldom out of it – silent, long-suffering, pleasure-pain, one-sided love that went on almost entirely in my head. In the world I grew up in we were reticent and shy about our feelings; humble, too, for we knew it was impossible for anyone to be drawn to us. (Some day I would be thin, graceful and attractive . . .) The safety of such adolescent love, up to the age of seventeen, was its charm. I was not ready for anything more practical. At the time I felt no need to put on paper my emotions.

My adult diaries do not tell all, nor do they include many emotional outbursts. I am not much given to that kind of indulgence. Re-reading them before writing about my memories – to check dates and sequences of events – I find I complained rather more than I realised. The odd thing is that I don't remember feeling disgruntled; perhaps I exorcised the sense of whatever it was that riled me by writing about it. But years later, all passion spent, the complaints and rare emotional entries make boring reading. Condensed conversations and recorded remarks are more rewarding to come upon. One of the pleasures of maturity is discarding false values. A continuing and developing thirst for discovering more enduring spiritual awareness has greater appeal.

The past no longer calls to me, even though I enjoyed most of it. Now that it is safely over, warm and dry-footed I can see my remote self with some detachment. I can also look back at the less happy times and pigeonhole them under the heading of Experience. Everything that is good (as Garnee knew) remains a present reality. I am glad I stuck to the daily practice of recording my doings. I enjoy reliving journeys and reading about meeting for the first time people who have turned into friends. In reading my old diaries I found much to remember with amusement, amazement and gratitude. I came upon items, some in daily entries, but most of them written at the end on the pages intended for accounts, that I was glad to see again.

Here are some of them:

The Welfare Care Committee woman I met at a school, where I gave prizes, had on her head the crab-shell she had eaten out of on her holiday in Madrid. She wore it on the back of her head with its tiny face and close-together eyes as a sort of climax on top. She said it made a good talking-point.

On television, Tortelier, the cellist, told about Anna Magdalena Bach saying to her husband: 'I think if everyone in the world was deaf you would still write as you do.' Bach said: 'It is not forbidden to hope that some day they may hear a little better.'

First line of a lyric sent to me by a fan, who wrote it and hoped I might have it set to music, and sing it on the radio: 'Woolly boots for baby Jesus.'

Teilhard de Chardin on liberty: 'The blessed constraint of not doing wrong.'

After I had done a broadcast about letter-writing, a listener copied for me the postcard sent to him by his ten-year-old son at boarding-school: 'Please send me a mouse-trap, a razor blade and some alum. I want to make a fur rug.'

Notice in a couchette on the train from Milan to Calais:
'This card is to faccilate control and to avid waisting your time.
PLEASE WIRTE CLAERLY

TANK YOU.'

My unseen friend K. M. sent me this quotation from a promising story written by her eight-year-old grand-daughter, Kate:
'Robert lived in a plain London house. He was a good boy on the whole but in the half no one could call him angelic. His sister Maria was brisk, firm and practical but agreeable to him. He liked to make balloons. When he was at work on one he did not care a fig for anything.'

In New York Dorothy Hammerstein's son Henry stepped into a lift up on the 38th floor which was so full of people that he was not able to turn round and face the doors. It was an eyeball-to-eyeball situation.
He couldn't resist saying: 'I expect you are wondering why I have got you all here.'

Misprint. Kingsley Amis quoted from a newspaper report on the funeral of one of the Salvation Army's Booth family: 'As the coffin was carried from the hearse to the train at Victoria Station a large crow sang *Abide with me*.'

Overheard in Brighton: 'He kisses me as if he was practising the trumpet.'

I am not alone in my dislike of being told a dirty story by a smutty-minded teller. But the fact is that a good dirty story – i.e. funny, concise and with an unexpected twist – told by a clean-minded teller does have an added dimension, and I would be less than honest if I didn't say that I enjoy it. Writing down such anecdotes is risky because it is difficult to indicate the tone of voice. In print a line that can be lightly floated on the air in conversation can turn to lead on the page. Here is an example of what I mean by a clean-dirty-story. It is essentially an English story.

Scene: A crowded railway carriage, of the old pattern, in which passengers sit facing each other. It is a very wet day. A small aggressive man gets in,

258

shakes his cap and raincoat over the other travellers and forces his way into a seat. He takes out a handkerchief and blows his nose in a long, detailed and exploratory manner. Then he clears his throat, elaborately, fortissimo, and also at some length. There is a blessed pause, broken by the man sitting opposite, who taps the offender on the knee and says quietly: 'And now perhaps you will kindly favour us with a fart.'

Overheard by me in Coventry Cathedral. 'It's meant for the young people of tomorrow. We are not supposed to understand it.'

Sybil [Thorndike] lunched and we discussed non-churchgoers, who are often more offended by jokes about religion than are the faithful. She told me that during rehearsals of *St Joan*, Bernard Shaw ticked off an actor for speaking of the Almighty in a holy voice. 'Don't say "God" like that,' said G. B. S. 'It sounds as if you are a non-believer!'

Dick [Addinsell] suddenly said: 'I want to talk about faith' (of which he always swore he had none). He told me that the affection of those he loves and who love him is beyond understanding. He asked me if I thought it came from a spiritual source.

To the Haymarket to see John Gielgud in his *Ages of Man* programme. The beauty of his voice moves me so terribly that I was looking through tears. So was he. I never saw a man cry so much. A lounge suit isn't right for Lear. Better when I closed my eyes. Not that any of that matters. He is a giant, and he does make me see the horses 'printing their proud hoofs i' the receiving earth'.

Tonight I mended a broken electric-light switch on the flex of a lamp, and I am filled with sinful pride. For over an hour I sat grunting over the niggling little screws, breathing deeply, wishing my fingers weren't so blunt. The moment when I put the lamp back into position, pushed in the plug and tried the switch was intense. It worked. No engineer building a bridge ever felt more satisfaction

Given to me by Jim Darling, this inscription comes from the Gothic church at Staunton Harrold in Leicestershire: 'In the year 1653, when all things sacred were throughout the nation either demollisht or profaned, Sir Robert Shirley, baronet, founded this church, whose singular grace it is to have done the best things in the worst times and hoped them in the most calamitous.'

Sent to me by an unknown fan from the Personal Column in an Indian newspaper, the *Madras Mail*: 'Safe in the arms of Jesus in a second-class carriage between Asansol and Calcutta.'

In the slack time when London buses are emptier than in rush hours I travelled with two young mums, each with a small child. The mums and I were seated by the door; the children were up in the very front of the bus. Their silence was suddenly noticed, and one of the mums called out:

'Clive – what you doin' under that seat?'

'I've found a litt'l 'ole and I'm puttin' me toffee paper down it.'

'Are you sticky? Wipe yourself on the seat then.'

[An evening at Virginia's] After dinner, before the men joined us, we discussed feet. Sheila [Talbot] said she could find with her toes alone any book in the Bible that we liked to choose. Ginny fetched a copy. Sheila removed her stocking. Slowly but surely she found Hosea.

[Signs of desperation] In a chemist's shop window: 'Why not give a sponge this Christmas?'

In a Hampstead bookshop: 'Children of progressive parents are kindly to be kept on leads.'

Noël Coward was interviewed by a nosey and ill-informed lady journalist about living in Switzerland. Did he have nice neighbours? Noël mentioned Joan Sutherland and other starry locals and said: 'I'm seeing Yehudi this very afternoon.' 'Yehudi who?' 'Yehudi Bankhead.'

Clemence Dane: 'I like almost everyone except the conceited. Vanity can be lovable, is approachable, but conceit is a total barrier.'

I discovered quite lately that the story of Pavlova in Edinburgh is not known to younger generations.

Pavlova had just finished dancing her famous Dying Swan. Slowly, gracefully, tragically she sank to the floor, her arms forming the creature's neck, as the music – and the Swan – died away. An awed silence filled the theatre. Before the applause broke out a refined Scots voice said in a chatty tone: 'She's *offly* laike Mrs Wishart.'

A piece of graffiti, also familiar.

'My mother made me a homosexual.'
Below this in a different hand.
'If I gave her the wool do you think she'd make me one?'

Garson Kanin [who wrote, among other successful movies, *Born Yesterday*] told me of an ex-variety star who failed in a straight play and knew exactly why. 'I can't act sideways.' [Nor can I. It is the penalty of solo performers.]

A misquotation: 'Bubble bubble, toilet trouble.'

About space.

I have no sense of panic about space. It has always been there. God fills it and I am happy to leave it as it is.

My cousin Ann Holmes had tea with Flora Russell, a friend of our grand-mother. She is now ninety-nine. Told Ann the reason Granny put her boots on first when dressing in the morning was because she always did imaginary skipping in her bedroom after her cold bath. And when our Aunt Rachel came to tell her she had become engaged to be married, Granny, still in bed, said: 'Wait until I've put on my boots before you tell me about it.'

Mrs Warre Cornish said to her daughter Charlotte: 'Even after a Channel crossing, I say to myself, "I am English; I was born in wedlock; and I am on dry land." '

Viola wrote to me from a summer music-school at Dartington. 'The ladies [of the choir] worry greatly about their intervals. A tenor has been found trying to get into the lotus position behind a hedge.'

In a friend's bathroom these lines, framed, are placed where she can always see them:

> Thou shalt know Him
> When He comes
> Not by any din of drums
> Nor the vantage of His airs
> Nor by anything He wears
> Neither by His crown
> Nor His gown
> For His presence known shall be
> By the holy harmony
> That His coming makes in me.
>
> Anon *circa* 1500

CHAPTER FIFTEEN

The Circle Grows Smaller

ONE FORM of holiday I swore I would never take is a cruise. The idea of being trapped at sea with a crowd of people bent on killing time, having a 'jolly' and dressing up for gala evenings, and feeling compelled to be a joiner whether one wishes to or not – none of it is for me, or for Reggie. As do small islands, ships make me want to get off and walk. But when Geoffrey Platt wrote to us from America, a year or so after his wife Helen died, to suggest that we might join him, with Helen's sister Priscilla and her husband Pen Hallowell (all very old friends of ours) and Gardner Cox and Alice Holbrook, he made it sound so attractive that we, too, booked to go on the same Swan Hellenic tour in 1976.

We had been to Greece once before in 1972, when Tommy and Mary came with us, and we hired a self-drive car. Delphi was, in all senses, the high spot of that tour and remains so. We were all stunned by its potent atmosphere. Perhaps it had something to do with the altitude and the clarity of the air. It was a still, warm day, slightly overcast, and the sound of nightingales, cuckoos and the staccato conversation of distant goats filled the great gorge we looked out on, when we opened the shuttered windows of our rooms. The hotel was built against the wall of the cliff-side below the road, so that the reception hall was at street-level and we took a lift three floors down to get to our bedrooms. The next morning when we climbed up to the forum, went up higher to the theatre and higher still to the stadium, the same music filled our ears, and the scent of herbs, particularly thyme, assailed our nostrils. Flowers were in profusion, from nine-foot lemon-yellow fennel plants to tiny brilliant sapphire-blue pimpernel. Why does Delphi, now feel so peaceful, and indeed in the spiritual sense so 'holy'? I found it a mind-expanding place of hope and confidence. A place of benevolence. For me it is the most remarkable of all the places I have ever seen. And in the loveliest setting. We saw it again in 1978 on a pouring wet day, and the wonder was still there.

The Circle Grows Smaller

We had heard about these Swan Hellenic Cruises – about the small ship on which you sleep for two weeks as you sail from port to port with congenial like-minded passengers, and with distinguished lecturers on board to inform you about the history of the fascinating places you are going to explore. 'You become a parcel,' we were told by old hands who had done the trip before. 'Swan does all the organising for you, takes care of your passport once you leave Gatwick airport and doesn't give it back until you return.' Letters flew between Prissy and me about what clothes to take. Would it be dressy? Cold, warm, wet? We settled for trousers and a variety of tops by day, long skirts by night, raincoats, sweaters and above all flat-heeled, rubber-soled, very roomy shoes to climb up and down the rocky ruins. We chose well and needed everything we took with us.

It was April, when we flew to Athens to join the M.T.S. *Orpheus*, a small Greek ship painted buff-yellow and white. It was spring-flower time all over the Mediterranean. The two weeks proved to be the holiday of a lifetime, topped only by a second two weeks a couple of years later, when a trust set up by my mother's father before his death in 1918 finally matured and was distributed to his grandchildren. The share that came to me allowed us to bring Mary and Tommy over from America and take them with us on the second cruise.

It was while we were at sea between distant points, such as Venice, say, and Olympia, that the lecturers gave us longer lectures about the ancient peoples, and the places we were going to visit. They spoke of mythological and historical Greece. (I continued to be confused over this even after lucid talks by Peter Fraser.) They told us about Greek philosophy, art and sport, and before we got to Asia Minor we learned about Byzantium, Constantine and modern Turkey. I couldn't take a searching examination on any of it, but at the time it lit up the places we saw. For a moment I was almost able to sort out the difference between Ionic and Doric architecture. It was possible to lie on one's bunk in the cabin and hear the lectures piped through over the radio system, but the groups Reggie and I were with, on both cruises, preferred to attend school in person. As I had done when I was on the Pilkington Committee I made drawings of faces, while I listened. Attentive faces make good models, and I enjoyed myself, working with an ink-pencil in a small sketch-book. I kept this in my handbag and was able to add a few outdoor sketches of fellow-passengers, perched on fallen columns or the steps of temples, as they heard the introductory talks given on the sites. Though I was out of practice on the first tour and no better on the second, the drawings are for me a kind of shorthand diary and remind me of the people and the places.

As well as Delphi I treasure Ephesus because, as we sat in the theatre waiting for the sun to come up over the horizon and warm us, Lord Wolfenden read to us from Acts 19 and instantly brought alive the story of the silversmiths who demonstrated against St Paul in defence of their livelihood – the making of idols of the goddess Diana.

Assos, also in Asia Minor, is my other special 'pleasant place' we went to on our second cruise. It is a tiny hill-village perilously cling-ing to a high rocky peak on top of which is a flat open space where the Greeks built a temple to Athena. We went there with a small group (one busload) as an alternative to visiting Troy, which Reggie and I had both seen on the first trip. It was a pretty afternoon with a pale sun, and the oak forests, through which we drove on the up-and-down-hill road, were just coming into leaf the colour of honey amber; the trees were hung with amber tassels. For some miles before we got there we had glimpses of Assos standing out against the sky, as the bus took us along the switchback way. It stopped in the village square half-way up the peak, and we walked, puffing in my case, up a very steep roughly cobbled street between old cottages, past an historic ruined mosque up to the flat open space at the top, the site of the temple. Not a lot to see except the outline, but the place had a magic about it because it was so remote, so high, the day windless and there was a positive, blessed silence. Some small, quiet children followed us and offered little sprigs of mint. I searched my pockets for sweets – I almost always have some in my bag or pocket – but for once I had none, and, though I think pennies would have been more welcome, I had none of those either, and Reggie by now had gone on the steep cliff walk with the rest of the party to see the great wall still so well preserved. After cautiously looking over the edge, at the buried jetty of the ancient harbour six hundred feet below, where Paul is supposed to have landed, I sat on a stone and found growing in the short grasses at my feet a tiny bright red ranunculus, with a black eye and a frilly green collar, delightfully called *Adonis*. I was happy to sit there for five minutes more breathing in the by-now-familiar scents of mint and greenery, and thinking with pleasure of the remoteness of where I found myself.

My particular joy was the wild flowers. Like the light in Greece one had heard about, the legendary flowers were something I wanted to see. Unlike our sadly sprayed countryside, Greece and Turkey are still carpeted, pied, dotted and wreathed in flowers. I have only seen those

Singing 'They'll Never Believe Me' in the Theatre at Delphi

lands in the green time; biscuit-coloured landscape comes later, and I don't want to see it. Green Greece is a revelation. The flowers come up wherever there is a fistful of earth, enough to hold a root. They come up through paving-stones, hang from rock crevices, fill ditches, cover banks and spread like a tightly patterned Liberty cotton over all the open spaces. On the island of Delos, after I had climbed up and down the marvellous ruins, I settled myself under a warm stone wall and on one page made separate little water-colour portraits of eight or nine small flowers that I could reach from where I sat. After an afternoon at three thousand feet on Mount Parnes, near Athens, where we went on a botanical expedition, I did the same thing back in my cabin, recording four kinds of dwarf iris – some whiskered and one widow – orchids, single-petalled clover, yellow daisies, white daisies, and a dramatic fragile dark brown and green striped fritillary. V. Sackville-West, in her poem about the Kentish Weald called *The Land*, refers to English fritillaries as 'sullen and foreign looking . . . like Egyptian girls'. Those on Mount Parnes are more mysterious and

shyer. There was also a tough yellow buttercup with a furry stem –
doubtless as a protection from the cold – and violets blue and violas
palest yellow.

Chris Brickell was the botanical lecturer on both of our cruises. He
led expeditions and afterwards arranged a display of the flowers found,
identified by name so that those of us who were interested and were
not already informed could learn which flowers we had seen. As the
days went on he and his attractive wife, like a pair of Pied Pipers,
collected more and more flower-finders for the enjoyable botanical
trips.

I recommend this kind of cruise in which you sleep in the same bed
for two weeks, but can get off the ship and walk on land almost every
day. The comfort of not having to pack up and move on every few
days, as we would have had to do on a land trip, made the tour restful.
The walking took place when we reached the ancient sites after journeys
in big coaches that we always found lined up awaiting us at every port.
For those two weeks life was certainly strenuous, not a moment wasted.
We noticed that even the quite elderly accomplished the early starts
and long days and not only survived but were obviously pleased at
all they had achieved. And no one *has* to go on all the trips. There is the
dear ship where one can stay on deck and rest. Our particular group
went on every expedition, gasping occasionally, but infinitely rewarded. I hadn't taken so much exercise for years. It was a gruelling
programme, but somehow we didn't notice it much until it was over
and we were back at home; and by that time we had so much to remember, re-think and enjoy that the unaccustomed exercise became
part of the good time.

Our second Swan tour took us to Sicily, where Viola and I had
spent a week in 1944 working in two hospitals, one in Catania and the
other in Syracuse. Memories of those strange times when we sometimes
worked in five wards a day and were stretched as we had never been
before or since swept over me. The place looked no more prosperous
and just as rain-soaked as when we had been there. I thought how
much Viola would have enjoyed all we had been seeing on the tour and
about which she knew so much more than I did. She had been brought
up on the classics by her clergyman father, who was also a naturalist,
and one of her dreams had been to go to Greece. A few years after the
war she and I flew to what was then called Northern Rhodesia, invited
by my brother-in-law Harry Grenfell, at that time Mayor of Lusaka, to
open a new theatre. Our plane had engine trouble; we were grounded

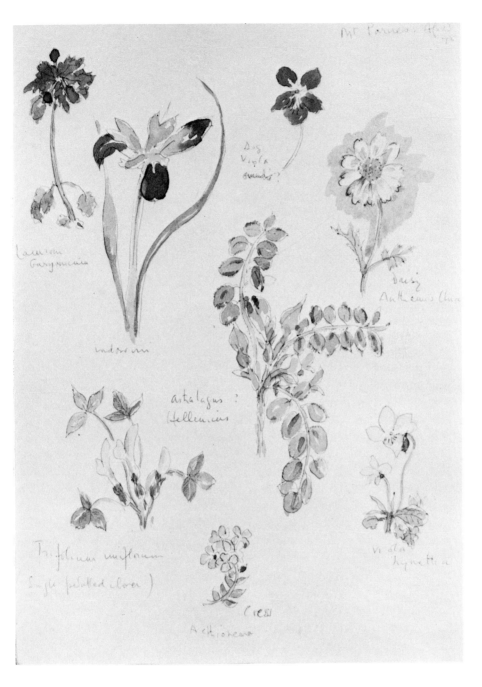

Some of the flowers found on Mount Parnes

Jean Cowan

in Athens for eighteen unexpected hours; the airline put us into a hotel for some sleep, and then organized a sightseeing bus, with a guide, to take us round the city and to the Acropolis. Viola's delight at being there was good to see. She walked through the Parthenon (in those days one was still allowed to do this) and looked out to sea, her eyes shining. We were both silenced by the stiff climb and the fact that here we were on the *Acropolis* in Athens – in *Greece*. It was the only time she went there.

Viola died in 1974 of a sudden but prolonged illness that left her totally paralysed, except for her eyes. For a creature of light and swiftness of mind and body – no one could vanish so quickly, particularly after a concert, as she did – and for a pianist whose chief way of communicating was through her hands, this was an appalling tragedy. In the last years, when she could no longer manage on her own, she went to live in what she called her Cabin, an extension out at the back of a blue-painted terrace house in Crabbe Street, Aldeburgh, with Jean and Christopher Cowan, who had become her close friends. There she was cherished and devotedly cared for in the long, narrow room that looked out into a small enclosed back-garden where grew a lavish white hydrangea bush. Tall as a tree, it put out flower clusters as big as a child's head. Although she was mostly confined to her room, when she was well enough Jean took her for drives to remote, marshy or wooded places where they watched birds. Viola's interests remained varied and continued to range far and wide. Her musical friends still consulted her, and she occasionally managed to give a coaching or two. The rest of us came to see her for her many individual quirks and qualities, and her humour. Being with her there was never like visiting a sick-room, though there were times of terrible anguish

Viola Tunnard

that most of us did not see. Our visits to the Cabin were a pleasure and a refreshment. Her strength of character and her gaiety made all who saw her at that time respect and admire, with awe, her increasing bravery.

There was no more soft saccharine sweetness or resignation about Viola in her illness than there had been when she was well. She was fairly autocratic, clear in her tastes and wishes, and astringent in her views. She ruled her own roost; but an increasing gentleness born of a new kind of strength became evident, and her appreciation of all that Jean did for her (and it was considerable and enjoyed, I know, out of love for Viola) and of the support given in turn by other devoted helpers was real; and she made it plain. She never lost her perspective nor her sense of humour, and if one needed evidence of the indestructibility of man's spiritual identity it was to be seen and felt in her presence.

With every visit I found her facial beauty increased. When I first knew her I told her she had just the right face for playing the piano. 'Big nose,' she said. No, I told her, just the satisfying disposition of good features that add up and, seen in profile, are noble. 'Pooh', she said. In her enforced stillness and with growing serenity she became more beautiful.

The last time I was with her, a few days before she died, we spent a quiet afternoon talking about the good times we had shared. We both knew she would soon be on her way. I said, 'I wish I could set you free.' By this time she did not find it easy to speak. There was a pause – and what she then said to me is the most precious thing she ever gave me. 'Perhaps,' she said, 'I am free already.' If this had been said to me by anybody else in similar circumstances I might have wondered whether they were saying it to comfort me. But never in all our long friendship had Viola ever been less than honest with me; I knew that she had discovered something I, too, was beginning to understand, and that is that no matter what happens to one's material body it does not, cannot, touch the spiritual identity that is our eternal being.

Soon after my parents died – within two years of each other – I had an experience that is not, I believe, uncommon where there is loving and liking. It was as if each in turn was restored to my memory at the height of their powers, lively, funny and pleasing. All the last sad pictures receded and disappeared, and instead I saw them, and continue to see them, at their most characteristic and best. And that is how I remember Viola – alert, funny, contributive, brilliant, brave and strong. Also original, and, and, as always, elusive. That was one of her great attractions.

In January 1978 a performance of Bach's B minor mass was given at the Priory church of St Bartholomew the Great by Janet Baker, Peter Pears, April Cantelo, Bryan Drake and many other of her musician friends 'as a tribute to her memory and to provide a memorial to her by endowing bursaries at the Britten–Pears School for Advanced Musical Studies' at the Maltings, Snape, near Aldeburgh. The orchestra conducted by Richard Marlow and led by Kenneth Sillito, included many well-known soloists – Richard Adeney, Cecil Aronowitz, James Blades, Janet Craxton and Philip Jones were some of them. The three cellists were Olga Hegedus, whom Viola had known since the early days of the war, Keith Harvey and Martin Lovett, of the Amadeus Quartet. Other friends wrote appreciations of her for the programme. Margery Sharp who, with her husband Geoffrey Castle, has a house on the front at Aldeburgh, came to know Viola only a few months before her death. She wrote that the Cabin

was an enchanting room with an oriel window, vaguely Pre-Raphaelite . . . At first she [Viola] sat in a padded chair opposite the bed whereon I, cross-legged, enjoyed the softness of a furry rug; then it was I in the chair and she on, then in, the bed. We laughed a lot. Indeed, as she became more and more physically incapacitated, the gaiety of Viola's spirit became more and more marked; then its serenity. She faced death, I will not say with insouciance, but with such happy equanimity that when the day after our last visit we heard she had gone, we felt almost a grievance against her for having left before telling us more of what she obviously knew, the right way to die.

Our immediate circle has grown smaller. Victor's and Dick's departure, within a few years of each other, made a huge gap. Both had been very much part of my professional theatre life, but that was over, and it is as my very close friends that they are missed. At one time the three of us – and Virginia – talked daily to one another on the telephone. She and I still do. As they grew older and went out less Dick and Victor spoke at more frequent intervals every day and evening.

For some years before his death Victor had been chair-bound. As Viola had done, he managed to keep a lively interest in what was happening in the world, in music, in the theatre and in books. But most of all his interest lay in his friends. He had a devoted circle of close friends, and with each one he somehow achieved a special relationship, precious and concerned. Somehow he had time for us all, and the one-to-one closeness of these relationships was real. After Dick his dearest friend was Virginia, and more and more she became indispensable to him. She lived in the same street and had a key to let herself into his flat when his housekeeper was out. She did a great many jobs for him, shopping, organising the re-decorating of his rooms and generally giving him her time. As one who benefits from her imaginative kindness, apparently casual so that it appears effortless, I know just what this can mean. Victor could be quite demanding and peremptory, and there were times when Virginia objected to some chore he wished her to undertake; but not often. He was excellent company, responsive, quick-witted and with a sense of humour capable of mocking not only his friends but himself. He could be a considerable tease and was sometimes critical and caustic and took swipes at those of us in his inner ring whom he thought were acting 'uppish'.

Victor never had a garden of his own, but his appreciation of flowers was considerable, and friends from the country brought him special bunches. London friends, without gardens, knowing his taste for specie roses and exotic lilies found these at specialist florists, to give him pleasure. He always arranged the flowers himself, a big operation involving sheets of newspaper all around his chair, buckets of water and a selection of vases to choose from. He did the job superbly.

Going to see Victor in his second-floor flat overlooking Hyde Park, where for so long Evelyn Vallely nursed him, was always rewarding. Later she went to look after Dick. She gave them patient and loving care and both were devoted to her. When my visits were over I realised how very little had been said about his own situation. To give oneself as wholeheartedly to each encounter as Victor did, eagerly asking questions and demanding detailed answers, is a rare accomplishment. His interest was genuine, his concern for one's well-being real. Not only did he have a special relationship with his friends, but he had the right – or thought he had the right – to bully them from time to time. It never occurred to any of us, I think, to tread gently in a verbal battle; he was fully capable of holding his own. One of his characteristic replies to the question, 'How are you?' was 'Absolutely smashing', followed immediately by 'Next question'. I always came away from seeing him feeling stimulated; and full of admiration.

After Victor's death Dick began to withdraw. This was sad and bewildering for those who were fond of him, and it seemed as if the man we knew as an attractive, strong, very idiosyncratic individual (complicated is perhaps a simpler way of putting it) more aware of the nuances of relationships and more talented than most other people, was no longer present.

We continued to speak on the telephone from time to time but he would not let me visit him. 'I don't want you to see me like this.' But shortly before his death he said he would like me to come to his Cheyne Walk flat, and, although I found him altered and thinner, his strange medieval looks were tranquil, and the long-boned El Greco hands lying still outside the bedclothes were as beautiful as they had always been. At this last meeting all the recent sense of withdrawal was gone. We spoke briefly of our mutual love and I said I would always cherish all the good times we had shared, and he said, 'Yes – *yes*.' After he died, Patrick Woodcock, his old friend and doctor who was also his executor, told me Dick had left me the bronze cast of his right hand that had first belonged to Clemence Dane. It stands on top of a bow-fronted chest-of-drawers in the passage in our flat where I see it every day.

Writing about the shining goodness of my friends makes me realise how fortunate I am to have known such people. I do *like* my friends. Their infinite variety and their continuing affection is something to record with a great deal of pleasure, and I do so not only out of gratitude but as a salute to them all. What I miss when they are gone is the sharing, particularly of jokes and ideas. It was good to tell things to Victor, and I continue to find myself thinking – as I do about Viola, Barbara Bevan and my father – oh, I must remember to tell them this or that. Knowing how much they would have appreciated certain anecdotes is part of the continuing joy in remembering them. Reading, just now, through an old diary to remind myself of times and places, I found an entry that I know would have given them as much pleasure as it gave me to see it again:

'Libby Douglas-Home's "daily" told her that last night she had had a dream in which she heard the ferrule fall off Princess Margaret's umbrella.'

CHAPTER SIXTEEN

All Change

THE very last performance of songs and monologues that I gave was decidedly 'special'. In the spring of 1973 Lord Plunket telephoned from Buckingham Palace to say that the Queen wondered whether I would consider doing a programme, in June at Windsor Castle, for her guests on the occasion of the Waterloo Dinner – a function that takes place every year in Ascot week. Thank you, I said, I'd love to. A few days later he telephoned again. The Queen, he said, thought I might prefer not to dine before giving a performance; nevertheless if Reggie and I would like to come to dinner she would be pleased to have us. As a rule I never went out before doing a show, but I do not often get invitations to dine with my Sovereign – nor does Reggie – and I did not hesitate to accept for us both. Then I remembered that of course Bill would be coming to Windsor with me. 'I expect the Queen will ask him, too,' said Lord Plunket. Later he told me that when he mentioned Bill to Her Majesty she asked if he had a wife; if so she must be asked as well. With pleasure the four of us ringed the date, 21 June, in our engagement books.

The Duke of Wellington, I believe, is always invited to the Waterloo Dinner; it is the occasion on which, by tradition he gives the Queen, as a token of his right to maintain his royally bestowed lands, a replica of his own personal standard. This is a small banner made of white satin worked in gold thread. That summer was the first time the present Duke, who had lately succeeded his father, was to deliver his tribute, and it seems the obligation had slipped his memory until a day or two before the banner was due to be presented. Busy fingers in London were put to stitching it, and I was told that it was delivered by taxicab just before the dinner. I like to believe this is a true story. I wonder what the Queen does with the banner. Perhaps it is returned to the Duke under cover to be used again the following year, otherwise there must be quite a pile-up somewhere in the Castle.

Every detail of that warm summer day and evening stays sharply in my mind. I had asked if I might have Diana with me to look after the lighting and generally run the programme, and she went to Windsor in the morning and saw that the Green Drawing-Room, where we were to perform, was arranged as we needed it. Stage lights were borrowed from the local repertory theatre, and Diana directed where they should go, and had the piano put in the right place on the low platform, which was set within a wide bow-windowed alcove, voluminously curtained in bright dark green silk damask that made a good background for my new flame-pink Thai silk dress. After Victor Stiebel's retirement all my stage dresses were made by Clive, and this was the last and one of the very prettiest. Its stand-up fold-over collar was lined in moss-green silk; so were the slit ends of the long sleeves and the front panel of the wrap-around skirt.

Reggie hadn't worn a white tie and tails for a very long time and Virginia advised him to rehearse in case his shape had changed since he had last put on his finery. He was positive he hadn't changed an iota, but to be on the safe side he bought a new hard collar, a size larger than he used to wear. All was well with the tails and the stiff shirt. He couldn't be bothered to try on his white waistcoat, but the night before the party I persuaded him to look at it, just for safety. I was called in to see whether I could fasten the buckle at the back, but the strap wouldn't meet it by at least an inch and a half. Drama. All I could find in my work-box was a small end of limp white tape, but by doubling it up I contrived a practical strap. At least he was able to breathe without danger of bursting his buttons. He said he was surprised to find how uncomfortable such clothes were, and was amused to see that Prince Philip had taken to wearing a soft silk shirt with his hard collar and white tie – a practical and sensible man.

I hired a car to take me to Windsor in the afternoon. When I got there Diana was still setting up the lights, and I stood while she focussed them on me. I sang a bar or two to try out the sound and liked it. Helpful men were arranging gold chairs in two semicircles behind the armchairs where the Queen and other members of the Royal Family were going to sit. Beside the Queen's chair stood a little table for a carafe of water and some chocolate mints. (I didn't notice her take either during the performance.) Reggie's niece, Susan Hussey, who is one of the Queen's Ladies-in-Waiting, was on duty and let me use her rooms to rest and change in. Sue is tall, dark, elegant, domesticated, kind to her uncle and aunt and a creature of spirit and understanding. That afternoon she was at the races with the Royal party. I hung out my dresses – I had decided to wear two, the pink to play in, and for dinner a bright dark green Thai silk exactly the same colour as the Green Drawing-Room curtains – before lying down to go through words and doze off in between. I came out of my doze to hear the sound of many cars driving up towards the castle. Sue's windows faced Windsor Great Park. It looked very lush and green in the summery haze. I got to the window as a procession headed by the Queen's car passed by, everyone dressed in their best for Ascot.

The Lady-in-Waiting's rooms are below a long curved corridor hung with Gainsboroughs, Zoffanys, Canalettos and a lot more pictures there wasn't time to identify, as Reggie, the Blezards, Sue and I made our way to the main part of the Castle. We stopped for a moment to look at two big glass cabinets filled with a display of Royal orders, British and foreign, their coloured ribbons theatrically bright under interior lights. But it was the flowers everywhere that gave me the most pleasure. At intervals, all the way along the curved corridor, stood eight-foot-tall standard fuchsias, like young trees, in every permutation of pink and purple, red, white and magenta, all at their exact point of perfection, with plenty of fat buds hanging among the already opened bell-flowers. I remembered as a child being forbidden to pop the fuchsia buds on my grandmother's bushes at Chorleywood, and as a measure of maturity, and to celebrate the occasion, I popped a couple of the Queen's buds as I passed by. At the top of a shallow flight of steps – I never sorted out the different levels of the castle – near a collection of fascinating Holbein portraits that made us stop and look, there was an exuberant flower arrangement, on a scale that made me gasp – giant rhododendron heads of the palest possible pink, white and cream, mixed with great star explosions of double white peonies with lemon yellow stamens. And in the White and Gold Dining-Room the whole length of the table at which all seventy of us sat was decorated with a repeat pattern of low bowls of yet more pastel-coloured flowers – roses, white, cream and pale yellow; white daisies; carnations, cream and white; and for a touch of colour, an occasional sharp coral-apricot rosebud. The visual pleasures, as they had been the only other time we had been to the castle, were endless. I was so busy looking at the pictures, the flowers, the other guests and finally, when they joined us in the Pink Drawing-Room, at the Queen and her party, that I have now forgotten the details of the procession into the Dining-Room. I know I enjoyed the journey, and remember feeling as if I were in a ballet. The table not only looked pretty with its many flowers, and at each place a five-piece setting of George III Waterford glass, but the food pleased the eye as well. It was just right for a summer occasion; it, too, was almost entirely pastel-coloured; cold avocado soup (pale green), hot salmon-trout (pale pink), veal in a delectable sauce with tiny new potatoes, baby carrots (cream, ivory and pale orange), and the exception to this delicate palette, leaf-spinach echoing the dark green of my dress and the silk damask curtains in the Green Drawing-Room. Then came pineapple ice-cream, piled up in hollow pineapple shells, with the kind of sponge fingers I most like – squidgy. I badly wanted to have a good tuck-in, but resolutely I took only sample-sized helpings and sacrificed greed to the performance ahead.

Towards the end of dinner there was the wailing sound of bagpipes tuning up. I looked across the table at Bill. He was wincing. In spite of having a great-great-grandfather from Dundee, I am not usually moved by the music of the pipes. But, as the party of at least a dozen Scots Guardsmen, in full dress, swung into the Dining-Room at a brisk tempo, their kilts swinging from side to side in perfect unison, I was both stirred and impressed. The volume was deafening. I was glad when they eventually swung out again. As Bill and I agreed later, we could only admire anything so brilliantly performed. We were also, as mere Sassenachs, amused at such goings-on.

When the ladies left the Dining-Room I couldn't join them for coffee because I had to race the long distance of the corridor and down the stairs to Sue's room to change my dress and get back to the White Drawing-Room, where Bill and I were to wait until the moment came for our entrance. I got there still smoothing my hair and patting my dress as Bill tore past me. For his solo spot in the programme he was including his Victorian epic in words and music, *The Battle March of Delhi*, and had left in Sue's room the tattered printed copy of the piece originally found in an old music-stool in his father's house. It was an essential 'prop'; breathing heavily he returned with it at the precise moment that we were summoned to appear.

Through Sue the Queen had asked me to perform certain items she had seen me do on television. All the numbers were comedy; that is what the Queen specifically wanted the programme to be. This made it difficult to plan; for variety I always introduced 'straight' numbers to make a contrast to the funny ones, and without some sentiment or drama I thought it must be a monotonous list. However orders is orders, and I put together the programme as commanded.

Here, for the record, is what I performed:

Eng. Lit. III (The last of the three sketches about the Vice Chancellor's wife).

Unsuitable (A mature woman in a hat who gets 'sent' by jazz rhythms).

Two Speeches (A grand lady opening the wing of an Old People's Home, and a best man at a wedding).

Five Encores (Pastiches of the kind of songs you might hear at a school concert, after dinner in a drawing-room, at a Wigmore Hall recital, at a Festival Hall recital, and after a Masonic dinner).

A Terrible Worrier (An old Bucks woman who wins a rabbit in a raffle).

Hymn (Thoughts going through the mind of a woman in church as she remembers she has left, at home, some chicken stock simmering on the stove).

Nursery School Teacher: Story Time.

Opera Duet (With Bill, another musical pastiche).

Olde Tyme Dancing ('Stately as a galleon I sail across the floor').

After I had done the programme the party moved next door to the Pink Drawing-Room for drinks. Diana joined us. I was so hungry that my stomach rumbled. Either I looked as famished as I felt, or else Prince Philip heard the rumbles, because he ordered sandwiches for me. As if by magic a plate of the most refined chicken sandwiches I have ever seen appeared. They were very thin, very damp and of a deliciousness that was irresistible. How was it possible to cut new bread to such paper-thinness? Generously I offered the plate to Bill, who told me he had done very well at dinner and had the grace to restrain himself to two. I finished the rest with no difficulty.

In the days of Queen Mary's court there were supposed to be many rules about what women wore. Black was certainly frowned upon, if it was not actually forbidden; long sleeves in the evening were considered too informal. On this occasion the Queen, the Queen Mother and Princess Margaret all wore white, with sashes and tiaras. Their dresses were far from informal and all had long sleeves. Prince Philip and the Duke of Beaufort were a sight to see in their knee-breeches and the Garter – very becoming on a trim leg, and both were well equipped. The whole occasion was gloriously grand. An anachronism at the present time? If so I welcome it.

So long as we have a monarchy and there are castles, pomp and ceremonies of traditional pattern (and considering the hazards raised by some presidents in recent history I hope we will be blessed – yes, blessed – with our kind of monarchy for ever and ever) let everything be managed with the superb order that only the British now seem capable of achieving. May these occasions be done in the grandest manner, may they be performances of real style to lift the heart, gladden the eye, and nourish the spirit. As a production the Waterloo Dinner could not have been bettered.

In her own hand the Queen wrote a two-page letter to thank me for the performance. She hoped they had not been a very 'stuffed shirt' audience. (They had been ideal.) And she went on to say friendly things that led me to suppose she had enjoyed the occasion. Bill and I certainly did; and so did Joan and Reggie.

After that I retired from the boards, without a vestige of regret. It had been a wonderfully exciting and happy thirty-four years of performing, and I was grateful for it, but glad to stop. Do I miss the audiences and the applause? Not for a single minute. The time was right for a change of pace. Perhaps the moment had come to start writing a book of memoirs.

For years in common with others in my profession I had been regularly invited by different publishers, on both sides of the Atlantic, to consider writing the story of my life. A typical letter read: 'We have had a splendid idea – why don't you write a book of memoirs? We can help you with it.' I imagined this sinister phrase meant ghost-writing, and my positive reaction was 'Not on your Nelly!' It was writing verse for *Punch*, and light articles for women's magazines, and then the radio critic's job in the *Observer* that started me off as an earner. This preceded my career as an entertainer, and when that began I wrote all the material, except for three numbers, that I performed on stage over the next thirty-four years. If a book was going to be written about me and my life I was going to be the writer.

Because at that time I had no immediate intention of trying to write a book I felt I could ask Rupert Hart-Davis, an old friend, who then had his own publishing house, how I should answer these letters. 'Tell them,' he said, 'that you are already bespoken to me.' If some day I did write a book, and he liked it he would publish it. This possibility set me up; for all the books Rupert produced were quality products, not only to read but also to look at and handle. By the time I felt I was ready to begin writing Rupert had retired to live in Yorkshire, but his advice 'to get it all down' and not to worry about the editing until all the material was gathered in, was helpful; so throughout the long time it took me to write the book were his encouragement and his friendly interest.

It was while I was in South Africa, staying at Harold Grenfell's house on the hill, in Messina, that I began to work on *Joyce Grenfell Requests the Pleasure*. I was on my own a good deal of the time, because Harold and Reggie spent the middle of the week working at the company's head office in Johannesburg. The weather was piping hot. By eight-thirty in the morning I was seated under the arbour by the swimming-pool, and there I stayed until the midday sun came through the leaves and drove me into the house, where there was a breeze through the hall as well as a ceiling-fan to stir the air. I decided that primarily I wanted to write about the people I loved who had influenced my life for good. There were plenty of them. There were one or two others whose influence had worked in a reverse way, showing me how not to behave. They, too, had served me well. I began to make notes. Memories of my childhood and adolescence were clear; I didn't need any reminders. I not only remembered people, clothes, scents, rooms and places, but the precise feeling of being three – eight – twelve, and so on.

Looking back at the Walter Mitty daydreams of my early youth, when I fancied being famous but never got around to deciding what to be famous for, I am touched by their hopeless optimism. I was always the wrong shape for dancing – ballet dancing, I mean. When I took part in the dancing first act finale of the revue *Tuppence Coloured* I made a mess of it. The entire company led by me, and dressed in a variety of pinks and clashing reds, did a rumba around the stage, but I could never get the hang of changing the arm movements at the same time as I changed the foot movements. A good deal of giggling went on from Elisabeth Welch and the rest of the line as they followed my strangely un-South-American lead. But in the ballroom I did rather better. Indeed at a charity ball, a week before our wedding, Reggie and I won a waltzing competition and were awarded an armchair with a wickerwork back.

As time went on I swapped all my Walter Mitty-ings for tentative – again unspecified – literary aspirations; but as I wasn't much of a speller and was confused by grammar – what is a past participle? – and had not yet produced an original idea, this daydream went the way of the others; but not completely. Ever since I had had verses accepted by *Punch* and worked on the *Observer*, I had put in my passport, under 'occupation', the brave word 'writer'. When I went on the stage I changed this to 'writer-entertainer' – in that order. 'Journalist' seemed presumptuous; I thought 'writer' was a more modest, cover-all noun. By using it I planted a tiny waiting seed of ambition. I never had any theatrical ambition in the sense of setting-up a target and working towards it – before I knew where I was I found myself in the theatre, and once there it was enough to be doing whatever next came my way. I have always had a sense of all-is-well, and trusted it. But tucked away at the back of my mind was the idea of some day writing a book. The only true ambition I have ever had was to be a good writer. I kept the idea warm, waiting for the far-away right time.

Literature was what I was interested in. The writing I admired belonged to that category; it had recognisable and individual style and read easily, because it was clear. Most of it, I now realise, was written by women – Jane Austen, Rebecca West, Elizabeth Bowen are some of the enduring names that have stayed on my list. Theirs was the kind of writing I read and still re-read with unchanging pleasure.

Because I admired good writing, I tried too hard. What came out was a long way from literature; it was self-conscious, over-careful, dehydrated and without character or flavour. Worse than that, it had no recognisable tone of voice. Did I have a tone of voice? My only continuous practice of putting words to paper had been in the weekly diary-letters I had written to my mother in America (Tommy sent them back to me after she died) over the eleven years when we were separated from 1937 to 1946, and in the letters I had written to Virginia ever since we were about fifteen and one of us was away from London. These were unedited communications; they rambled on, were sometimes graphic, occasionally funny, sad, 'holy', thoughtful. Their main merit was their liveliness. Virginia told me they read as I spoke. It is amusing to compare how differently, in the war, I described the same incident to my mother in America and to Virginia, then living in Bristol to be near Tony who was with an anti-aircraft battery. Because I knew my ma was agonised about my being in and near London under the bombing, I was gentle about what I told her, played down the unpleasantness of the raids and made light of the damage done. To Virginia, undergoing her own noisy nights in the West Country, I was not so delicate. You would hardly think the letters were about the same events; or from the same pen.

When Victor Stiebel wrote *South African Childhood* he was much helped by Lorna Andrade, who for many years had worked with Osbert Sitwell and before that with another author, A. E. W. Mason. She became Victor's friend. Tentatively I asked him if he thought she might be willing to help me. 'Ask her,' he said. Late in the autumn of 1973 she came to have luncheon with me to talk about the possibility of helping me with my book.

Lorna is attractive to look at, slight, with thick grey curling hair, and a small secret smile that hovers before she lets it break through. She has the figure and agility of a girl. The first time she came to Elm Park Gardens she didn't notice the lift in the corner of the entrance hall, and ran up three flights of stairs and was not out of breath when she reached the top. She is shy, intelligent, well-read and full of diverse interests. At first I was a little frightened of her. I knew her experience had been with real authors, and I didn't have a great deal of confidence in the much worked-over pages in long-hand that I was about to show her. I think she may have been as wary of me as I was of her, but we soon found a meeting-place, and my respect for her judgement and appreciation for the care and help she gives me is hard to exaggerate. Not only does she check every proper name, place and form of address (as well as my erratic grammar and spelling) but she finds me any information I need. She belongs to the London Library and uses it well on my behalf. Lorna never bullies me; indeed she prefaces her questions about phrases I've used that are unfamiliar to her, by saying she is sure I am right but she wants to be certain that what I have written is what I intended. I remember she had never heard of some of the Americanisms I used, such as 'barber-shop harmonies', 'visiting firemen', and 'buck and wing'. She often made me rethink, which was salutary, and I readily rewrote when I was convinced that she was right. But I stood firm if what I had written *was* what I meant to say.

All through the writing of my first book Reggie helped by doing preliminary editing. Without telling me what he was going to do he took two of the early chapters, had them xeroxed, and then, without changing my words, cut up the pages, rearranged the order of sentences, paragraphs and sometimes whole pages, and stuck it all together with Sellotape in a more coherent pattern. At first I was a little taken aback by this bold move, but as I read through what he had done I knew the chapters had a better flow, and read more easily. He had never before tried anything of this kind, but found he had a feeling for editing and enjoyed it. From that time on I gladly accepted his help; it is friendly

Lorna Andrade

and practical to have a resident editor in the house. The final version of the book was a joint family affair. So is this one.

In the end Rupert read the completed manuscript through at least three times – a kindness and privilege of which I am fully aware and for which I am very grateful. He introduced me to Richard Simon, who became my agent and showed the book to Alan Maclean of Macmillan, who accepted it, and chose Richard Garnett to be my official editor. This was pleasing because, before he went to Macmillan, Richard had worked for many years at Hart-Davis, and like Rupert, he has a true feeling for books and cares deeply about the quality of paper, the type and the placing of illustrations as well as bindings and titles.

The look of a book and the way it handles mean much to me. I am wholly delighted by the look and the feel of *Joyce Grenfell Requests the Pleasure*. It is even more handsome than I dreamed it could be. I can say that without boasting, because, apart from choosing the colour for the binding, I had nothing to do with the book's appearance beyond expressing approval when Richard showed me what he proposed. The photograph on the dust-jacket – a candid camera-shot cheerfully and toothily exact – is apparently unmistakable. My mother would not have liked it. She always wished me to appear at an advantage, but the picture chosen by Richard was the right one for the job. It did a lot to draw attention to the book, because it made people (and me) laugh. In regard to its contents, I feel – as I felt when a poem or anything else I had written turned out well – no sense of personal responsibility. Indeed when a piece comes off I look upon it with some awe. Where has it come from? At first with my book I knew exactly where it had come from – a great deal of hard work, and the pleasure of remembering much that had been good – and I couldn't dissociate myself from it. Then I got used to it and let it go.

It took me three years, off and on, to write the book, and when it was finished I discovered my work was only half done. First came the novelty of reading galley proofs. This began as a pleasure. I was used to seeing myself in newsprint and magazines, but to see my words set out in what would eventually be the pages of a book was a new and exciting experience. The sentences I had wrestled with had settled down; the whole thing looked strange and independent, and I felt pleasantly removed from it. But going through the two-foot-six-long galleys was a slow and demanding job, and the novelty soon wore off. Reggie checked them, too; so, very kindly, did Rupert, and, of course, the book's editor, Richard Garnett. Every time any of us read the proofs new and different mistakes were found. The biggest and worst blob of all could only have been recognised by Reggie or me. We had been through the early typescript countless times before it was set up in print; separately we had read the galleys, and sitting side by side at the dining-room table, we went through them again for one final look. It was only then, a day or two before they were to go to the printer, that Reggie noticed I had called his mother, who died when he was five and whom he barely remembered, by the name of her sister, Sybil. Shaken by this lapse we began again at page one for just one more read-through. In spite of all our care, when the book appeared yet more mistakes came to light. As a member of the panel of B.B.C. 2's television quiz *Face the Music* I might be supposed to know a little something about composers and their works, but I let through three fat and obvious musical bloomers, and I blushed with shame.

Inside the poster:

Joyce Grenfell
Requests the Pleasure

on Thursday
September 16th 12.30-1.30pm

Signing-session

I had never thought about the promotion of books. Well-established authors may not have to do any promoting; it is certain that the Brontës – admittedly they had genius – rarely left their moorland village, and their books continue to sell all over the world. But for lesser writers promoting is now part of the selling game, and, like travelling salesmen, which is exactly what they are, they are sent out into the highways and byways of book-buying areas to draw attention to their products. I enjoyed the programme arranged for me – interviews on radio, television and with the press; literary luncheons and dinners with signing-sessions to follow; as well as other signing-sessions in bookshops. All these things were set up for me to do not only in Britain, but also in South Africa, Australia and later, for another publishing house, in the United States of America.

I was surprised to find myself on separate occasions sharing after-dinner speaking with three ex-prime ministers, all of whom had books published in the same season as I had. I appeared twice with Alec Douglas-Home and once each with Edward Heath and Harold Wilson. Promoting one's wares is a levelling business; I couldn't decide whether I had been elevated, or they had condescended. I don't imagine that any of us remembers much of what the others talked about. I noticed that those of us who were not on our feet delivering our homilies were busily making sure we could read last-minute additions to our prepared texts. If we had already spoken the relief of sitting down appeared to deafen us. Not too many axes were ground by the politicians but, with one exception, the commodity in short supply was charm.

Writing the talks – they were not speeches – for the literary gatherings took time and invention. I am not a speaker. I am a talker, that is to say I often, as a real speaker does not, get entangled with my syntax and end sentences on unsuitable words like 'of' and 'with'. I always mapped out a plan for every talk, and made myself prompt-cards with key words in capitals, and sometimes wrote out in full whole sentences I wanted to be sure to get right. And like everyone else I tended to get new ideas *en route*, and digress from the original plan. Sometimes this was more successful than if I had stuck to my notes, but it is usually wiser not to be too self-indulgent about improvising. To get me started I spoke of the disadvantage of having a face made familiar by film and television; because I am larger than I appear on the screen, when I turn up in the flesh, I am not quite what was expected. 'I'd no idea you were so b—, I mean so tall.' And there is the added problem of identification. I seem to have the kind of face that reminds people of someone else. When I played in hospitals and camps during the war I was often told how like I was to the viewer's Aunt Ada, or a woman he had once known who worked in a Woolworth's in Basingstoke. Jeanette Macdonald was another possessor of noticeable teeth of whom I put the lads in mind. Coming off the night-train from Manchester, after recording a *Face the Music* programme, I waited by the gate to meet the hired-car driver who was to take me home from Euston. It was a bleak morning. The wait was long. A small man, in a sad mackintosh, with very red hair, passed to and fro staring at me. At last he couldn't stand the strain and came over. 'Are ye no Ceesily Courtnaidge?' I had to disappoint him. My favourite misidentification occurred during the year of the Queen's Silver Jubilee. I was on one of many committees set up to celebrate the event and had put on tidy clothes and – now rare for me – a hat to attend a meeting. High on a scaffolding, two men were painting a house, as I walked by. 'That's Dame Sybil,' said one, inaccurately, to the other. I looked up. 'It isn't, 'I said. 'No – that's right. You're the woman on the music – you know – er – what's it called . . . ?' *'Face the Music,'* I said. 'That's it! You're right – and you are – ?' 'Joyce Grenfell.' Slight pause while he took in an unfamiliar name. 'I see.' The face was known to him, but he had never heard the name. When dear Sybil Thorndike died, two or three years earlier, she had been ninety-four years old.

The signing in bookshops was my biggest surprise. I did not expect very many people would turn up to buy my book or wish to have it signed, and on a boiling hot Saturday in June, with the finals at Wimbledon being shown on television, they didn't, but in other places they came in complimentary numbers. This was heart-warming, to put it mildly. For an entertainer – or anyway for this entertainer – meeting the public is not a hardship and, circus horse that I am, I responded to the opportunity of meeting the audience that had hitherto remained on the other side of the footlights. It was another new experience to meet so many people who seemed to look on me as an old family friend; this made the occasions a pleasure. Perhaps rather too many remembered me from their childhood, and now brought with them their grand-children to look upon an historic part of granny's past (me), but it was friendly – if sobering. I was flattered by the long memories of loyal fans, even when they got it wrong and had me confused with Beatrice Lillie or Beryl Reid. This muddle happens to all of us in the business. 'I'll never forget you in that sketch about the Girl Guides.' (I have never done a sketch about Girl Guides.) 'I don't suppose you'll ever forget the time you came to Pontypridd.' (I have never been to Pontypridd.) It was particularly pleasing to meet again men and women whom Viola and I had entertained in those hospital wards and isolated unit tours we made during the war.

I had never been to anyone else's signing session, and I didn't know what was expected of me. Was I supposed to sit at a table waiting and hoping, and, when asked to sign, simply put my name on the page? It seemed an arrogant assumption that my name written baldly like that had any value. I dislike the sight of an illegible flourish of a name scrawled *at an angle*. It looks pretentious and inconsidered and, from my observation of the few books I have seen signed by authors, the greater the writer the simpler and neater, and *straighter*, the sig-nature. I try to keep my own straight but under pressure it tends to gallop unless reined in. I decided that the least I could do was look the buyer in the eye and acknowledge his existence. In the end I found that each signing turned into a small encounter and, although this took longer, it was friendlier and less lofty than an impersonal autograph across a blank page.

Most of the signing sessions I did took place in the autumn in Britain, South Africa and Australia; all with Christmas in mind. This is the kind of dialogue the Book Buyer and I engaged in.

J.G. Hello.

B.B. Hello.

J.G. Are you going to keep the book or give it to someone?

B.B. Well, I thought I'd give it to my mother – for Christmas.

J.G. What do you call her?

B.B. Er – well – Mum.

J.G. Do you want me to put 'To Mum' and, as I don't know her, her name in brackets, and then with love from you and good wishes from me?

B.B. That sounds all right.

J.G. And her name is . . . ?

B.B. Isabel.

J.G. Isabel what? You see I don't know her . . .

B.B. Oh – I see – Isabel Chutterworth.

J.G. And Happy Christmas?

B.B. Yes. Good idea.

J.G. What is your name?

B.B. Brian . . . better put Bri.

J.G. 'With love from Bri and all good wishes from Joyce Grenfell.'

B.B. 'Thanks – nice – [and depending on age and sex] lovely – super – smashing.'

'Could you put something funny?' was a daunting request, and somehow I got out of it with a plea of no time to think of anything. Occasionally I was asked to write a cryptic message.

B.B. I'd like you to put 'Remember Solihull, July 1976. Love Weary Willie.'

J.G. And good wishes from me?

B.B. Oh – well – yes – better put that.

Joyce Grenfell Requests the Pleasure was published in England in September 1976. It was to be on sale in South Africa a month later, and shortly after that in Australia. Reggie and I had long looked forward to the return visit to Australia we had planned for December. We arranged to fly there via South Africa, where, after Reggie had attended some

Messina meetings, I would do book-promoting occasions in Johannes-burg, Cape Town and Durban. These were fewer and smaller than at home but just as heart-warming. By now I had had my baptism of fire and had found the formula for book-signing; but interviews always have to be played 'off the cuff'. As a performer I was used to that. All the same there were surprises. More than once, in Britain and overseas, I was faced by an interviewer who had not read my book, which we were supposed to be discussing. Until this happened – the first time it was a young man from one of the top Sunday newspapers in London who hadn't done his homework – I had not fully realised how sharply accurate is the sketch I wrote about the mature and literate wife of the Vice-Chancellor of an Oxbridge University, who finds her-self in exactly this situation. She is articulate, kindly, with an Oxbridge voice. She cannot pronounce the letter *r*. After some uneasy flounder-ings by the young interviewer she asks him: 'I wonder . . . Have you read my book, Mr Wimble . . ? No, I *do* know how difficult it is to find time to read what one really wants to . . . No – no – I don't mind in the *least*. No. It's only that . . . since you *have* so *very* kindly invited me to come on to your television programme in order to discuss my book, I thought you *might just possibly* have read it . . .'

Truth to tell I was pleased, considering how many new books come out daily, to find how thoroughly most of the journalists, T.V. and radio interviewers, *had* done their homework.

In Johannesburg an old friend, Kim Shippey, well known as a broad-caster all over South Africa, was a great help in arranging for me to be heard on radio and seen on S.A.B.C. television. In South Africa it is generally supposed that women are the book-buyers, and groups of them meet regularly for sandwiches and coffee to discuss and decide which books on the current list they will most enjoy. At one such morning gathering I met Mary Renault, whose novels set in ancient Greece I have long admired. I was glad to be able to say so. It turned out that she was a fan of my old movies. These, and occasional radio programmes transcribed by the B.B.C., are the only means by which British entertainers and actors can be known in South Africa.

We flew from Johannesburg to Perth late in November. It had been seven years since we were last in Australia and both of us looked for-ward to our return with the sort of tingle I used to feel as the holidays came nearer. We landed at some unearthly hour, as a line of orange in the dark night sky showed us where the sun would soon rise. We got out of the hot and heavy plane and stood on Australian soil. The air was clear and cool, and, loaded with packages and coats, I spread out my arms to express my pleasure at being back. The night-man at the motel facing the Swan River was, even at that early hour, tidy in a city suit, and he helped us lug our bags to the lift and along a covered balcony to our room on the top floor. We thought we were far too excited to sleep, but decided that a little rest was a good idea, and without bothering to unpack more than our night things got into our beds. We woke six hours later, by which time the sun was high in the sky, shining on apparently endless miles of low red roofs spreading to the horizon across the river.

Everywhere that I did book-promoting Macmillan provided the most agreeable publicity department people to look after and guide me. In Australia it was a young Englishman who met us in Perth, where he had arrived ahead of us to arrange my engagements. I said I thought I might, when we were both about twelve years old, have been in the same Girl Guide Company as his mother. 'I think,' he said courteously, 'it was possibly my grandmother.' So it proved. He was therefore young enough to be my grandson, and one of the most companionable young men that either Reggie or I had ever met; apparently unconscious of age or background; friendly, funny, natural, kind, imaginative and considerate. He was all these things not only to the visiting author and her husband, but to everyone he met; a free citizen of the world. He was also good at his job, and apparently enjoyed doing it.

All the book-jobs in Perth were fitted into one crowded day, so that in the evening we could go to Mandurah, where my school-friend Cynthia Robinson had moved into a Spanish-style house she had just built on the edge of the sea. It was she who sent me the box of strange Western Australian wild flowers the year I first went to Australia. We spent three restoring and restful days with Cynthia, and she and I shared diverting memories of our school days, in particular about a girl called Mary – or was she Martha – no, Margaret – no she *must* have been Mary – whom we hadn't much liked because she sneaked, and who was eventually expelled. We recalled that she used to *eat* her toothpaste in bed in the dormitory; but we decided that couldn't be the reason for her sudden departure, and now we would never know why she left. Reggie tolerated our elderly enjoyment of such trivia without too much obvious ennui.

We were present at a poignant scene on the day when the nearby farm, where Cynthia and her late husband Angus had lived for so long and brought up their six children, was cleared of its furniture and left ready for the new owners. The son who had taken on the running of the place was emigrating to Denmark with his Danish fiancée; another son had come over to collect some of the family furniture. The rooms once so full of children and memories stood empty. It cannot have been an easy time for any of them, especially Cynthia, but her calm and courage, and her concern for the young people, helped to make the last, difficult moments easier for everyone. 'We were always very happy there,' she said as we drove away.

We flew on to 'promote' in Adelaide, Sydney, Brisbane and Melbourne. For the three days I was working in Sydney, and after I'd finished the book-jobs, Nancy and Vincent Fairfax lent us their attractive garden flat, made out of the original kitchen and other service rooms, under the house and terrace. We found an ice-box filled with groceries; a desk with stamps and air-letters ready for our use; flowers and fruits and magazines – a great welcome. There we could be completely self-contained, but with a good deal of comings and goings between upstairs and downstairs.

The publishers gave a launching party for *Joyce Grenfell Requests the Pleasure* – for me to meet the press and book trade – in one of the vast purple-carpeted foyers of the Opera House. Distances at the Opera House make journeys within the National Theatre on the South Bank seem like tiny strolls; there are stairs and more stairs and long approaches out in the windy air, and I could not describe the place as comfortably convenient. We were there in summer; what can it be like negotiating those external areas in the bleak midwinter?

We had been taken over the Opera House in its early building stages seven years before, but we had not seen it finished until the evening of my 'launching'. And we had not been into any of the auditoriums until, on our return from Melbourne, Nancy and Vincent took us to a pre-Christmas concert 'for children of all ages'. A few days later they generously took us to see a performance of the Australian Ballet Company's enchanting production of *Eugene Onegin*, a piece worthy of the unique building. On the whole, we decided that the Opera House is, as George Robey said of a belch, 'better out than in'.

In Melbourne, where I was to tape the long-running Sunday night radio programme *Guest of Honour* that is relayed all over Australia, I was paid one of the best, if oblique, compliments I have ever had. It came, at a book-signing session, from an elderly woman wearing an Ena Sharples hair-net and an overlong tweed coat – it was a hot summer's day. English, I said to myself, probably from the North. She didn't buy a book, she just stood against the wall having a good look. When I had finished signing and the crowd had left, she came over to the table and said, in a voice that still had its original Yorkshire vowels: 'You're just like yourself – ordinary.'

At another signing, in the same city, we found Myrtle who had taken such good care of us when we had originally stayed at the Windsor Hotel, waiting outside the door of the bookshop to greet us. She said she was now retired and had read in the press that I'd be there that afternoon. She was looking her best in a big royal blue velvet hat. She said she was sorry she couldn't stay; she just wanted to come and see us again.

Every morning while we were there I telephoned Pamela Stiebel who lives just outside Melbourne, and whom I knew before I met her brother Victor. We are both early starters, and we rang each other at an earlier hour than many people might consider civilised. It was good to talk quietly before the day got started. At about seven a.m. Pam asked me what I was going to talk about that morning when I recorded *Guest of Honour*. 'I've no idea,' I said. 'It's an interview.' 'Are you sure?' said Pam. 'It's never been an interview before; it's always a scripted talk on a specific subject.' My heart bounced. I looked again at my typed list of promotional jobs; all it said was the name of the programme, the address of the A.B.C. studio and the time of recording – ten a.m. that day. Three hours to go and no script.

Now and then, if I am in a relaxed mood, I don't mind that kind of surprise. I rather like the stimulus of having to think quickly; but more important I also know answers always exist to be found – if one is ready to receive them. I sat up in bed, the better to concentrate, and suddenly I remembered that in a folder in my book-bag I had the outline of a chapter, I had been working on when we were in South Africa, on the subject of friendship. While Reggie shaved in the bathroom I read the pages out loud, improvising as I went. The reading took me exactly thirteen minutes. I was allotted fourteen for the broadcast; allowing for the inevitable expansion in performance, this was just about right.

I made copious notes about the improvised additions, and at the studio I told the producer what had happened. He asked if I was willing to have a go at recording. If it worked we would keep it; if it didn't I would have to write a script and somehow find time to record it later. When the red light came on everything fell into place. As I went along I had some new and useful ideas, and it seems it all came out smoothly; the producer was pleased. And I was grateful. Very. If I had known I had to write a script for *Guest of Honour* I think 'friendship' is the subject I should have chosen, because, as I have already said, it is in Australia that I have found it especially nourishing and giving.

The book-promoting tour that had begun in England, continued in South Africa and taken me on to Australia, finished early in December, and then it was time to see some of our friends. There is a special relish about going back to houses where we have been happy, and for Reggie and me there are several such houses in Australia. The one that has become our Australian home-from-home, is Elaine in Sydney, where we stay with Nancy and Vincent Fairfax.

Trying to describe a house built in the uncertain architectural style of the early twentieth century is not easy. Elaine is such a house. It is a big family 'mansion' with terraces, a balcony and a verandah. Modern improvements have simplified the grandeur, and pale paint has lightened the heaviness and made the house cheerful and welcoming. The land on which it stands slopes suddenly, and when you make the tricky turn-in, at the gate off the main road above it, the gravel drive is surprisingly steep as it curves by a high hedge thickly planted with white azaleas – a bridal sight in spring – to the levelled square before the front door. The garden, too, is steep with hilly paths and steps leading down to a grass tennis-court, and beyond that to a door in the wall that opens on to a little beach and the harbour. Elaine is a happy house – a worn-out phrase, but I don't know another way of giving it an accurate accolade.

We returned there for Christmas. At first we again stayed in the self-contained garden flat, but when Nancy and Vincent's elder daughter Sally White arrived with her husband and children, we moved out of the flat for them and went up into the house proper. Wherever we stayed under the Fairfax roof suited us, and the view from the guest-room balcony was even better than from the garden flat. It was difficult to realise we were in a busy city as we looked out over the garden and through and above the tall trees at the ever-present harbour. Nancy provided us with the wherewithal to get our own breakfast (I bless all hostesses and hotels that make this possible), and we took it out on to the balcony and enjoyed it as we watched early morning Harbour traffic going by.

This was the first hot-weather Christmas Reggie and I had ever spent together. I had had two warm-weather Christmases during concert tours with Viola, one in India during the war and the other, a spring-like one, in the Canal Zone of Suez after the war. In Sydney it was high summer, and the sight of chemists' shop-windows decorated with tufts of cotton-wool snow, and perspiring Father Christmases in the big stores, panting and dripping under their beards and scarlet costumes looked to us both strange and comic.

The night before Christmas I asked Nancy if I might provide a treasure hunt for the moment when luncheon was over, crackers had been pulled, presents opened and a surprise diversion could be useful. I still like playing the treasure hunt game as much as ever, and getting it ready is the best part. I got together twelve small familiar objects and, early that morning before anyone was about, I hid them in the living-room in places where they could be seen, without anything having to be touched, by the smallest child or the tallest grown-up. I thought the two most successful hidings were a banana and a small round white peppermint. The first was the more difficult to camouflage, but it was a very straight banana and I taped it between two bits of carved decoration on an antique barometer hanging on the wall. The mint was hard to see stuck on the head of a china figure where it looked like a tiny white beret.

On Christmas Day it was all hands to the plough, in preparation for a big family lunch party. Nancy and her daughter Ruth were in the kitchen. Four grandchildren and their parents, with Reggie and Vincent, sorted silver and glasses, brought in extra chairs and got ready the tables. I finished off twenty-four place-cards with coloured felt-tipped pens just as I always did for our Christmas Day luncheons at home. When all was ready some of the party played tennis on the grass court below the house; Reggie and Vincent sat back in deep chairs on the terrace; and Nancy, the grandchildren and I went for a pre-luncheon dip in the harbour.

The tide was high and the water surprisingly clear for a landlocked sea. It lapped the shores of the little curved beach where the pale sands were clean and smooth. The children thought I was a very funny swimmer. I hate getting my hair wet, never wear a bathing-cap unless the waves are high, and apart from a few gentle breast-strokes just to prove I do know how to swim, I spend most of my bathing time sitting *on* the water with my head high as a duck. This talent delighted them, and gave them giggles. Of course it is nothing more than a form of floating; with a few scissor-movements of the legs to keep me in place, I can sit almost bolt upright *ad infinitum*.

With Nancy on Christmas morning

After luncheon – the traditional foods didn't seem out of place, and chilled brandy butter goes splendidly with Christmas pudding in any weather – Reggie and I stole away to lie flat on our beds in a delightful daze from food, festivity and affection. I thought of my brother Tommy and his family in America, of Virginia in London, and felt a stab of homesickness, coupled with a slight feeling of guilt at having such an irresponsible and care-free Christmas, while they were having winter weather. And Virginia was also taking on our regular Christmas party guests at a luncheon of her own. A good time was had by all, as I later learned. Earlier in the day Virginia's telephone call from London came through dead on time, and we had a perfect connection. She was ten hours behind us, so for her it was still Christmas Eve. We told each other in the clear projected tones one uses to cover long distances by telephone about our weathers and our hopes for each other's happy Christmases.

'Did you get my Christmas card?'

'Yes – did you get mine?'

295

I think it takes more practice than either of us had to get the best out of three minutes' telephone time.

Our good day ended quietly with cold left-overs, just as it always does at home; on television there was an undemanding and unauthentic Olde Englishe Christmastide variety show, conceived in California and brought forth in Great Britain, starring Julie Andrews. It had been a happy, different and affectionate Christmas with a dear and loving family.

Flying home with a stop-over in South Africa, I thought about the way the lines have continued to fall unto me in pleasant places. This visit had been the best of all our times in Australia. I was retired from the stage and glad to be. I didn't miss the old life at all; in fact, and rather to my surprise, I loved *not* performing. The playing years had been an exciting and rewarding time, and I had a rich treasure of good things to remember. I had already started to work on the second volume of my autobiography.

I began to tot up the special 'first times' in my adult life. Apart from the most special of all – the day I married my husband – there was the first time in print; on stage; on radio; on film; on television and on a gramophone record. Which had been the *most* special, hard-to-believe, unexpected and astonishing of first times?

I had no difficulty in deciding the answer.

It was the first time I held in my hand the printed, bound and jacketed copy of my first book. A big moment. A new career had begun.

I remembered the last lines of a song I wrote with Dick:

> There is no such thing as time,
> Only this very minute
> And I'm in it.
> Thank the Lord.

Index

Figures in italics (*43*) indicate pages on which illustrations appear.

Index

Index

Index

Index